My Other Self
Sexual fantasies, fetishes and kinks

By

Angela Lewis PhD

My Other Self
Sexual fantasies, fetishes and kinks

A copy of this publication can be found in the National Library of Australia.

ISBN: 978-1-921791-28-4 (pbk.)

Published by Book Pal
www.bookpal.com.au

Author's Note:
While this is a work of non-fiction, names and other identifying data relating to persons in this book have been changed to protect their privacy. In some instances events have been reshaped and composite characters created in order to protect these and other individuals.

Disclaimer:
The author and publisher do not advocate practising any of the activities listed herein. Many are dangerous and some lethal. People who choose to do so, do it at their own risk, and the reader retains all responsibility for choosing to apply any material presented herein to his or her life.

Cover design and photo © Angela Lewis
www.myotherself.com.au

Any ladle's sweet that dishes out some gravy.

Contents

Acknowledgements

One thing I didn't expect out of this journey was to make new friends and meet so many wonderful people. In particular I would like to thank (among many, many others) Mistresses Michelle and Amanda, Goddess Alexa, Nik and Jo of Muki's Kitchen, Ataraxia from The International Association of Rubberists, the beautiful Ms Arinda Storm Weaver for her help on nails, hair and smoking, Miss Emma, Summer Ray and Baby Mikey for their advice on adult babies and diaper lovers, Michelle for sharing her special story on intersex and Charles, Marc and Joel for their input on male submissiveness—to Joel a very special thank you for being my long-standing sounding board on all the things that make up the world of domination and submission, your help was invaluable.

I thank Tony and DC for their advice on the interests of casting and disability, Helen for an entrée and perspective on Furry that I would never have been able to access without her guidance, Duamutef for educating me on all things vore, Eboni for talking to me about pee play and cross-dressing, and Jinxypie and all the husbands (in particular Sam) who gave their time so freely on the subject of cuckolding. To my editor: it took time to find someone who was prepared to put prejudices aside and take on this project, but Margaret Johnson 'The Book Doctor' stepped up to that plate! I would also like to thank my dear friends Barbara Stapleton, Sue O'Neil and Andrew Rixon for all their help and advice and in pushing me to completion.

Heartfelt thanks go to the love of my life for simply being, as well as to my son who was a teenager when I started this, and to his credit accepted with good grace that his own mother could write such a book.

Preface

"Let's have sex with the cat and then torture it,"
says the sadist.
"Let's have sex with the cat, torture it and then kill
it!" shouts the murderer.
"Let's have sex with the cat, torture it, kill it and
then have sex with it again," continues the necro-
phile.
"Let's have sex with the cat, torture it, kill it, have
sex with it again and burn it," says the pyroma-
niac.
There is silence, and then the masochist says:
"Meow."

—email doing the rounds in 2008

One of the most common questions I was asked by friends
and colleagues during this research was "but why?" And this
often went with raised eyebrows and a puzzled look. The
answer is quite simply because I wanted to know. My
knowledge base in this area wasn't that extensive, given I'm a
heterosexual woman brought up in suburban Australia, so my
sex life—I freely admit—has been so-called normal and lacked
experimentation (in BDSM circles known as vanilla). After
writing a small article on fat fetishism for the Counselling
Australia journal a few years ago, and meeting Nik and Jo, a
lovely couple from the cannibal fantasy community (no, I
didn't get eaten!), it dawned on me that there was a whole lot
going on that I had simply not encountered. I learned so much
while researching all the different ways people express
themselves sexually, but the best lesson was to open my heart
and mind to other people's normal.

One thing that I need to make clear from the start is that
this is not a how-to manual, nor does it aim to recruit anybody
to a so-called deviant lifestyle; rather it is about providing

information without censorship or implied judgment—because at the end of the day I'm simply telling the story of all the different ways people enjoy sex and erotica. While there is no definitive data that quantifies the incidence of so-called kinky sex, research suggests it is practised by 10-15% of the adult population (Brame 2000) and 14% of American men and 11% of women (Kleinplatz and Moser 2007, Janus and Janus 1993); figures that health care professionals can ill-afford to ignore or dismiss as marginal.

The data for this book was collected by reviewing literature in related fields, visiting websites, joining forums and online groups and entering into conversation and correspondence with those I met along the way. This included people from Australia, America, UK, Czech Republic, Germany and Austria (being bilingual proved to be a huge bonus). It does not rely on pro-forma questionnaires, scales and mean averages; instead it shares an honest account of what people were willing to divulge in the ways they wished to divulge it. While I initially used a pseudonym (as is common practice for most online groups), I always explained why I was participating when making comments or asking questions and never portrayed myself as anyone other than who I was—but I very quickly ended up using my real name and real contact details because I realised that if I wanted honesty, I had to be completely transparent myself. Being brave enough to use my own identity was the best thing I could have done because, before I knew it, I was guest blogger on a cuckolding site and page administrator for a diaper lovers' Facebook page—and people began to trust and actually approach me.

Talking about what they do and how they do it to a complete stranger while trusting that I would not misrepresent their lives so I could write something sensational, required a (rather large) leap of faith. However many people took that risk and in sharing their thoughts, experiences and feelings with me, made this book possible. Real names and other identifying data have of course been changed for the obvious reason of protecting the privacy of all those who participated; so if you are reading something and think "oh that must be Mike I work with", you'll be wrong because in some instances I've taken the added precaution of reshaping events and characters to further protect participants.

This work has become collaboration in a way I could only have dreamed was possible. Most of the sections were reviewed by people from the relevant communities—and some were pickier than others about what I wrote and how I presented their narratives which resulted in lots of time and rewrites—but we all stuck at it to ensure that what you will read is authentic and factual and tells people's stories as they wanted them told. My thanks go to each and every one of them for giving me their time, trust and honesty. Without their seal of approval this work would be nothing.

Introduction

Abnormal sex is what others do that you wouldn't
enjoy.

—Money, 1986

It seems that human beings can be aroused by almost anything—in fact there were times during my research when it
seemed that sticking 'philia' at the end of any word was a
legitimate way of creating a new fetish. John Money in the
1986 publication *Lovemaps*, (which he hoped would become a
forerunner in the world of sexuality and erotica—
unfortunately it did not), named a number in this very fashion,
including apotemnophilia, chorephilia and kleptophilia:
respectively sexual arousal from the thought of having an
amputation, sexual arousal from dancing and sexual arousal
from stealing.[1]

Through the ages individuals of different races, genders
and sexual orientations have experienced discrimination,
distrust and hatred because of misinformation, lack of
knowledge and lack of discussion. While times have changed,
people who practice kinky (i.e. non-mainstream) sex largely
continue to experience discrimination in ways that previously
disenfranchised groups, such as homosexuals, are only too
familiar with.

Most of us accept that someone may call himself say 'a leg
man' to indicate his preference for a body part, but that isn't
generally considered a fetish though it could well be. Many
people (both men and women) have preferences for various
rituals and practices that work for them when having sex, but
unless the ritual involves a bizarre object or practice, that is

---

[1] See Money's 1988 publication *Gay, Straight and in-Between* for his
full list of paraphilias.

1

also generally considered to be ok. Yet for those with any type of erotic or sexual interest outside the current socially acceptable parameters, sexual activity and how it is practised often has to be secretive, with many practitioners constantly on guard against exposing their true nature and desires. For many this can result in their lives being full of anxiety, secretiveness and even loneliness, a theme that I came across many times. This is how Nik from Muki's Kitchen describes growing up and coming to terms with his fascination with cannibal fantasy:

> How all of this felt during most of my life...in a word, lonely. There was no Internet when I was growing up and this is not the sort of subject any-one would feel comfortable talking about (face-to-face) with anyone else. Especially not a confused kid and definitely not with my parents! For most of my life, I thought I was a complete freak and probably a borderline nut-job. It's embarrassing, scary, and very lonely.

Luckily for people like Nik this situation has eased since the cyber-revolution brought us the Internet, which has provided a level of access to erotic communities and information about kinks and deviant sex that is almost mind-blowing. This has not only resulted in a tremendous cultural and social transformation, but has created a very simple way for people whose sexual interests are not mainstream to connect with others who share their interests—and discover that in the words of Dafyd from *Little Britain*, they are "not the only gay in the village". German sexologist Volkmar Sigush claims this revolution has allowed what he terms 'neosexualities' such as homosexuality, bisexuality, voyeurism, exhibitionism and other forms of sexuality previously declared pathological or perverted, to become more accepted by society. This has understandably been a lifeline for many people who silently agonised about the assumption that they were the only person on the planet who needed to have their genitals crushed with a stiletto before they could think about climaxing.

As Siemens (2008) remarked in regard to learning, perhaps one of the most significant contributions the Internet has made to society is the forced consideration of perspectives and opinions outside our own. Each hyperlink allows us a simple access point to a new perspective, which we can choose to take advantage of...or not. However, as some of us have discovered, there are problems with finding specific information and like-minded souls on the Internet. Searching for anything related to sex frequently links to aggressive online marketers trying to sell products, sexual services or images, and the searcher is bombarded with lewd advertisements and pop-ups. Locating actual information online becomes a tiresome needle-and-haystack problem—and as I discovered, no matter how rigorous a security system you employ, may also result in damage to your computer system.

Given the interest and curiosity that most people have in how others express themselves sexually, you would also think that this field would attract academic researchers in droves; however, this is not the case and in my experience most available research is found in academic journals that the average person cannot access. As Dr. Michael Wiederman, book editor of the *Journal of Sex Research* remarks, lack of research may be due to the assumption that researchers investigate topics that interest them, and as a result stay away from this field as they don't want to be thought of as sexual deviants!

Because there are so many erotic interests that people enjoy I've chosen as many as possible, but acknowledge this is by no means the complete picture.[2] Some interests are more obscure than others, while others have large community groups, resulting in a range of available information. In terms of how I catalogued the activities, it is simply divided into sections based on what I personally felt made sense.

---

[2] Given that restrictions on time and space mean this book does not cover all the erotic interests that people have, readers may also be interested in Brenda Love's comprehensive 1992 publication, *Encyclopaedia of Unusual Sex Practices*.

What Makes It Perverted or Kinky?

Everyone has three lives: a public life, a private life, and a secret life.

—Gabriel García Márquez[3]

The way a person expresses their sexual desires is as unique as the way they speak, sing, or think. As the old saying goes, "one man's meat is another man's poison", and so it is with what is termed abnormal sexual behaviour. A perversion (or kink in the vernacular), is usually any type of sexual act that is outside of the generally accepted norm of sexual behaviour in a community at a particular time in history. This is basically a moving feast, as norms of behaviour are culturally defined, so what is considered 'deviant' also changes through generations. The moral boundary between what people consider to be normal behaviour and what is considered abnormal or perverse has no straight line, as generations struggle with their moral geographies. Just as dress lengths have changed through the centuries, sexual fashions have also undergone large revolutions.

In Ancient Greece for example, no distinction was made between heterosexual and homosexual activity, while from the fall of Rome to the 15th century Christian Church leaders considered sex of any kind to be a sin, and 19th century Western medicine considered masturbation to be a mental illness requiring medical treatment. The struggle over what is deemed sexually acceptable continues, with Iran in 2008 still considering it illegal for unmarried men and women to dance together, while it was not until 1998 that the US State of Maryland amended a law that prohibited anal sex between consenting adults. Homosexuality (once considered to be highly deviant in most parts of the world) was still classified

---

[3] *100 Years of Solitude* (1998).

as a disorder by the American Psychiatric Association (APA) until 1973; now they describe it as a "normal variation", despite homosexuality continuing to remain punishable by lashing or stoning in a number of Islamic countries.[4]

While there is no way of predicting what sexual interests or acceptable parameters may arise (or indeed vanish) in the future, and despite changing cultural mores, the standard for so-called normal sex still tends to be based on conventional, reproductive or recreational sex between a man and a woman. Depending on where you live and what your religious persuasion is, anything outside that definition could be considered by some communities as sinful, illegal or immoral.

The terms fetish, deviance or perversion are the most common and widely understood layman's terms used to broadly describe attraction to any non-mainstream sexual practices. In the literature on sexology and psychology, the term paraphilia generally replaces the words perversion or fetish and is considered the more correct term to describe sexual arousal in response to objects or situations deemed socially or sexually unusual. Paraphilia is a term created from the Greek prefix para meaning around or beside and philia, which is one of the ancient Greek words for love. When combined, these words give us the term paraphilia, which is literally translated as 'to one side of love', or 'beside love'.[5] As we are talking about lust and sex, you might be wondering what love has to do with it—as did Moser (2001) who proposed the term paralagnia (lagnia translates to lust) to be more accurate—but sexologist John Money's (1980) preference for

---

[4] Internet search for Sharia Law (Islamic law) and homosexuality for more information, or see the entry under Wikipedia at: http://en.wikipedia.org/wiki/Shari%27a#Homosexuality.
[5] However as Malin and Saleh (2007) argue, the term paraphilia may well end up as an unintentional pejorative, given how easily people misunderstand the term and make the mnemonic link to the word pedophilia, thus wrongly confusing it with child molestation.

using the term paraphilia remains the industry standard to describe unusual sexual interests in a non-pejorative way.

The Fourth Diagnostic and Statistical Manual of Mental Disorders (DSM-IV) published by the American Psychiatric Association[6] has become the world standard for evaluation and diagnosis of mental health. This manual has also chosen to use the term paraphilia to refer to a general category of recurrent, intense, sexually arousing fantasies, urges or behaviours. The DSM-IV defines paraphilias as revolving around the themes of (1) objects or nonhuman animals (2) humiliation or suffering of the person or partner or (3) nonconsenting persons.[7] In the DSM-IV definition, paraphilic behaviours have several common characteristics, including that the behaviours or urges show an established pattern of at least six months duration, that they are sexually motivated and that it results in what they term "clinically important distress or impairs work, social or personal functioning". Of course only the person with the paraphilic desire or interest can be the judge of whether their behaviour hampers or impairs how they function. Eight paraphilias garner DSM-IV diagnoses (exhibitionism, fetishism, frotteurism, pedophilia, sexual masochism, sexual sadism, transvestic fetishism and voyeurism), with a large variety clumped under a ninth category called 'Paraphilia NOS' (NOS signifying not otherwise specified); a residual category created to contain all other paraphilias and where all the more interesting ones live.

---

[6] American Psychiatric Association (APA) (2000).

[7] Morrison (2006, p.360).

Doesn't Everybody Sleep on Rubber Sheets: What are Fetishes?

Latex and leather and red satin sashes.
Candles and handcuffs and black rubber lashes.
Being whipped, being bitten, being tied up with strings,
These are a few of me favourite things.[8]

In common speech any fixation on a singular inanimate object, body part, body feature or sexual practice is called a fetish, so it has a wide array of applications. In terms of its original meaning, Merriam-Webster's Dictionary gives us three choices:

- an object (as a small stone carving of an animal) believed to have magical power to protect or aid its owner;

- any thing or activity to which one is irrationally devoted;

- an object or bodily part whose real or fantasized presence is psychologically necessary for sexual gratification and that is an object of fixation to the extent that it may interfere with complete sexual expression.

The original meaning of the term fetish was an amulet or charm, which was believed to have supernatural powers. This talisman was then worshipped because of its magical powers. We rarely use this definition of fetish anymore, instead applying the term generally, as people are said to have a fetish for anything they have a serious interest in, such as collecting fine wines, going running daily, having to wear a new pair of socks each day, or only dating red haired women. More often than not, a fetish is called a fetish only by people who do not

---

[8] Poetry on www.kinysexpuppet.com, sung to tune of the song 'My Favourite Things' from the *Sound of Music*.

share the same level of interest and to whom this interest seems inexplicable or weird. The person devoted to a thing or activity in this way would rarely use this term to describe their interest. This is part of the reason that hard data in terms of numbers is difficult to ascertain. As Kafka (2009) observes in reviewing existing case studies, many men who self identify as fetishists do not necessarily report what he terms 'clinical impairment' in association with their fetish or fetish-associated behaviours—in other words it doesn't bother them and they happily go about their lives.

A move to lumping fetish in with 'weirdness' started around the nineteenth century, when the French psychologist Alfred Binet (1857-1911) used the term to describe certain kinds of unusual male sexual activity. Also during this time, one of the first sexologists (Krafft-Ebing 1886), deemed fetishism to be a pathology, because it was frequently associated with deviant sexual practices and perversions as defined in those times. However, it is possible he made that link because his research was done by observing sexual variations in a Victorian mental asylum, so many of the people he observed were already mentally ill and perhaps did not really provide a fair cross section of the community.[9] Fetishists were originally described by Krafft-Ebing as men (never women) who specifically developed erotic attachments to objects rather than to people and who sought sexual gratification with and through that object, such as a boot, a glove or a piece of underwear. The prevalence and incidence of fetishism is unknown[10] but is still believed to be far more common in males,[11] though there are arguments that fetishism in women is simply ignored as it is deemed to be a taboo practice for the female gender.[12]

---

[9] Easton and Liszt (2000, p.23).

[10] Penix and Picket in Fisher & O'Donohue (2006).

[11] Money (1977): Kafka (2009).

[12] Gamman and Makinen, (1993).

There are many different kinds of fetishes and many of them are socially acceptable and commonplace—such as the use of seductive clothing or specific mementos. Common fetishistic objects today are clothing such as shoes or under-wear, garments made from rubber or leather, and matter related to the body such as excrement, hair or odours. The term has also been extended from the 18th century definition to include not only an attraction to an inanimate object, but also to specific parts of a person's body such as feet. As Chalkley and Powell (1983) found after a 20-year study of patients in the UK hospital system, fetishism is an extremely varied phe-nomenon in terms of both the fetish object itself and the activities in which the fetishist seeks to include the object. However, what remains constant is that fetishists experience a sexual thrill from kissing, touching, tasting or smelling the object, matter or body part. The object or body part is used while masturbating or included in partnered sex, often as a form of foreplay, while for those with a strong fetish attraction the object or body part takes primary focus during sex. It is generally accepted that most fetishes usually develop in early childhood[13] and then continue into adulthood. The criteria for fetishism according to the DSM-IV is as follows:

- Repeatedly for at least six months, the patient has intense sexual desires, fantasies or behavior concerning the use of inanimate objects (such as shoes or underwear).

- This results in clinically important distress or impairs work, social or personal functioning.

- The objects are not used solely in cross-dressing (as female clothing is used in Transvestic Fetishism) and are not equip-ment intended to stimulate the genitals (such as a vibrator).[14]

---

[13] Hopkins in Lubbe (2000); Kafka (2009); Munroe & Gauvain, (2001).
[14] Morrison (2006, p.365-365).

Theories of What Causes Sexual Difference

You only need to know WHY if you want to change things.
—female 33, who enjoys hurting willing sex partners

There are many theories that try to explain the origin of non-mainstream sexual behaviours; and while I overview some of them here, to date, there is no definitive and proven theory that explains why a person carries a particular sexual identity. I am not overly concerned with pin-pointing causes, nor am I able to attribute these differences to a particular theory (particularly as I am not a psychologist nor a psychiatrist), so this section merely provides some food for thought and offers some frameworks that people may find useful in theorising sexual desires.

Most psychoanalytic theories agree that so-called deviant or fetishistic behaviours begin in childhood or puberty.[15] This was confirmed many times over in the conversations I had with people in the course of researching this book. Many of them also spoke of being in a type of no man's land, alone with a kink or fetish that could not be talked about or shared, particularly in their younger years; this was a burden for many of them until they realised there were others with similar inclinations, thanks in no small part to the Internet, which was credited over and over again for allowing people to find their place in the world or to confirm they were not alone.

While there is no clear definitive answer to what causes paraphilias, an assumption made by pioneer sexologists such as Krafft-Ebing,[16] and still hangs over the minds of some

---

[15] See for example the work of Freud (1905) and Money (1977, 1980, 1986), both pioneers in the field and more recent work by Kafka.
[16] His major work was *Psychopathia Sexualis*, first published in 1886.

people today, is that those with a paraphilia are suffering some type of degeneracy caused by activities such as masturbation, mental illness or even unmarried sex. This may or may not be partnered with a belief that the person has been tainted by heredity (.e.g the mother was a prostitute, or the father was a drinker), neatly making genetics and environment responsible for creating paraphiliacs. There are even some studies that maintain that fetishes and paraphilic behaviours can be traced to epilepsy or dysfunction in the temporal lobe of the brain and that it can be cured by the use of medication.[17]

What is known is that men are more vulnerable to experiencing paraphilias, but as mentioned earlier in relation to fetishes, to date there are no exact statistics available on breakdowns or numbers[18] across the sexes, however some research suggests that the ratio of men to women is approximately 20:1.[19] Lack of data on numbers can also be attributed to many people with a paraphilia not seeking help as they simply go quietly about their daily lives. This may be because they don't see their interest as problematic or their silence comes from feeling embarrassed, guilty or ashamed. This has been further complicated by the introduction of mandatory reporting laws for certain sexual crimes which has anecdotally further decreased the number of individuals who voluntarily seek treatment and therefore make themselves known.

However as experts in the field maintain, non-mainstream sexual practices can only be considered a problem if they impair a person's social adjustment or stops them from having intimate relationships—and it cannot be assumed that all lovers of kink are distressed by their situation. As Massfungrl, (pseudonym of the husband in a swinging couple) says, "regardless of what we are both labelled, we do this for fun

---

[17] El-Bahri and Robertshaw (1998) in Lowenstein (2002).
[18] Malin, Fabin and Saleh (2007).
[19] APA (2000). *The Diagnostic and Statistical Manual of Mental Disorders.*

and for our relationship, and the labels really don't matter in the end".

Many in fact have made peace with who they are and their sexual choices fail to cause them anguish, so given the perception of stigmatism that remains around any type of sexual difference, it is more likely they remain private about their sexual interests so that the adverse reaction of others doesn't cause them problems. These aspects all contribute to the fact that there is relatively little in terms of published research in the area of paraphilias.

Freud: or Where's Your Penis Mum?

> No healthy person, it appears, can fail to make some addition that might be called perverse to the normal sexual aim.
> —Freud, 1905

Though Binet (1887) is acknowledged as the first to use the term fetish in the psychological sense, Sigmund Freud is more widely recognised in relation to the psychology of what is considered sexual perversion. Freud's school of modern psychology asserts that a fetish is imprinted as the result of an early traumatic experience. In Freud's view, a fetish originates when a male child realises his mother has no penis and mistakenly believes this to be female castration. Confronted with his mother's lack of a penis, the child represses this memory and latches onto some nearby object to take the place of this terrible sight, substituting this object for the missing penis. Freud's theory (highly outdated now), holds that the object in the child's gaze at this point (e.g. mother's high heels, the slipper in the child's hand), then becomes a sexualised object that triggers his sexual gratification for years to come. But Freud's theory does not explain why only some men develop a fetish, nor does it take into account the fact that women can develop fetishes as well as men. Both contemporary and feminist thinkers challenge the Freudian approach to sexuality and mental health, which ends up in the simple reduction of humanity's psychological troubles to an unproved assumption based on boys resenting their fathers and girls desiring theirs. Understandably Freud's phallocentric preoccupation has resulted in some feminists arguing that fetishism is classified as a perversion precisely because it disrupts the traditional penis-focused sexual mores of Western society. An Internet search on Freud will provide plenty of further reading for those interested.

Jung: I'm Being Followed By A Moonshadow...

Some people expend tremendous energy merely to be normal.
—Philosopher Albert Camus

Carl Jung was a Swiss psychiatrist who died in 1961. He was briefly mentored by Freud, as they followed parallel research paths into the theory of the unconscious mind. Where Freud fixed on the physical/animal nature as the primal driving force of mankind, Jung looked to the spiritual self as a more significant force. In Jungian psychology, the term 'persona' describes the face we present to the world, the public façade each of us adopts to hide our deep self and the things we do not like about ourselves. The flipside of the persona is called the shadow, and denotes the unconscious or repressed aspects of the mind that include weaknesses, shortcomings and instincts. The shadow also includes socially unacceptable aspects of human nature such as rage, jealousy, envy, lust, greed and pride. When a person manages to understand and integrate their unconscious aspects (the shadow aspect) into their conscious life, then the word 'individuation' is used to describe a person becoming fully conscious of who they are. Jung believed people became mature and fully integrated as adults only when they were able to tolerate, understand and assimilate these hidden areas of themselves, as this acceptance allows hidden strengths and creativity to bloom and to create what he termed 'a freedom of person'. Mardi Gras, Halloween and Brazilian Carnevale are examples of acceptable triggers of the shadow as these are socially tolerable periods in time when a person has permission to act out or visit the darker or less controlled sides of the imagination and self. Coming to terms with society's (and their own) expectation of how they should behave, while juggling the shadow aspect of themselves (that they might not want to acknowledge), is a struggle that many people who enjoy non-mainstream sexual practices may recognise in their own lives.[20]

Lovemaps

> Lovemaps! They're as common as faces, bodies and brains. Each one of us has one. Without it there would be no falling in love, no mating, and no breeding of the species. Lacking a name, however, the lovemap has existed in a conceptually unexplored territory of the mind, unknown to science and scholarly inquiry.
>
> —Money, 1986

John Money was a professor of medical psychology at an American university in the 1980s and did pioneering work on gender identity disorders and sexology. In the early 1980s he introduced the concept of what he named a lovemap. He

---

[20]For those interested in learning more, Internet searching on Jung's theory will yield a lot of information, as will reading Jung's *The Archetypes and The Collective Unconscious* (1954).

argued that in terms of emotional and sexual development, each person carries a mental ideal of love and lust, which he termed a lovemap, or as he formally defined it, "a developmental representation or template synchronously functional in the mind and the brain, depicting the idealised lover".[21]

Basically the lovemap can be described in layman's terms as a sex script of what turns a person on. According to Money, because this schemata of an individual's erotic fantasies and resultant practices is established in early puberty, it is difficult to alter once it has formed. He believed that when a person's lovemap becomes distorted or defaced in some way, the result is kinky or fetishist behaviour. He argued, for example, that a person can develop a paraphilic lovemap when they experience genital arousal from a non-sexual event. Money further maintained that as input into lovemaps enters the brain visually, and men have historically favoured visual stimuli, this accounts for more men than women having what he termed distorted lovemaps; which then account for their paraphilias as well as explaining why more men have them than women. For those interested in the lovemap concept, a list of Money's publications appears in the references.

Courtship Disorder

The original proposition by psychotherapist Havelock Ellis (1906) was that paraphilias were a symptom of arrested sexual development, occurring when a person fails to move through all the normal phases of courtship.[22] Sexologist and physician Kurt Freund[23] and various colleagues have

---

[21]Money (1986, p.43).

[22]Ellis and Brancala (1956).

[23]Freund was a Czech-Canadian best known for developing phallometry (the objective measurement of sexual arousal in males). See Freund (1990), Freund and Seto (1998), Freund, Sher and Hucker (1984).

continued work in this area, and put forward the theory that as human courtship is almost universally sequential, when a person stalls at a specific phase then they are likely to develop a specific paraphilia. The courtship sequence they proposed involved four phases: 1) finding a partner, 2) an affiliative phase involving smiling and talking to a potential partner, 3) a tactile phase in which physical contact is made and 4) the copulatory phase in which sexual intercourse occurs. In their model, if a phase is skipped or stalled then a person distorts that phase. So in their model they believe that voyeurism, for example, is a distortion of the finding phase, exhibitionism is a distortion of the affiliative phase, frotteurism is a distortion of the tactile phase and rape is a distortion of the sexual intercourse phase.

Cognitive Behavioural Theory

Where psychoanalysts such as Freud theorised that an individual with a paraphilia is repeating or reverting to a sexual habit which arose early in life and is often related to early childhood trauma, behaviourists believe a paraphilia occurs through a process of conditioning. In particular, they believe that paraphilias develop as a result of reinforcing the reward of the orgasm from a specific activity.[24] For example, non-sexual objects may become associated with intense sexual pleasure and if contact is repeated often enough, can result in the person preferring these circumstances to what is deemed 'normal' sexual contact.[25]

The anthropologist Desmond Morris described this type of process as malimprinting, which means imprinting by an organism (animal or human) that has not taken a traditional

[24]Tollison and Adams (1979).
[25]See also Binet's original work (1897) and later conditioning research by Rachman (1968).

path. For example, the baby duckling that is reared by humans then follows the human around thinking that this is his mother. If you apply this to fetishism and humans, a young person may experience his first sexual pleasure or orgasm while playing with his mother's fur coat or while rubbing up and down on a rubber floaty in the family pool one lazy summer. For some people, a subconscious link is then made between the sexual act and the use of the object or the circumstance. When people experience pleasure from a behaviour they are likely to repeat it, and the argument in this theory is that it becomes imprinted and part of their life-long behaviour.

This has much in common with Russian physiologist and experimental psychologist Ivan Pavlov's 1926 theory known as classical conditioning. Pavlov often experimented with animals, and during his research on the physiology of digestion in dogs he noted that rather than simply salivating in the presence of meat powder (an outcome he called the unconditioned response), the dogs began to salivate in the presence of the person who normally fed them. From this observation he predicted that, if a particular stimulus in the dog's surroundings was present when the dog was given meat powder, then this stimulus would become *associated* with food and cause salivation on its own. In his initial experiment, Pavlov used bells to call the dogs to their food and, after a few repetitions, the dogs started to salivate in response to the bell. So a neutral stimulus (in this case a bell), became a conditioned stimulus, thanks to the consistent pairing with an unconditioned stimulus (known as the conditioned response).

Psychologists Rachman and Hodgson used Pavlov's methodology to carry out an interesting experiment in the late 1960s with three male colleagues,[26] in which they demonstrated how sexual deviations could be created in adult male subjects. They set up a laboratory with monitors attached to each man's penis, intended to measure their sexual responses

---

[26]All of whom were heterosexuals with no history of fetishism.

to specific images. First they were shown photos of women's knee-length boots and each man remained neutral. Then they were shown erotic pictures of women, interspersed with images of the same knee-length boot. By the end of a series of conditioning sessions the men all got erections from pictures of the boots alone. Readers will be glad to hear that the scientists subsequently conducted further conditioning to return the men to their initial state of neutrality with regard to women's boots (phew!) .

Summary

While it is interesting to read about the different explanations offered for variations in humankind's sexuality, the fact remains that to date there is no definitive, neat and proven theory that explains why a person carries a particular sexual identity and exhibits certain behaviours. The more pragmatic lovers of kink have stopped looking for answers, instead subscribing to the view that you only really need to know if you want to change things about yourself—and it has been my experience that the overwhelming majority of those I spoke with do not wish to change anything about their sexuality:

> When I was a kid—a very long time ago—my well-meaning parents packed me off to a parade of shrinks to get rid of my fetish. All they succeeded in doing was reinforcing the notion that there was something wrong with me that needed 'fixing'. Finally, when I was 28 years old, it was finally suggested to me that I might be a hell of a lot happier if I just accepted my fetish and actually tried to enjoy it. Suddenly, the psychological weights I had been carrying since early childhood were lifted from my shoulders. I no longer needed to be 'fixed'—I was not sick—I was OK after all!

I found my 'ataraxia', the ancient Greek term for peace of mind. Rather than being overwhelmed by my fetish I embraced it. Sure, it's made mate-finding more challenging and there were still some bumps in the road because of it, but overall, I am no longer denying who I am, and that has made me a much, much happier person overall. (Ataxaria, 62 , male Rubberist)

If the Shoe Fits

Feet

They were the most beautiful feet I had ever seen. The arch was high and all together too suggestive, while the toes were long, tapered and painted in the most delicate shade of pearly pink which reminded me of a blushing vagina. All I could think about was when I could hold them in my hands.

A foot fetishist becomes sexually aroused when exposed to feet, in the same way that a conventional person may be when faced with genitalia or breasts. The clinical term for this interest is podophilia: podos (foot) and philia (love of). More than 95% of foot fetishists are men and their interest usually parallels their sexual orientation, so a heterosexual male is generally attracted to the feet of a heterosexual woman. Foot lovers are across all socio-economic groups, but anecdotally it has high appeal to blue collar men. Some folks get all the pleasure they need from looking at images of feet, fantasizing about them or reading erotic feet stories—with 'foot porn' reading something like this:

> Linda starts using both her feet to stroke Neil's dick. Neil moves down to the carpet where she rubs her foot over his body and face as she stands over him. She lets Neil suck on her toes, but only when she tells him that he can. Neil takes five toes in his mouth all at once and he feels like he has died and gone to heaven as she gently wiggles them against the roof of his mouth. (Reader story on a foot forum website)

21

But others need physical contact. Different individuals like to massage, caress, lick, suck, fondle, tickle, sniff or kiss feet. While the foot fetishist may enjoy having these things done to his own feet, he usually likes to give his attention to the feet of women. In China when foot binding was an acceptable practice, the tiny, bound female foot was considered highly erotic. The Chinese would start bandaging the feet of baby girls, turning the toes back except for the big toe. The extreme contraction of the foot would eventually cause a hollow space to form underneath.[27] As these bandaged feet were not really able to walk, the tissue became extremely soft and fleshy and for the Chinese male interested in feet, were viewed as a vagina equivalent. An invitation to touch or fondle the bound feet was considered a precursor to intimacy or a source of sexual gratification. Some Chinese men also had bound feet and these were as attractive to homosexuals as the female feet to heterosexuals. Today, most male podophiles take a submissive role in foot play, enjoying the idea of giving up their power and control to (literally) worship at a woman's feet.

Some foot lovers like to bypass conventional intercourse completely and give the foot a starring role during sex, known as a foot job. This is done by the woman using her feet to masturbate the man's penis in a similar way to using hands. When this is quite rough or vigorous it is sometimes called a 'hoof hugger'. A variation on this is 'pedalling', in which a woman manipulates the genitals of her partner in an up and down motion with her foot, like using the pedals on a car. According to the editorial director of France's *Foot Medicine and Surgery Journal,* the sole of the foot has thousands of nerve endings and is in fact one of the body's most sensitive tactile organs.[28] They keep a constant up-and-down pressure on the

---

[27]The resulting shape was known as a Lotus foot as it was thought to be shaped like a Lotus flower.
[28]Benamou (1996).

penis and change the rhythm by tapping or pressing hard. Those with particularly dexterous toes are able to move a foreskin backwards and forwards without using their hands. When the male foot is used on the female, the big toe is used as a substitute penis, either as foreplay or to take the place of conventional penetration. The well known publication *The Joy of Sex*[29] suggests that "the pad of the male big toe applied to the clitoris or the vulva generally is a magnificent erotic instrument".

As is the case with other forms of human desire, the podophile will have his own ideas of what is beautiful or attractive about certain feet. For example, some foot fetishists are fixated on physical aspects such as the size or shape of the foot, while others are more interested in the toenails or the footwear. Catching a glimpse of the sole of the foot can be particularly exciting, as this area is considered a highly private part of the person. Some foot lovers focus on the partner's toenails, which they may prefer long, short, manicured a certain way (e.g. squared or rounded) or painted a certain shade or colour, say only pinks or only reds. Others prefer all hair waxed or shaved from the toes. Another segment of the foot loving community find themselves excited by a specific skin texture on the foot (e.g. rough, smooth or callused), or have particular standards in relation to the degree of cleanliness. This can range from preferring pristine, sweet-smelling feet to being seduced by visible grime between the toes or dirty soles.

While some foot fetishists fancy feet bare, others prefer them in shoes, or as they term it, 'clothed', as well as preferring certain types of shoes—open-toed and high-heeled shoes are universal favourites. The definition of 'dressed up' may extend to socks or hosiery, so there is an overlap between loving feet and aligned fetishes such as nylons, pantyhose and

---

[29]Comfort, (1972 revised 2008).

shoes. Other fetishes such as tickling or bondage of the feet often accompany podophilia, and may overlap into the BDSM world.

Polls conducted by footfetishdirectory.com and retrieved in June 2009 showed that toes (at 53.3%) are a podophile's most favoured part of the foot, followed by the sole (at 31.3%). As to what they prefer to do with feet, the table below (also from footfetishdirectory.com) shows the results of interviewing 2,280 people on their preferences in foot-related activities:

Licking feet	28.9%
Getting a footjob	15.1%
Smelling feet	13.8%
Looking at feet	7.7%
Rubbing feet	3.2%
All of the above	31.4%

As a foot fetish and the closely-related shoe fetish are believed to be two of the most common sexual fetishes, it isn't surprising to find a wide variety of online foot erotica. This ranges from sites offering video clips on creamed feet, dirty feet, toes being painted, lesbians and feet, feet in pantyhose and feet in heels, flats or flip-flops, to sites specialising in feet of specific nationalities such as Czech feet or Asian feet. Foot porn for this market consists of women's feet being licked, sucked, tickled or massaged or showing the soles; and while there may be nudity or lewdness, the focus is always the foot. It is an area where amateur models regardless of age are sought after. Women are paid per shot for their various poses and for some of the popular models who may fill a few niches (e.g. attractive soles plus long toenails), it can become a way to earn a living.

Luckily for foot lovers there is also a lot of free online material. YouTube for example has a large range of feet-focused videos, featuring celebrities such as Victoria Beckham, Kylie Minogue and Carmen Electra, as well as a range of videos of 'amateur' feet. Some podophiles indulge their fantasy by stealth, innocently rubbing their feet on some part of another person, or 'accidentally' stepping on another's foot. Others spend time at venues where people are likely to be barefoot, such as yoga classes, swimming pools or the beach. A thirty-something male foot lover admitted he went on holiday to Asia twice a year, because that way he could go to several foot massage establishments daily. This gave him hours of quiet enjoyment, as he could lie back surrounded by relaxed, dozing women having their feet massaged:

> For US$7 an hour I can have the time of my life. Picture this: I'm lying back in a comfy chair, opposite me are rows of chairs and while there are guys, there are always women, naked feet facing me. I pretend to close my eyes, but I'm still looking and most times I get a great close up of a woman's soles for a whole hour. To top it off, it's mostly a woman massaging another woman's feet so I'm getting a little woman on woman sex play. And the cherry on this cake—while I'm having this visual feast, another woman is kneeling in front of me massaging my own feet! I don't mind telling you, it takes all my self control not to come on the spot.

One 40 year old woman reported breaking off a serious relationship because of her ex-boyfriend's interest in his own feet. The man (who was also in his forties) could not eat a meal without taking his shoes and socks off and fondling his foot with one hand while holding his fork with the other. Doing this is often a fetishist's version of masturbation and is known as a 'foot jack', but that was a piece of information I decided not to share with the woman telling me the story. Other foot fetishists have no problem sharing their masturbation techniques, as this 30-something man relates:

> I got sick of the usual foot jack using my hands on my bare foot. So I started experimenting and found I could bend my leg and then rub my dick on the heel of my foot. That was nice. Then I got into some yoga and now I've found that because I'm a bit more flexible I can bend my leg and get it so that the whole length of my sole rubs against my cock and I can just do my thing!

Clichéd as this sounds, for some people this fetish will determine their vocation, as they deliberately seek employment in areas such as shoe sales or podiatry.

In America there are any number of special events, parties and foot clubs catering to foot lovers. At these foot clubs, men pay an entry cover charge and are then free to negotiate with the attending women to partake in various forms of foot play. Ordinary women are invited to attend the parties at no charge, provided they are happy to have men worship their feet, while others are paid by the club to provide the service. The women who work at these parties are paid to have their feet kissed, licked, fondled and massaged with no sexual intercourse involved. For example, The Foot Worship Palace in New York currently charges US$200 for 'private foot worship' sessions — after a US$150 entrance fee is paid.[30]

It is a popular assumption in Freudian psychoanalysis that an initial attraction to feet occurs because this is often the first part of the parent a toddler touches, and because parents frequently play with a young child's feet. However, there is another theory that foot fetishism is caused by the feet and the genitals occupying adjacent areas of the somatosensory cortex of the brain, possibly entailing some neural 'cross-talk'

---

[30] Price correct at time of printing.

between the two areas.[31] A third, simpler explanation is that feet are less threatening than genitalia, and so become attractive to those with what is termed 'coital difficulty.'[32]

Famous podophiles include the American writer F. Scott Fitzgerald, author of *The Great Gatsby*, and the Russian writer Fedor Dostoevsky, author of *Crime and Punishment* and *The Brothers Karamazov*.

Related Interests

Trampling, masochism, giantesses, stockings, shoes.

Jargon and Search Terms

Arch cleavage—a high arch is considered very sexy.
Foot boy—male foot fetishist.
Foot buddies—mutual foot play.
Foot job—using the feet to masturbate a man's penis.
Foot worship—the attention lavished on a foot, which includes massaging, sucking or smelling.
Hoof hugger—a strong or vigorous foot job (see above).
Pedalling—using the foot in a pedal action to bring a person to climax.
Shrimping—sucking on someone's toes for sexual gratification.
Toe cleavage—naked toes and most specifically the gap between the big toe and second toe.
Further Search Terms: foot worship, footsies.

---

[31] See the theory of neurologist Ramachandran (2002).
[32] Love (1992).

Trampling

> The first time I wasn't prepared for the pain, just
> horny. She stepped right up on me with killer
> pumps, put her right heel directly in my navel and
> stepped full weight without mercy. I thought I was
> going to die.
>
> —Trampling fan, anonymous

Some foot fetishists enjoy what is called trampling, the practice of one person stepping, walking or stomping on another. This is done in a variety of ways, ranging from a gentle, sensual barefoot technique to the trampler wearing stilettos, boots or other forms of footwear deliberately chosen to inflict pain. It is overwhelmingly a male interest and for those in the BDSM scene, is an act performed by a Mistress, Domme or Prodomme[33] on the submissive partner, and signifies that he is beneath the dominant, literally and symbolically. Sex is not part of trampling, though the man may masturbate from the memory of the experience.

Online forums on the topic of trampling are full of discussions on how to deal with the pain, and aspects of safety. Many men freely admit that while they find the fantasy erotic, they simply cannot deal with the reality of a grown woman in high heels stepping on their torsos, no matter how much they crave it. A common way for men to create the feeling of being trampled without actually being so, is to be a human footstool. The man crouches in an all-fours position and the woman rests her feet or legs on his back. This is said to create a feeling of feet on the torso without the pressure or danger of a person's full body weight. But despite the pain and very real possibility of injury, some men such as 34 year old Dan who regularly

---

[33] Also known as a Foot Domme when she specialises in feet.

pays to have it done by a professional, find trampling a totally irresistible practice:

> I remember well the first time I did a trampling session. I had fooled around and done it with bare-foot girls, but this time I wanted to do it professionally. It's hard to describe the sensation, but agony is close. When she pressed with her heel I felt a bit like I was being impaled, but it was like an agony that was also ecstasy, it was such a unique pain. I could barely take it, but the reward was more than worth it as the pain was slowly overcome by pleasure of deep subspace. The pain never disappeared mind you, but it is unique once you get past the initial feeling that you are being killed. I needed Vodka and painkillers when I got home, but I'd still do it again.

Many men who enjoy this in adulthood report of having early experiences and memories of playing with other children who were larger or heavier and being sat on or crushed, which they attribute to the beginning of their fascination with trampling.

YouTube has a large range of videos on both trampling and pedalling. Most of these videos are fairly benign, with the pedalling being done on the ordinary foot pedals of cars, and it is left to the imagination of the viewer as to what the woman really has under her feet.

Related Interests

BDSM, giantesses, crush fetish, feet, stockings, shoes.

Jargon and Search Terms

Ball stomping—have a woman stand or press on a man's testicles.

Carpet—man who likes to be trampled, e.g. offering to be 'a carpet'.

Trampler—the person (usually female), who walks, stomps or tramples on the body of another.

Long Fingernails/Toenails

> You know you are a nail lover when your number one choice for a great hangout spot is a nail salon.

While this can be a fetish for either long toe or fingernails, long fingernails are by far the most popular. It is an interest shared fairly equally between men and women. The women who invest their time, effort and money into maintaining long nails generally do so for their own pleasure, and if they find themselves with an adoring league of male admirers or the opportunity to sell video clips of their nails, this is often just a pleasant by product of their interest.

Men who love long nails on women are generally so fixated on the nails that the overall appeal of the woman is of very little interest. This means that a 30 year old man will bypass a woman his own age who may be tall, slim, blond and beautiful if she has short nails, while being drawn to an overweight 60 year old purely because she has extremely long, painted fingernails. As a result, women with long nails will often choose to avoid relationships with men who consider themselves fans, as they feel they are being overlooked as a person in favour of their nails. Some men are so fixated on female fingernails that they consider women with short nails to have what they derisively call "man hands", maintaining they cannot be 'true' women without long nails. Their obsessive interest means they live for sightings of long-nailed women in movies (Glenn Close as Cruella Deville in *101 Dalmatians*, or Dolly Parton and Barbra Streisand in, well, anything), in magazines, at shopping malls and even checking out women driver's hands at the traffic lights. Nail forums are full of excited sightings of long nails on a cashier, tollbooth attendant or a casual hand resting on a steering wheel—and while requirements for nail shape, colour and cleanliness (or otherwise) vary according to personal taste, the common denominator is that the nail must be outrageously long, manicured and painted.

Nail lovers like Phil, whose wife has ordinary length nails and hates nail polish, admits he will watch late night shopping channel for hours on end or sit through the re-run of a late night movie he had no interest in, because he knows the presenter or the actress regularly sports good nails. Then he goes to bed and makes love to his unsuspecting wife while fantasising about the nails he finally spotted after hours in front of the TV.

Length is influenced by personal taste, but it is generally agreed that a woman's nails needs to be 2.5cm or over to be considered long. However men who are interested in being scratched say a shorter 1cm or so in length is best for this. Acrylic or natural is also open to personal preference, however real nails are more highly prized and the Asian market in particular demands natural nail content. Natural nails twist once they reach a certain length, so this is the mark of an authentic nail. Natural nails may have an over or underlay placed on them to keep them strong and less likely to break, however the Asian nail lovers even object to this.

The look of the nails always provides the initial attraction and while for some that is all that's needed, many nail lovers need a little more hands on action. Depending on the man he may enjoy stroking or touching the nails in preference to more sexual areas of the body, or as a prelude to sex he may enjoy watching or sharing the rituals of nail maintenance, such as filing or painting the woman's nails. When the nail is included in sex, the man may enjoy sucking or caressing the nails, take pleasure in them digging into his body or in being scratched, or even having them inserted into his body. This may be anally or into the penis via the urethra. Depending on the man's tolerance this can even be the thumbnail. Men who enjoy this but do not have a long-nailed or willing partner, purchase stick-on nails or buy the cast-off nails from fetish models and insert these themselves.

Many of the men who enjoy a nail fetish become sexually aroused by the smell and look of nail polish. For these folk it can be a great honour to paint a partner's nails; and they may also enjoy the ritual of watching the nail polish dry. Jess is a plump, motherly woman who always has beautifully mani-cured fingernails—which as I discovered, was not just vanity:

> If I want to turn my man on, I know I just have to unscrew a bottle of polish and wave it under his nose. He is complete putty then, because he knows I might just let him watch while I paint my finger-nails. If he has been really good we do the toenails too, which turns him on even more. Sometimes I pretend to change my mind and the sad look on his face is just priceless.

While male nail lovers have personal preferences on nail polish colour, fetish models say that red is the most popular, which can become tiresome when the models themselves have other colour preferences.

Arinda Storm Weaver is 48 and a self described BBW (big beautiful woman) who has recently undergone a double mastectomy—she is also a fetish model with outrageously long finger and toenails. Since her mastectomy 3 years ago, she has made her living selling video clips of her fingernails, feet, long hair and herself smoking. There is never any nudity, and for US$6.99 you might see 6 minutes of Arinda tapping her nails on a table. Arinda arrived at her new career completely by chance. She was suddenly divorced after nearly 20 years of marriage and then found herself alone and facing a double mastectomy. After experiencing hormonal changes her nails had a real growth spurt, so during her recuperation she played around on MySpace and put up a couple of photos of her nails—a source of pride—as she has always kept long and well maintained. Within a short period of time of uploading nail photos she was getting emails from men around the world, which snowballed to hours of email to answer every night after work and repeated clamouring for more photos of her nails. When one of her fans sent some of her photos to a premier nail lovers website, her career as a fetish model began in earnest and she remains highly sought after. Arinda describes the fingernail lovers as in her words "mostly takers as in they want things done to them," in comparison to the toenail or foot lovers who are happy to pamper or worship the feet and toes. Anecdotally the fingernail and toenail lovers are nominated as a well read and gentlemanly group who are mostly in white collar professions. In Arinda's experience, the toenail lovers are willing to spend more money than others she deals with, and will think nothing of flying her places to visit them.

There are a number of discussion forums for nails as well as video clips for sale and pay-per-view websites. Content varies from women in day to day activities (these concentrate on the hand or foot and are not generally focused on the face, body or any nudity), such as tapping their nails, smoking, putting on lipstick or painting their nails; to the same activities with semi-naked or naked models. Women with long toe or fingernails can make a modest income on selected websites by sending in their toe or fingernail shots and being paid an average of US$25 for a handful of photos. Some nail models also sell their worn false nails or clipped natural nails. They are priced according to length and finger, so a 2cm nail from a little finger would be more expensive than a 5cm thumbnail, which is considered the premium nail on a woman's hand. Men who purchase discarded false nails or fingernail clippings either treat these items as collectables—like figurines or stamps, or use them as sexual devices (see above).

Because the requirement is for super long nails (this can mean nails over 30cms or 12 inches long) which require both time and patience to grow, many Western models wear false nails. This also allows them to sell the worn nails on a more regular basis. Men who collect false nails generally prefer to first see a model wearing the nails on website or in a video before they purchase them. Men who have a fingernail fetish may also have a related smoking fetish and those with a particular interest in toenails will generally have a foot fetish.

The women that grow long nails generally do so because they love themselves with nails, and like Arinda find that their passion for long and beautifully maintained nails naturally dictates their lifestyle and partner choices.

Related Interests

Smoking, feet, smell.

Jargon and Search Terms

Houseboy—a submissive man who takes care of all household tasks for a LNB so that her nails do not get damaged.
LNB—long nail beauty, a woman with very long fingernails.
Naked—nails that are unpainted.
Screaming nails—scratching nails on glass or similar squeaky surfaces.

Shoes

Shoe fetishists have similar likes to foot fetishists. A person with a shoe fetish becomes irrationally fixated on shoes or other footwear to the extent that the footwear becomes the principle focus instead of the wearer. They are also sometimes referred to as retifists, after the 17th century French author, Retif de la Bretonne, who had a well-known fondness for shoes.[34]

While shoes do carry sexual connotations in mainstream culture for both men and women, this is not usually considered to be shoe fetishism. The shoe fetishist becomes aroused when his partner wears shoes he finds alluring or if the shoes are somehow present during sex. A well-known come-on or turn-on for both foot and shoe lovers is the shoe dangle, where the woman crosses her legs and dangles the shoe from her toes. Other behaviours considered sexually provocative are shoe twirling or constantly slipping the foot in and out of a shoe.

For some shoe lovers, sexual climax with a partner may not be possible unless they can see, touch or smell shoes during sex. For others it is possible to reach sexual climax simply by having contact with the shoe of choice. Whether another person is wearing the shoe or the shoe lover is alone with it, common practices include smelling, licking and caressing the shoe as one would an erotic body part. Interacting with the shoe in this way is known as shoe worship and depending on the man may include cleaning the soles with his

---

[34]At that time it was common for men rather than women to wear high-heeled shoes. The fashion is believed to have begun with Louis XIV who was a short man. Heel heights for men became flat again after the French Revolution in 1789 as men were called to fight and heels were kind of impractical for that task.

tongue, or fellating the stiletto heel. Women who provide
these services professionally are known as Foot Dommes. To
most shoe lovers the smell of the shoe is reported to be as
powerful and sexual as the smell of a vagina can be to a
heterosexual man—and to a shoe fetishist, is sometimes even
preferable As one shoe lover explains:

> The foot has always been a phallic symbol and the
> shoe is therefore a symbol of the vulva. The male-
> female relationship between the foot and the shoe
> is obvious, ancient and very universal. The shoe is
> simply a hole and into the hole the foot slips. The
> foot of course simulates the penis slipping into the
> vagina.

Some shoe fetishists masturbate with their own shoes.
This is done by leaving the shoe on the foot, bending the leg,
and rubbing the penis along the edge of the shoe. Charles
Baudelaire the French poet, Casanova the famous womaniser
and Goethe the German poet were all shoe fetishists.

Shoe fetishists often fixate on extreme style shoes, which
may be specifically designed as either fetish or haute couture
wear; and many report a preference for women's high heels.[35]
High-heeled shoes or boots help to elongate the calf and create
a longer-legged appearance, which is generally considered to
be sexually attractive. High heels don't actually serve any
purpose, but most women's wardrobes contain at least one
pair. They were invented in Venice in the 16th century and
some were as high as 20 inches (50 centimetres). Shoes—in
particular boots—with some type of fur on them are considered particularly sexy, as in the imagination of the fetishist the
fur takes the place of pubic hair.

---

[35]A specific attraction only to high heeled shoes is known as
altocalciphilia.

One well-worn theory of shoe fetishism is that in many cultures an infant's experience of his mother may involve crawling around her feet, so he sees a lot of women's shoes. The theory goes that if sexual behaviour is imprinted at this time, it may lead to feet or shoes becoming the primary object of arousal.

Related Interests

Feet, trampling, stockings, smell, Femdom.

Jargon and Search Terms

Arch cleavage—a high arch is considered very sexy.
Shoe play/shoe tease—when the woman does things such as dangling a shoe from her toes, rocks her foot in the shoe or slides her foot in and out of it.
Shoe worship—licking or sucking the shoe and/or heel.

Stockings, Pantyhose

> You can see through it, but not completely—this makes it enticing, it builds anticipation and teases you by showing the shape but not the skin. Delicious.

Both shoe and foot fetishists may also have a fascination with stockings or pantyhose. Some foot fetishists have a preference for foot play when the foot is clad in nylon, finding it sexier to fondle, lick or kiss the partner's foot when she is wearing stockings. Men who enjoy hosiery report they are variously attracted to the polished, glamorous look of a woman in nylons and to what is described as the "silky and pleasing texture" of the fabric and how it defines and beautifies a woman's legs so they appear smooth and without blemishes.

Some men with a fondness for pantyhose report having a fascination with the gusset and how it sits so close to the woman's vagina. Many stocking fetishists enjoy the theatre of a woman donning or removing her stockings, or appreciate the level of glamour and sophistication hosiery adds to the wearer. Others prefer the partner to keep hosiery on during lovemaking, as the stocking and suspenders or stay-ups evoke thrills related to the woman's semi-nakedness. Many men report specifically enjoying the feeling of the nylon or silk-clad leg rubbing against their own skin during sex.

Men with a serious interest in stockings are very knowledgeable about brands, shades and deniers and usually have specific preferences in this respect as well as personal predilections in respect to fishnet, nylon, pure silk, glossy, seamed, stay-ups, lace-tops or reinforced heel or toe. There are many online forums specifically for discussing stockings and pantyhose and it is common to find it crossing over to foot worship sites.

As a subset of this interest, some men (without necessarily being cross-dressers) purchase stockings and pantyhose for themselves. Their enjoyment comes from handling the garments, masturbating with them or wearing them under their clothes. This has become such a burgeoning market that many hosiery chains are manufacturing sizes and cuts of pantyhose to suit the male body.

Related Interests

Feet, shoes, stockings, voyeurism.

Jargon and Search Terms

Pantyhose job—utilising feet or legs wearing pantyhose to bring a partner to climax.

Bite Me!

Mouth

A mouth fetish is a preoccupation with the (usually) female mouth. This interest can be as simple as enjoying watching a woman eat, yawn, or put on lipstick in a public place. It can also be a preoccupation with sexual acts involving a woman's mouth or experiencing sexual enjoyment from gazing into a woman's open mouth as part of consensual play. Mouth porn does not require nudity and examples might be a woman deliberately chewing food, dribbling saliva or simply opening her mouth wide for inspection:

> My wife knows only too well how I feel about women's mouths. Sometimes she toys with me and knowingly chews with her mouth open when we're in public. Other times when we are alone she will be more explicit. She'll look me in the eye and fill her mouth with something soft like cantaloupe or pear. Then she'll open it and show me the mashed up food, deliberately letting it dribble out of the corners. If I'm really in her good books she gives me oral sex with the food still in her mouth. It's so good I couldn't even describe it. (50-something male, personal exchange).

Catching a glimpse of the uvula is considered particularly exciting. The uvula is the small piece of tissue that dangles at the back of the throat and is visible when someone says "aah". Discussion forum contributors regularly debate the merits and attractiveness of various women's uvulas as well as sharing sightings of any so-called 'cute' ones. It is possible (though rare) to have the uvula pierced with a decorative ring similar to an earring. An attraction to the mouth (or a desire to show it) may be related to a belief that the woman is being deeply intimate in sharing a part of her body that is normally hidden. For others the interest may be tied to a Vore fantasy as they imagine being eaten by another being (see Voreaphilia). The Internet has made it easy to purchase and view all manner of mouth images or video clips, with an advertisement for one reading:

> Karyna has something to show you. It is her stretched out mouth. She really opens it up wide and then says 'ahh'. Watch me as I get my finger in there to press her tongue down to give you the best view imaginable of way down her throat.

Safety

There are health risks related to swallowing an uvula ring if it comes loose.

Related Interests

Tongue, teeth, dentistry, smoking, voreaphilia.

Tongue

> Susie starts off by wiggling her long, pink, wet tongue around. She then opens wide letting the spit dribble off its cute little tip in the process.
> —online advertisement for a tongue video

The majority of websites and discussion forums related to the human tongue specifically concentrate on female tongues, and there is an obvious crossover with mouth fetishism. Tongue porn, while it does include fellatio, licking and kissing, always includes images and videos of women involved in relatively benign activities such as eating—often food that requires licking or opening wide to show it in the mouth and on the tongue.

Tongue lovers are sexually excited by a tongue in the same way others react to genitals or breasts, and use Internet forums to share stories, swap pictures and buy videos. Discussions involve sharing the sighting of a lovely tongue or debating the merits of width, length and dexterity, and a woman's ability to curl or manipulate her tongue in unusual ways is always greatly admired. For this reason tongue fetishists are also very interested in the length of the sublingual frenulum, the membrane that attaches the tongue to the floor of the mouth, and its length influences the tongue's dexterity.

While just the glimpse of what is deemed a 'cute tongue' might be enough to get some tongue lovers aroused, aesthetic standards change according to personal taste. This varies from being attracted to tongues which are pierced or unpierced, rounded or pointy, pale coloured or rosy red, or stained from eating sweets or fruits. Variances aside, a long tongue is universally admired in this community, so methods of tongue lengthening are often discussed. Contributors to forums advise that lengthening can be accomplished by doing tongue yoga exercises or by manual manipulation known as milking, where the tongue is kneaded and massaged then pulled and twisted for a few minutes. A more radical way of achieving a long tongue is by having the sublingual frenulum cut by a doctor. While this will not actually lengthen the tongue, it will enhance its mobility, giving the illusion of length.

People who have a particular interest in tongues may also enjoy giving or receiving what are known as tongue jobs. In a tongue job, one person sucks or fellates the other's tongue as would be done to a penis. Conventional oral sex (often in preference to genital sex) is very popular, given the opportunity the tongue has to take a major role in proceedings.

Related Interests

Mouth, teeth, dentistry.

Teeth

Grandma, what big teeth you have...

A teeth fetish, also known as odontophilia: odonto (tooth) and philia (love of), refers to sexual arousal from teeth. This ranges from attraction to overly large teeth, very small teeth, crooked teeth or gapped front teeth, to having a preference for someone who wears braces, to getting aroused by watching a woman brush her teeth. It can even extend to an interest in tooth extractions or dentistry (see Dentistry below). An attraction to teeth is shared by both men and women. Non-standard teeth are particularly admired as they make a person different or more accessible. Some female celebrities who are admired on odontophilia Internet forums for their unusual or non-perfect teeth (giving the perception that a person is 'real') are Patricia Arquette, Lauren Hutton, Jewel and Kirsten Dunst, while the male singer Seal is considered by many women to have a highly sexy front gap. Gapped front teeth, while admired by both sexes, are considered particularly sexy by many women. A contributor to an Internet forum described how she specifically sought out gap-toothed men, because she particularly enjoyed what she called 'teeth sex'. This is the act of sliding the tongue between the other person's tooth gap in a simulation of genital sex. Women inserting some or part of their anatomy into the body of a man reverses the norm, so the novelty of simulating sex in this manner may be an unconscious part of the attraction.

Having a preference for biting in sex play is also related to teeth, as some people simply have a thing for teeth in terms of how they will look or feel when used to nip skin. Arousal from

42

biting or playful nipping on erogenous zones by humans is known as odaxelagnia. The actress Marilyn Monroe enjoyed biting and was said to be accomplished at drawing blood from the lips of her bed partners. Many animals are also known to enjoy nipping and biting as a form of arousal.

The Kinsey Reports[36] found that 55% of females and 50% of males responded erotically to being bitten, and the ancient Indian love manual, *The Kama Sutra* recommends it as an ideal form of foreplay. Biting can be taken to extremes, with some sex workers specialising in inflicting deep bites that break the skin. Men who report enjoying this type of painful biting are often powerful, well-paid individuals who attribute the pleasure to the brief moment when they lose control, as well as the shock to their system that both the pain and the novelty provokes

Related Interests

Mouth, dentistry, voreaphilia.

Jargon and Search Terms

Tooth cleavage—the gap between the front teeth.
Tooth sex—running the tongue between a tooth gap in simulation of sex.

Safety

Medical practitioners warn that any form of play in which the skin is broken and blood is involved carries inherent health risks in the form of communicable diseases such as HIV or Hepatitis.

---

[36]The Kinsey Reports (1948) and (1953) were considered highly controversial at the time of publication as they challenged conventional beliefs about human sexuality and discussed subjects that had previously been taboo in the 1950s.

Dentistry

> Sandra shows you her teeth with amalgam fillings,
> composite fillings and carious teeth—what a
> mouthful, I counted at least 9!
>
> —Advertisement pay-for-view dental website

The French novelist and infamous sexual pervert the Marquis de Sade went a little further than most with his interest in teeth, as it's said he enjoyed pulling out women's teeth prior to having sexual relationships with them.[37] It is possible that if he lived today he might be a member of a dental fetish group. Thanks to the Internet, discussion forums and websites exist on the topic of all things dental, including women showcasing their crowns, caps, fillings and tooth cavities, as people with a dental fetish enjoy the view inside the mouth. Unlike mainstream pornographic websites or magazines, most sexual dentistry models are shown from the neck up with no requirement for nudity or beauty, as the focus of interest is teeth that have had dental work. Preferred visuals are close-ups of the inside of the mouth and teeth, so the woman's face may never be seen. Her mouth will be wide open to allow the clearest possible view of crowns, caps and fillings; and the shots are mostly quite clinical. Unlike the teeth fetishist, the dental fetishist finds the teeth (in terms of shape, appearance, etc) of little interest unless they have some obvious dental work or require fillings.

Mouth braces are a specialist branch of dental fetish, with the overriding focus not on the teeth but in details of the braces. Most of the websites catering to this interest (with names such as 'metal mouth, 'brace babe' and 'brace face') operate as pay-per-view for videos and photos of attractive

---

[37]Sade (1935, reprint 1994).

girls in braces, getting measured for braces or getting braces fitted. As is the case with the general dentistry websites, images focus on the open mouth and not the body, but do include the face as it is related to the smiling or open mouth. Of interest are aspects such as whether the braces are metal, plastic, coloured or clear and whether they are on the top or bottom teeth. Braces lovers like to live vicariously and enjoy reading stories about girls having their braces fitted or visiting the orthodontist to have their braces tightened, adjusted or cleaned. There are also sites that marry a love for braces with pornographic imagery. These include oral sex performed by a girl or woman wearing braces, women with metal dildos next to their metal mouths or women cleaning their braces while naked.

Some erotic dentistry lovers have a corresponding interest in dental apparatus and enjoy seeing and discussing actual dental procedures. Erotic images in this case might be of a woman in a dentist's chair with various dental implements hanging out of her mouth, or of an attractive woman dressed as a dental nurse holding dental equipment.

Related Interests

Medical play, mouth.

Jargon and Search Terms

Braces babe—an attractive girl wearing braces.
Metal mouth, brace face—woman with braces.

Smoking

> I did not have sex with that woman.
> —Ex-US President Bill Clinton

Capnolagnia: kapnos (smoke[38]) and lagnia (lust) describes sexual arousal from watching those of the opposite (or preferred) sex smoke. Having a mental connection between images of smoking and sexual excitement is commonly a male interest. It does not describe a person who has a smoking addiction. The global media exposure of ex-President Clinton's novel use of a cigar as a dildo has heightened awareness that some folks consider cigarettes, cigars and smoking to be sexy. It is an interest with both a large Internet presence and a long history. American and European cinema (particularly the black and white films of the 1930s and 1940s) frequently construct a subtle type of sexual air around smoking. The German actress Marlene Dietrich was often seen posing provocatively with a cigarette, and who could forget Humphrey Bogart with a curl of smoke around his lips in the classic movie *Casablanca*? People who enjoy watching others smoke have varied preferences including:

- The inhale: an attraction to watching a woman bring a slim, white cigarette or plump, brown cigar to red lips, followed by watching her lips pursing and her cheeks hollowing as she draws in smoke. How the inhale is performed is also of interest. This can range from a pump, which describes taking a full drag to the lungs, or a double pump (taking two full drags in a row without exhaling), to simple dragging—the classic placing of the cigarette be-

---

[38]To be absolutely correct, the term kapnos refers to carbon dioxide, but is commonly used to designate the word smoke.

tween the lips and sealing them so the smoke may be drawn from the filter to the mouth.

- The exhale: other men find how the woman exhales her cigarette smoke to be particularly sensual. Preferences range from seeing women French inhaling, which is inhaling smoke that is in the mouth back through the nose (and over the lips) then exhaling through the nostrils, blowing smoke rings, or blowing a tight stream, which is an exhale pushed through lips which are barely separated.

- The manner in which the cigarette is held. For example, does the woman play with it, caress it with her lips, crook her fingers, tap the ash a particular way or use a cigarette holder?

- What women smoke: this varies from women smoking standard long white cigarettes or cigarettes with white or brown filters, to women who smoke strong cigarettes, women who roll their own, women who smoke cigarillos, women who smoke cigars and so on. Women smoking unfiltered cigarettes is particularly popular with the German market.

Despite the fact that smoking is socially unacceptable in most Western countries, the smoking fetish remains popular. The attraction to female smokers varies from men who make a sexual connotation of "cigarette as penis" in which the cigarette between a woman's lips suggests to them she wants a cock in her mouth, those who find the pout of her lips reminiscent of a vagina, and others who perceive a woman smoker as a rebellious risk taker or an independent spirit.

Smoking fetishists also enjoy activities such as 'being smoked', which involves having large amounts of smoke deliberately blown into their faces, being given oral sex while the woman smokes (known as the smoky BJ) and forced smoking when the man is held or in some way restrained while the woman blows smoke directly into his mouth, as this contributor to a smoking forum describes:

> She exhales straight into my mouth, so I can absorb her second hand smoke. The last time was the best. She was really brutal about it, exhaling hard into my mouth and making me take 2 or 3 drags at once. It was like I was smoking double, and she knew it. She got so turned on making me smoke twice as hard as her she gave me the last drag, then put her hand straight into her pants and made herself come.

Some smoking fetishists consider the smell of exhaled smoke from a woman's cigarette to be particularly sexy, maintaining that the smell of a woman's exhaled cigarette takes on a different and very pleasant smell after it has mingled with her feminine essence (see also Olfactophilia). Another reason for finding exhaled female cigarette smoke sexy is a belief that once the smoke has been inside an attractive woman it has somehow become imbued with her femininity or feminine spirit, and this is what makes it sexually exciting. It is very easy to purchase women's used cigarette butts on the Internet and men who purchase the used butts enjoy tasting them, sniffing them or holding them while masturbating.

Ashtray play in which the woman uses the man's open mouth as a literal ashtray or has him kneel in front of her so she may use his cupped hands for her ash and butts is common as well as 'dabbing', slang for the act of quickly touching the lit cigarette skin or clothing. However both of these acts are also practised as forms of domination and submission without necessarily being a part of a smoking fetish. Some smoking lovers enjoy watching woman put a lit cigarette to small insects while imagining it is their bodies being burnt (see also Crush Fetish), however videos harming living things are illegal in many countries.

Internet sites, videos and magazines catering to an interest in smoking run the gamut from showcasing clothed women smoking or posing with a cigarette to women blowing smoke into other men's or women's faces or genitals, women smoking while masturbating, masturbating with cigars, smoking while having sex, or smoking while giving oral sex.

Arinda is an older fetish model who sells clips of herself smoking as well as clips of her very long toe and fingernails and her long hair. Simple video clips of her smoking a cigarette without nudity or lewdness are her best selling items. She often makes clips based on what customers suggest, so that might be smoking in the car, smoking while quietly seated at a table or ones such as *Arinda Smokes: In The Snow*, costing US$5.99 and consisting of Arinda standing outside smoking a cigarette while snow falls gently. To a casual observer the clip is of an ordinary woman quietly enjoying a solitary cigarette. To the man who loves to watch a woman smoke, the act of Arinda dragging on the cigarette, the pout of her mouth, the exhale of smoke into the cold air and even knowing the brand she smokes are considered highly erotic.

Some smoking fetishists also have a balloon fetish, happily combining both interests by watching someone pop balloons with a lit cigarette. Videos, clips and stories catering to this combination are also freely available on the Internet:

> Mina chain smokes Marlboro Light 100s and keeps accidentally popping the balloons, which seem to be everywhere. Eventually Mina tells her guy 'for every minute that you keep me waiting, I'm going to pop one of these balloons'. True to her word, Mina's cig pops his latex lovelies with her all-whites, punishing him for keeping her waiting. She fearlessly pops all but two, with cigarette in hand,

between her lips, and even with her Bic lighter. For fans of smoking and balloons, this video is sure to satisfy![39]

Related Interests

Balloons, domination and submission, smell.

Jargon and Search Terms

Ashtray play—when a woman uses a man's open mouth or cupped hands as an ashtray.
Dabbing—quickly and lightly touching a lit cigarette to the body or clothing.
Smoked—to blow massive amounts of exhaled smoke onto another's face.
Smoky mouth—pornography that includes girls smoking.
Snap inhale—a method of inhaling where one opens his/her mouth, shows the smoke then quickly inhales, sucking all the smoke in. This is normally done by lifting the tongue up then opening the mouth and snapping the tongue down while inhaling.
Further Search terms: Forced inhalation.

---

[39]For sale on the balloon fetish site: www.theballoonfetishvideo.com.

Bless You

Nose

> As you can see, the tip is the part of my sexy nose
> that sort of reaches out from my face, striving to-
> wards *you*, I think. My long nose bridge and my
> nostril wings work so hard to hold up my nose tip
> for you to touch it. I wish *so much* that my tongue
> was long enough for me to lick my own tip with it.
> —advertisement for a pay-for-view website

Nasophilia: (naso) nose and (philia) love of, describes
sexual arousal from seeing or touching another person's nose.
Being turned on by noses is an interest shared by both men
and women. While nose lovers focus on the nose, they still
take into account the other person's overall look or their own
sexual orientation.

People with a nose fetish have specific preferences for
what they find attractive ranging from a long nose, a large
nose, a hook nose, an upturned nose, a nose with very large or
small nostrils or even a specific type of bridge. For some
people it is enough to look at images of their preferred style of
nose, or to join online groups to discuss sightings of what they
consider a sexy nose. Online forums[40] hold discussions about
noses in general and celebrities with sexy noses, and provide a
venue to share pictures of both men and women with long or
large noses. Some nose fetishists also enjoy viewing digitally
altered pictures of noses which have been made to appear
more pronounced, which is known as 'morphing' (think
Pinocchio's nose), as well as staged pictures of women with

---

[40] See for example the websites of The Big Nose Appreciation Page
(http://www.cyberium.net/bnguy/)
and Pinocchia (http://forums.pinocchia.com/).

some type of small implement sticking out of their noses—say a tampon, toy gun or cigarette. Nudity or pornography is generally not associated with an interest in noses, but when it is, the nose is always included, for example in a shot next to a penis or a breast. Most nasal mucus fetish sites include nudity as a standard, and this is discussed further under Mucus below.

Including the nose in foreplay or sex is referred to as noseplay. It may include touching, stroking or massaging the nose tip or nose bridge, licking the nose (known as nose kissing), sticking the tongue or fingers into a nostril, or sucking the nose and consuming nasal mucus. All of these activities are broadly known as 'a rim job'. Noseplay can also include using the nose as a penis, nose blowing (as a simulation of ejaculation) and watching someone sneezing, as this woman describes:

> If I really want to turn my hubby on I pretend to have an itchy nose and ask him to scratch it for me—he almost blows his load when he is doing it. While I find it all a bit hilarious, it makes him happy, so I figure why not...

Nose fetishists are almost universally opposed to rhinoplasty[41] because it removes many of the features that they find desirable. Celebrities such as Sarah Michelle Gellar, the singer Enya and the royal Mary, Crown Princess of Denmark, are especially loved by this community because they refuse to have their noses fixed.

Related Interests

Sneezing, nasal mucus.

---

[41] Alteration of the nose by surgery.

Jargon and Search Terms

A Pinocchio—a large nose.
Flower buds—nostril holes.
Morphing—digitally altered pictures of noses made to appear more pronounced.
Wings—the sides of the nose.

Nasal Mucus

Mucophagy is the term used to describe the consumption of human nasal mucus for erotic pleasure. It is done by one partner licking the mucus from the other's nostrils by digging it out with a finger then eating it, or by one partner blowing her nose and then allowing the mucus to be licked from her face. The partner can also deliberately sneeze into the mouth of the other, as described below by a young Asian man:

> She said, "watch my nose, I am going to sneeze into your mouth and I want you to eat the honey". I opened my mouth and she came close with wide spread nostrils. I was so excited and pleased to know I was getting her delicious honey. With her two fingers she pressed her nose and sneezed so hard that heaps of thick, white fluid came out from her two flower bud nostril holes. It went straight into my open mouth. I held it on my tongue for as long as I could, then I swallowed it with full pleasure.

Mucus is often a subset of the nose fetish but it can be an interest of its own. As is the case with the consumption of other bodily fluids such as menstrual blood, this practice may be used to demonstrate total acceptance, commitment, submission, worship or love of the partner.

Safety

This practice carries inherent health risks of contracting illness or disease from contact with bodily fluids.

Jargon and Search Terms

Nose juice, nose honey—nasal mucus.
Snot girls—girls on the Internet or in magazine shoots who simulate or engage in real play with nasal mucus.
Further search terms: booger girls, booger play, snot play.

Sneezing

A sneezing fetish is a sexual attraction to seeing or hearing another person sneeze.[42] The attraction can be attributed to a number of triggers: for some it is related to a nurturing impulse, as it gives a person the opportunity to take care of someone who is sick or has allergies. For others the attraction is in the loss of control that sneezing represents, which is seen as an allegory of orgasm. Watching a partner sneeze and go through all the stages—the build up to the sneeze, the expulsion and the release on completion of the sneeze—are highly sexy to a sneeze lover. Others are attracted to the momentary vulnerability of the person while sneezing, so their enjoyment comes from witnessing the person lose control:

> I don't know what it is, but at that moment when a woman sneezes she loses all self control. She can't talk, she can't do anything else but sneeze and that

---

[42]This interest parallels sexual orientation and the person sneezing must also be sexually attractive to the sneeze fetishist.

sneeze represents her complete lack of control in the same way a woman can lose herself temporarily in an orgasm. I get to share and witness that moment. It's magic.

Some men are attracted by watching a woman sneeze while gargling, as this exaggerates what is expelled; while others are fascinated with what the woman uses — a handkerchief, a tissue or her hand. Whilst most sneeze fetishists prefer witnessing spontaneous sneezing, there are some who are aroused by sneezing brought on by some type of deliberate irritation or stimulus. Some popular methods of inducing sneezing are inhaling pepper or inserting different implements such as cotton buds into the nostril; however, doing this is potentially dangerous.

Sneeze fetishists can be quite specific in their requirements, having particular likes and dislikes around vocalisation (e.g. soft, medium or loud), wetness of the sneeze (e.g. dry, average or wet), target of the sneeze (e.g. into hands, tissue or uncovered) and induced or genuine sneezes, with 'genuine' being more prized by the true fetishist. Repetitive sneezes are also highly regarded, with most fetishists enjoying hearing or seeing continuous sneezes or sneezing fits. One sneezing website I visited offered 165 different sound recordings of sneezing; each with a description, such as "the strong sneeze", "the wet sneeze", "the nasal sneeze", "the explosive sneeze", or "the little girl sneeze". In stories about sneezing, the climax of the story is always the sneeze itself, and to that end sneeze erotica goes to a great deal of trouble to describe the sneeze, including the textual representation of the sound with descriptive phonetic spelling, eg "ah-ah-ah-choo", "ha-choo", or "huh-choo", when there are no audio clips available.

Safety

Sticking anything up your nose or inhaling irritants can be dangerous.

Jargon and Search Terms

Hanky girls—women who deliberately sneeze for erotic purposes.
Inducing—inducing sneezes by using irritating substances.

Rapunzel, Rapunzel...

An enchantment with hair includes hair on the head, no hair, body hair, body hair removal and the rituals surrounding these practices.

Hair

> I am a Master Barber and ladies I'm looking for women who love to cut, style and chat all things hair.
>
> —Online singles advertisement

Trichophilia: (trichos) hair and (philia) love of, more commonly known as hair fetishism, is a need to see or touch human hair for sexual arousal. While this can be body hair, it is most commonly hair on the head. Many feminists consider long hair on a woman symbolic of being tied down or tethered, but hair fetishists treat it with reverence, respect and awe. Hair as a sexual device is well known in media, and a woman playing with her hair while holding eye contact with a man is globally recognised as a sexual signal. American author Ernest Hemingway is said to have had a lifelong erotic obsession with hair, and frequently found ways to slip references to hair into his novels.[43]

Erotic hair activities vary according to personal tastes. Many hair enthusiasts include hair in foreplay, fondling, smelling or brushing it as a prelude to sex. Other common activities include braiding or cutting hair, masturbating with or ejaculating into the partner's hair, or the simple ritual of washing then drying the partner's hair, as this married man in his late sixties describes:

---

[43]Eby (1999).

My beautiful wife is totally cool about me washing her hair, massaging her scalp and then drying it—in fact she loves it. But she acts like she is doing me a really big favour when she gives me this privilege. I don't mind, in fact I prefer her having this attitude as it has ensured that for the last 36 years it has remained our special ritual and not just an act of cleansing.

Hair in sex play usually needs to be long, particularly for a hair blow job, when the woman fills her mouth with her hair and then fellates her partner. When the woman wraps her hair around his penis and he masturbates with it, this is known as a 'silky'. If the woman's hair is not long, the man may simply ejaculate into her hair or enjoy pulling her hair during sex. A novel way of having 'hair sex' (which evidently works best with longer and thicker hair) is to put the hair into a loose ponytail. The man then slides his penis into the middle of the ponytail and simulates sex. The penis is held snug by the loose elastic and the man holds his hand around the ponytail so that his penis is encased in hair.

There are special Internet dating sites[44] which help people to locate a love interest fitting a preferred hair profile, such as a prospective partner with long, short or curly hair, or hair that is a specific colour or style. Some hair fetishists also look for partners who enjoy specific hair play activities, such as hair styling, colouring, perming and even cutting.

Mutual hair cutting is considered to be one of the ultimate experiences of those who enjoy erotic hair-play. Describing her pleasure in this practice, one woman said it was something she only enjoyed when in a relationship, as it involves a high degree of trust and intimacy. For her it was a deeply erotic thing which she only shared with that special someone. Many

---

[44]See for example www.hairpersonals.com.

women, particularly in the lesbian community, report a fascination for mutual hair cutting (in particular of long hair) as part of foreplay:

> Look I just can't explain it. Hacking through hair is just such an addictive thing. The sound, the 'crunch, crunch crunch' of scissors on hair sends me wild, whether that is me cutting my own hair, my partner's hair or she cutting mine.

A man in his late fifties posting to a hair lover's forum explains his interest in mutual haircutting:

> If you have never tried it don't knock it. I can't count how many times it has sparked a weekend long bedroom marathon with my dear, late wife. We were married for 30 years and it was something we never stopped enjoying, even the build up to growing the hair we would later cut for each other.

The allure of cutting hair either by stealth or with permission has been around for some time. In the early nineteen hundreds sexologist Havelock Ellis conducted a case study on what he termed "a young man of good family" who developed "an impulse to cut off girls' braids and would gaze admiringly at the long tresses and then clip them off with great rapidity"; he did this in some fifty cases before he was caught and imprisoned.[45] In a review of what he terms neurotic behaviour, another early sexologist and psychoanalyst Otto Fenichel, described the braid cutter as a

---

[45]Ellis & Bracala (1975).

common type of sadist, maintaining that the braid was a depiction of the penis.[46]

Non-sexual hair videos focusing on long hair being brushed, shampooed or styled, contain no nudity or sex whatsoever but are as popular as the more pornographic ones for sale. Middle-aged Arinda Storm Weaver (who is also a smoking and nail fetish model), successfully sells simple, short videos focusing on the day to day care of her very long blond hair. Her three minute clip titled *Hair Care Outside* sells for US$3.99:

> After a fresh shampooing, I went outside to give
> my hair a nice brushing in the open air. I do hope
> you enjoy watching it sway back and forth.

Hair erotica includes all the activities that hair fetishists enjoy, such as hair masturbation and ejaculation into hair, as well as haircuts, hairdressing or head shaving. There are many websites selling clips and videos which portray hair in a pornographic way, as this teaser for one such clip promises:

> Not only can you see my silk wrapped around his
> cock, but you can hear me as I suck the cum from
> my hair afterwards.

Baldness is considered a part of hair fetishism. While this may sound like an oxymoron, an interest in the partner being bald is tied in with erotic fantasies and activities related to head shaving or hair cutting, and is not exclusively related to having a partner who is genetically bald. The activities leading to a bald head are often as prized as the end result of enjoying the look and feel of the partner's head:

---

[46]Fenichel (1945).

> I really like braiding hair, ponytails, brushing, shampooing...but I really want to be bald, this is my secret dream, to meet a pretty lady who will buzz and shave me! (Lesbian seeking a partner on Hairpersonals.com).

It is not unusual for a woman to prefer a bald heterosexual partner, however online personal sites also list large numbers of lesbians searching for bald female partners, as well as heterosexual men looking for women who either want to go bald or are bald by choice. For lovers of a bald head, shaving the partner's head is considered the Holy Grail of hair activities. For that reason hair porn that marries head shaving with sex is extremely popular.

Trichophilia is often confused with the medical condition Trichotillomania (TTM), an impulse control disorder in which the sufferer has an urge to repeatedly pull out body hair, including scalp, facial, nose or pubic hair, eyelashes or eyebrows.

Jargon and Search Terms

A silky—when hair is wrapped around the penis for masturbation.
Hair BJ—giving oral sex with hair in the mouth.
Silk—hair.

Hair: Pubic and Underarm

> Hey baby, get over here, I really fancy some pit.

An attraction to pubic and body hair is a separate area of hair interest. There is a wide array of pornography available that focuses on women with a lot of pubic hair, as well as erotic writing related to men's fantasies or real-life experiences with hirsute women. It is very easy to find websites and discussion forums that focus on glimpses of body hair on celebrities, such as the hair between Alicia Key's breasts, the hair on Tyra Bank's calves, Beyonce's underarm re-growth shadow or even the stray hairs on Madonna's top lip. Lovers of body hair have preferences for where the hair is located, so that might be hairy thighs, forearms, back, chest or nipples— the small square of hair that appears above the buttocks on some women is affectionately known as "the welcome mat". It is probably more unusual than commonplace for male Westerners to admit to a liking for hairy partners, and may well be a type of backlash against the current fashion that mandates women wax, shave or depilate their pubic areas away:

> It was a real treat in this day of shaved pussies to run my fingers through a thick, black mat of pubic hair—you forget how a real woman is supposed to feel—like a woman, and not like some pretend little girl. (Male, mid twenties)

> Seeing some pubes coming out of the side of underwear or a bikini is just a bit left of centre, if you know what I mean. When my wife hasn't waxed for a while she gets these stray hairs sticking out— but I have learned to say nothing and just enjoy the view, because it embarrasses her and before you know it she will be waxing it all off and my fun is over! (Male, late forties).

An attraction to hairiness is not just limited to men, as some women are also particularly attracted to men with hairy bodies, finding it a sign of virility or masculinity. Angie is now 43 but still clearly remembers the first time she realised hairy men attracted her. She was 15 years old and on her way to school walked past a bus-stop where a number of older Catholic school-boys waited every morning. One of them was of Italian descent and even with his school tie done up had visible black hairs peeping over his collar:

> It was a shock, it was so sexual. But in a way that confused me. I never spoke to this boy but I could barely tear my eyes away from him and I lived for the days I would spot him. I'm in my forties now, but if I catch a glimpse of a bit of hair curling over the top of a loosely buttoned business shirt...pick me up from the floor because I've died and gone to heaven. Neck, chest, underarms—give me a big, hairy bear anytime!

When the particular attraction is underarm hair this is known as hircusophilia or axillism (axilla) armpit and (ism) act. For some men this provokes an erotic response because a display of underarm hair is connected to thoughts of pubic hair—as one man describes it, looking at underarm hair makes one think of "a woman's other soft and hairy mound". While some people find enough enjoyment just in looking at hairy armpits[47], others get an erotic charge from inhaling the scent of sweat and pheromones emanating from underarm hair. Others take it a step further and enjoy licking the armpit area or for masturbation , finding it an ideal pseudo sex organ:

> I think that hairy armpits on women are such a turn-on. I guess for me it's like having two extra pubic areas to play with—what a great bonus, I just want to suck those puppies dry!

---

[47] Many underarm lovers prefer the term underarm, as it has sexier connotations than 'armpit'.

Underarm sex is practiced more commonly in Latin American and European countries where underarm hair is culturally acceptable. It is also a viable way for couples in devoutly religious countries to have a form of guilt- and disease-free sex. Those who enjoy it report benefits that include being able to easily vary the pressure and action, and say that the stimulation of the hair rubbing the penis closely approximates vaginal sex. One person I spoke with described the best time to have armpit sex as within a day or so of the woman shaving, when a fine regrowth of hair created a light and pleasurable friction.

An attraction to armpits is shared by the heterosexual and gay communities.[48] Underarm erotica includes stories, videos and images of masturbating in, licking, kissing or showing off armpits and there are various preferences that range from hairy or stubbly to plump, young, thin or old armpits. Devotees on armpit forums enjoy discussing the merits of various types of underarms, including hair length, colour, texture and smell, as well as sharing sightings and experiences. As one man commented:

> I think that there is NOTHING more exciting than
> a woman with hairy pits. A hairy woman in a tank
> top with her arms above her head is just magical,
> and the best surprise is when I catch sight of it un-
> expectedly.

A love of underarm hair is also not limited to men. There is a Facebook group run by a woman called 'Sweat baby sweat. Men's armpits get me excited and a little bit high' and in her introduction she writes:

---

[48]See for example www.armpit-sex.com.

Men's armpits are beautiful, their armpit hair tends to be sparse and wispy and soft, the skin also soft from where it's never been shaved...

Of the 85 members on the day I visited, approximately half were women (or purporting to be women). Underarm smell is often a large part of this interest and in this respect it can cross over to olfactophilia (a fetish for smells).

For some men the attraction to a hairy body, in particular underarms, lies in a perception that the woman has a strong, rebellious or adventurous spirit, or that she is exotic and interesting, not conforming to current Western standards. In Europe, where many women would not consider having hairless underarms, this topic would not even merit discussion, as for them it is 'business as usual'. Other men report being turned off or repelled by hairless women, believing their appearance too child-like to be considered erotic (particularly when the hairless area is genital).

In his writing on human sexuality Freud[49] theorised that there was "no doubt" that women wore fur because it reminded them of pubic hair (Doraphiliacs take note!) and the painter and Tahitian enthusiast Paul Gauguin was evidently so enamoured of pubic hair that he kept a few from each of his lovers as keepsakes.

Jargon and Search Terms

A Jackson Five—hairy armpits, in reference to the singing group 'The Jackson Five' who all had large afro hairstyles.
An axminster— a very hairy pubic area (from the brand name of a popular carpet).
Au naturel—women who don't shave or depilate their bodies.
Bagpiping—the act of masturbating with a partner's underarm.

---

[49]Freud (1905).

Bear trapper's hat—lush or thick pubic hair.
Boob pubes—hair around the nipples.
Furrie ladies—women with lots of body hair.
Sweaty caves—sweaty, hairy underarms.
Treasure trails—long pubic hair.
Winter-warmer/fur burger—hairy pubic area.

Hairlessness (Genitalia)

> I love the feel of shaved genitals both mine and my partner's. I enjoy going down on him when he is hair free and could do this for hours. I also feel so much more sexy when I'm hair free.

When a person is aroused by or has a preference for hairless genitalia, this is known as being acomoclitic. This is not exclusively a male preference as many women prefer being with a man who has removed his pubic hair, believing that hairlessness is 'cleaner' or because they enjoy the novelty of the situation. One beautician I spoke with says that every summer they encounter more men requesting genital waxing, known colloquially as manscaping or 'husking the corn'. As a result, her salon has recently employed a male waxer as some female beauticians do not feel comfortable with, or proficient in waxing male genitals. As this man relates, hair removal is not just a young man's game:

> I'm in my fifties and I've been removing my body-hair for about 15 years now. I either shave or wax my balls, my shaft, the bush, my ass and my chest. The wife loves it, it feels great and it has rejuvenated our sex-life. It might be just me, but I feel my penis looks bigger this way and that makes me feel more confident sexually and therefore makes me more self-assured in bed.

In America during the 1950s it was considered improper to publish photos or show films in which women's pubic hair could be seen. To get around this censorship rule, filmmakers and publishers of erotic material featured women without pubic hair, so a lack of pubic hair signalled that the woman was a porn star, a stripper or an erotic dancer. In the nineties a preference for little or no pubic hair became fashionable in the West—although Brazil's swimwear has long dictated brevity as mandatory for pubic hair styles. As a result, the routine removal of pubic hair by the average housewife means that partially or completely depilated genitalia has become so commonplace that the practice is no longer considered unusual.

Waxing for women can include the bikini line, pubic crest or triangle, mons, external labia and perineum. The ordinary bikini wax takes the hair away from the sides of the bikini, i.e. any hair that is visible from the sides and top of the panty line, while the Brazilian wax goes a step further, removing hair from the labia, perineum and bum crack. As there is no age limit on waxing your pubic area, beauticians report girls as young as 14 requesting complete removal of their pubic hair. A male Brazilian wax includes waxing of all or some of the bikini line, penis shaft, scrotum, perineum, and pubic crest.[50]

Removing the hair from the pubic triangle is not part of the standard Brazilian wax. If the pubic triangle is included this may be called a triple X (or just xxx), a hollywood wax, a full Brazilian or the sphinx. If only a small amount of pubic hair is left, there are various styles such as the landing strip, the teardrop or a heart-shape. Most people who try Brazilian waxing tend to become fans, citing benefits such as feeling much cleaner, enhanced sensitivity in the genital area, "feeling sexier" or believing it spices up their sex lives.

---

[50] The tuft of hair above the penis.

For the most part people who remove body hair do it as part of their regular maintenance schedule, either alone in the bathroom or at a beauty salon. But for some the act of pubic hair removal is of itself a sexual thrill. In this case the universal choice is shaving, and with it comes a whole ritual related to hair removal. As these comments show, the act of shaving can be an integral part of sex, with either the woman being shaved or both partners shaving each other:

> The hubby and I like to shave each other's privates. He likes some left like a landing strip, but I prefer it all off. It definitely adds spice to regular sex, and we look forward to it when we have a shaving night booked. I get so turned on when he lathers me up and starts rubbing in the shaving cream or oil and the drag of a razor blade against that sensitive skin can't be beat. Afterwards we both really like it when we feel the freshly shaved skin upon skin....what a heavenly feeling. Great for masturbation too—not to mention oral!

Katie is in her thirties and says she has engineered shaving into foreplay with her partners since she began having sex. She generally finds new partners open to it, if not a little surprised by her request. As she always keeps herself shaved (and not waxed) she says it makes it easy to bring the topic up, as the hair grows back fairly quickly and needs maintenance:

> I just love the delicious feeling of the razor gliding so close to my lips. I have my favourite brands— there is no point buying some rubbishy plastic one as they are more prone to nicking. You really have to trust your partner to be careful and pay attention, so the first time with a new man there is a kind of virginal aspect to it as I lay there quietly and he carefully and gently ministers to me. They

are universally very careful as they are so scared of cutting me, so this makes the first shave with a new partner the most memorable. Once I get to know them better I let them do my butt-crack, but mostly I get a trusted girlfriend to take care of this, as I can't really do it properly myself. And trust me, if you don't keep doing it, the itch back there of new hair growing will drive you nuts!

Some female sex workers allow clients to shave them for a fee prior to sex, and for the customers who enjoy this, it is considered to be the most erotic part of the service.

Safety

Waxing done by trained professionals is considered the safest way of removing pubic hair, as putting hot wax on your own genital area could lead to accidents and shaving can leave a person prone to cuts and infections, as well as creating itchy regrowth in what is a sensitive area.

Jargon and Search Terms

Husking the corn—slang for waxing the penis.
Manscaping—waxing or shaving the male pubic area.
Smoothie—someone who has no pubic hair.
White tiger—slang for a woman without pubic hair.

Thanks for the Mammaries

Have ye beheld (with much delight)
A red rose peeping through a white?
Or ever mark'd the pretty beam
A strawberry shows half-drown'd in cream ?
Or seen rich rubies blushing through
A pure smooth pearl and orient too?
So like to this, nay all the rest,
Is each neat niplet of her breast.

　　　　　—*The Nipples of Julia's Breast*, Herrick (1634)

Breasts

Mammagynophilia: mamma (mammaries), gyno (woman) and philia (love of) most commonly known as breast fetishism, describes a pronounced sexual interest in female breasts focusing on either the look, shape, size or texture. Unsurprisingly, it is believed to be the most common sexual obsession for men around the world, so it can be difficult to work out if it is a preference rather than a fetish. In clinical literature of the 19th century, a focus on breasts was considered a form of paraphilia, but in recent times it is considered normal except when a preoccupation with breasts overshadows the relationship with a partner.[51] For some breast lovers visual presentation is highly important, so the breast must be dressed or presented in a particular way (e.g. in a nursing bra, with nipple rings or in lace and ribbons); while for others it is more important that the breasts are a specific size or shape, such as large, small, flat or rounded. This can be so important that sex may not be possible unless the breasts fulfil these requirements. Other men have little interest in the breast itself, but have distinct preferences with regard to nipple shape, size

---

[51]Lattierer (1998).

(puffy, or flat), colour (very dark to pale) and presentation (tattooed or pierced areole). When the fascination centres on nipples it can also extend to a requirement for inverted nipples, unusually long or thick nipples, or even lactating nipples.

For others the important aspect is not the appearance but that the breasts are the focal point of the sex act. Mammary intercourse is commonly referred to as a tit wank, tug job or titty fuck. It is done by the man placing his penis between the woman's breasts, which are then squeezed together, and the man slides his penis up and down between the breasts to mimic intercourse. This is a popular way for couples in devoutly religious countries to participate in a disease and guilt-free form of sex.

Breast fetishism may be linked to lactophilia, a sexual interest in human breast milk. As well, there can be some crossover to balloon fetishism, as the breast is considered to have similar traits to that of a latex balloon, given its shape, malleability, softness and how the balloon also has a 'teat'.

Jargon and Search Terms

Airbags—breast implants.
Between the hills—sex between the breasts.
Champagne glass tits—breasts that look like the silhouette of a champagne glass.
Cute-obagos—term used to describe natural breasts, which are 'cute' and deemed not too big and not too small.
Globe tits—breasts that look like the silhouette of a perfect hemisphere and because of their perfection are generally the product of surgery.
Puffies—swollen, long or large nipples.
Yummybagos—breasts that are considered particularly attractive.
Udders—lactating breasts.

Related Interests

Adult baby, adult nursing, human cows, balloons.

Adult Nursing

> I haven't lactated in about 6 years but I loved the
> feeling of nursing. My husband wasn't into adult
> nursing back then, but maybe I can twist his arm
> and get him to try it again. If not, well maybe there
> is someone out there who would like to try it with
> me?
>
> —Advertisement on an Internet site

Lactophilia: (lacto) milk, and philia (love of)[52] also known
as erotic lactation, adult nursing and milk fetish, is a term for
sexual arousal caused by lactating breasts. Men and women
who engage in adult breastfeeding are said to be in an adult
nursing relationship (ANR) and sexual pleasure from this
activity is reported as mutual. Those who enjoy adult nursing
say it leads to a very close and mutually dependent relationship as a regular and frequent schedule must be maintained
both in order to stimulate continued milk production and
relieve engorgement. Women who are not pregnant or
lactating naturally, but want to begin or maintain an adult
nursing relationship, often take drugs and herbs known to
bring on lactation. Women who manage to bring on milk say
that aside from taking supplements, it takes prolonged
massage and manual manipulation of the breasts several times
a day as well as the use of breast pumps in order to induce
lactation. Because it requires a great deal of perseverance to
lactate, women who have recently breastfed a child and wish

---

[52]This is also sometimes referred to as galactophilia.

to continue with adult partners generally find the transition to feeding an adult easiest.

Interest in erotic lactation commonly develops after a baby has been breastfed in the home and men stumble across it when they help a partner relieve engorgement. If one or either partner finds it sexually arousing the practice continues after the child is weaned. There is little research on why some grown men choose to suckle other than for sexual stimulation; but online chat room conversations reveal that for some there is a direct link to the feelings of warmth, safety and love they associate with being breastfed as infants. Adult breastfeeding may also be associated with infantilism (adult baby play).

While most people who enjoy an ANR relationship describe it as a monogamous, consensual and mutually beneficial practice, some men report feeling ashamed about enjoying breast feeding as they feel it places them in an inferior, submissive role. Harry has been with his current partner for six years and has two grown children from a previous marriage. He discovered adult breastfeeding after the birth of the first child with his new partner. It began by accident as she was loath to wean their child, despite the fact that he was approaching his third birthday. She had tried to stop evening feeds but her breasts ached at night as her milk production continued. Harry didn't want her to continue feeding the toddler given the boy's age, so he found himself as he puts it, "helping her out", but has yet to come to terms with his new interest:

> To be honest, most times I hate myself after I have breastfed. I want to do it; it turns me on, but leaning into my partner's chest and suckling changes the dynamic. While I don't think of her as my mother, the fact that she is holding and feeding me from her body is all very strange. But because the best climaxes of my life are when one of us mas-

turbates me while I suck down that milk, it makes
it worth the weird head trip afterwards.

Many women report experiencing a feeling of power from
seeing their partner 'dependant' on their breasts, and enjoy the
role reversal of being the dominant partner. While breastfeeding creates a sexual element because of psychological factors, it
can also allow the woman to experience highly erotic sensations as a direct result of the strong suckling. In a study
conducted in 1999, approximately 33% to 50% of mothers
found breast feeding erotic, and among them 25% felt guilty
because of this reaction.[53]

A number of Internet sites facilitate contact between
women who either are lactating or wish to lactate and men
who are seeking milk, with approximately half the advertisements placed by women. As well, there are professional
brothel services that cater to adult nursing males. The UK
comedy hit *Little Britain* (2005, 2008) featured a character called
Harvey who was a 30-something engaged man who insisted
his mother breastfeed him in all manner of public venues and
on social occasions.

For couples who do not have the time, patience or perseverance to start and maintain lactation, a fantasy version of
this type of play is achieved by dripping cream onto the
woman's nipples and then sucking or licking it off.

Related Interests

Adult baby, breasts.

Jargon and Search Terms

ABR—adult breast feeding relationship.
ANR—adult nursing relationship.

---

[53]Levin (2006).

Lactation prostitution[54]—breast feeding services offered in brothels by lactating women.

Milkman—a man who gets erotic pleasure from suckling a woman's breasts.

Wet-nurse/Milkmaid—a nursing woman.

---

[54]Giles (2004).

Body Type

Fat Admirers

> Fat girls give the best head because they're **always** hungry.
>
> —Encyclopediadramatica.com

Fat admirer (FA for short) is a term used for male heterosexuals who are sexually attracted to large partners. Research shows that fat admiration is overwhelmingly a male interest;[55] however, women can also be FAs and are referred to as FFAs (female fat admirers). The Internet has helped the culture of fat admiration blossom into a world-wide community, with members' interests ranging from size acceptance and seeking fat life partners to fat-pornography and force-feeding fantasies. The homosexual community also shares this interest and here the fat admirer is known as a chubby chaser[56] and the fat person as a 'bear'. Most gay chasers tend to favour a physique that centres on a large belly and a small penis, although the average FA—whether gay or straight—is generally of medium size himself.

Activities FAs enjoy include choosing to date or have relationships exclusively with fat women, preparing meals and snacks and watching the overweight partner eat, measuring or weighing the partner, seeking out images and stories related to fat women and accessing pornography or erotica centred on fat people. Because social disapproval of fat women remains strong in Western society, some FAs keep their admiration as an online fantasy and never actually date an overweight partner, or if they do date it is frequently a clandestine relationship kept away from friends and family.

---

[55]Blickenstorfer (1996).
[56]Though this term is sometimes also used by heterosexuals to describe themselves.

Fat admiration has become so popular that many main-stream online dating sites now have links for BBWs—big, beautiful women. Online erotica and pornography centred on the large woman is also prolific, with a diverse audience base, of whom many are Western men and not just the stereotypical African cultures.[57]

Fat admirers are universally fascinated by the way a fat body moves, feels and looks. Some FAs describe touching fat as very soothing, and love the feeling of sinking into the other person's layers of fat. For some it is a nice reminder of being a small child pressed against the mother's breast. Others are turned on by the novelty of the woman's physical weight and girth, and love grabbing handfuls of buttock or thigh:

> I love her skin, it is heavy, soft and silky. When she lays flat her breasts spill down to her back and her thighs spread over most of the bed, so there is barely any room for me. I feel like I am lying in a soft creamy pool of flesh…(Contributor to a FA forum)

While some men say the major turn-on is touching such a large amount of silky, soft or spongy skin, FAs and their partners also acknowledge that folds of fat and skin bring their own challenges in the way of sweat and body odour building up in the folds, skin mottling in an unattractive way and chafing and rashes or ulcers forming as a result of so many fat layers. It is such an issue that most fat admiration websites host discussions around skin problems, allowing members to swap advice on what creams and lotions work best in these situations.

---

[57]A recent American movie *Phat Girls* (2006) also dealt with these themes in a comedy which was based on the pursuit of plus-sized American women by Nigerian men.

While non-FAs perceive fat as a barrier to sex, either physically or aesthetically, FAs see this very differently. Because a large belly or fat thighs may impede access to the woman's genitals, FAs find it a turn-on to accommodate the fat and gain access to the woman's vagina, but sex with a fat partner can present challenges or require uncommon techniques. As one fat admirer explained to me, if the woman is extremely overweight her labia also increase proportionally, so unless the man has a long penis, penetration is very shallow and sex occurs mainly with the vaginal lips. Position problems are likely to be more of an issue to the woman than to the man, because unless the man finds a way of accessing her vagina satisfactorily, the woman may have a diminished experience. This does not generally pose a problem to the man, because even if he does not end up having conventional intercourse, he gets enough stimulation from rubbing or masturbating against the woman's curves and mounds. Tammy, a self described "pear shaped fat woman", offers the following advice on the Dimensions magazine web site, which bills itself as celebrating the fat lifestyle:

> Intercourse isn't always necessary. I have so many places on my body that are soft and moist and smooth that a man can make love to, especially if we have no protection and can't practice safe sex vaginally. I had one lover who thought just being under my stomach was heaven and could climax almost immediately. Many men, non-FAs included, also like it between the breasts.[58]

Another problem specific to 'big love' is that the woman's fat thighs or belly can make a condom slip off, especially after climax, making safe sex practices precarious. Fat lovers need to be aware of this, and take appropriate care.

---

[58]www.dimensionsmagazine.com.

While many fat women are cautious during love-making and fear that they may hurt a lover with their bulk, a large number of FAs talk about the turn-on of feeling a fat woman's weight on top of them. Some FAs are therefore interested in BBW facesitting or smothering, which involves images or play based on the woman sitting on or otherwise squashing her partner, particularly enveloping his head, with her buttocks; as well as enjoying the Giantess fantasy.

Related Interests

Giantess fantasy, fat feeders, smothering, facesitting, ass worship.

Jargon and Search Terms

A plumper—an affectionate term for a fat person.
Apron or belly apron—the belly when it becomes large and overhanging and looks like an apron.
Bear—a fat gay man.
BBW—big, beautiful woman.
BBBW—big beautiful black woman.
Child of size—a fat person.
SSBBW—exceptionally large (super size) woman.
Table muscle—Gay slang for the belly.

Fat Feeders

> Try frying chicken in a batter and flour, taking it
> out again, battering it and flouring it and frying it
> again. VERY fattening hee hee hee. Also if you
> want soda, you can remove the fizz by putting
> sugar into it so it doesn't fill her up and she can
> drink more—and an added bonus—all those lovely
> extra cals from the sugar! Happy gaining.
> —Rubens Fat Feeder website

The feeder culture is about encouraging a partner to gorge
themselves on food so that they become as fat as possible. Men
who want to feed women are known as feeders, and women
who like to be fed and have a goal of continued expansion are
called feedees. This is generally a consensual practice, with the
man purchasing, preparing and feeding the woman with the
goal of obvious weight gain. The gay equivalents are encou-
rager for feeder and gainer for feedee.

As well as experiencing erotic pleasure from feeding their
partners and watching them eat, feeders get enormous
pleasure from weighing and measuring their partners, and
wax lyrical about bloated bellies and the excitement of
witnessing a woman's flesh expand. As one man remarked, "a
big belly is the loveliest pillow of all and I get to make my own
pillow as big and soft as I want it!"

The feedee often has a genetic potential to be plump, and
for some women such as 25 year old Jenna who at 170cms
weighs over 127 kilos, there can be a sense of relief in finally
being allowed to enjoy food without feeling guilty or judged:

> Sometimes people stare at me when I sit down to
> the table and have 4 plates of food in front of me,
> but I no longer care. I've always been a big girl and

always struggled with it, but the turning point came for me when I met someone who thinks I am beautiful because I'm big. Nothing turns him on more than seeing me chow down on some delicious, crispy calamari and fries. Its really helped me to accept my size and stop feeling guilty because I love to eat. I'm going home with my man after dinner—which is more than the stick insects giving me the evil eyes can say!

Fat women can also enjoy a feeling of power from having their every need attended to and being worshipped for their size. As any feeder will tell you, his woman's sensual needs are of paramount importance, so food is brought to her and fed to her, and her feet or belly are massaged; after which she is admired for her girth and beauty. However there is huge potential for harm and abuse of the fed partner, especially if the goal is the complete or partial immobilisation of the feedee, which puts the woman into a form of perpetual bondage as she becomes a prisoner in her own body.

Even when feedees are not immobilised, the fatter they become the more reliant they must be on their feeders not only to feed them, but to support them in every way—including basic hygiene such as washing and toileting—leaving the women with very little free agency. For these reasons, many in the FA community are troubled by feeder relationships, describing them as predatory, misogynistic and dangerous. They make the very valid argument that once a woman is in a state of physical helplessness due to her weight, it is difficult to reverse the situation, stop the 'play' and quickly revert to a normal life.

Feeding is not confined to a feeder/feedee relationship, as many men and women get pleasure from gaining weight themselves and act as self-feeders. There are many websites and groups dedicated to gaining weight and discussing it, allowing people to enjoy their interest within a supportive community. Fantasy Feeder[59] (FF to its fans) is one of the largest, containing forums, stories and photographs related to fat and weight. Discussion forums for online communities are on topics such as 'How much McDonalds can you eat in one sitting?' and 'Eating until you are totally full'. While some women consider actively gaining weight liberating or a challenge to stereotypes, for others like twenty-something Belle it is simply about the hedonistic enjoyment of consuming food:

> So tonight I was kind of hungry — as usual! So of course I had to order some food and I think I went a little overboard. I had 2 orders of chicken in black bean sauce, a full order of fried rice, 6 crab sticks, 4 egg rolls, a wonton soup and 4 of those almond cookie things. Oh and plus about a litre of cola. It was so much food but it tasted great — I really love Chinese food. Right now my tummy feels tight and full which is just wonderful.

Some participants in the culture of feeding enjoy force-feeding a partner; however, this is deemed unacceptable even by feeder standards, as many believe those women are forced into these practices because of their physical helplessness. In force-feeding, the feedee is held or tied down and then fed with the aid of some type of tube or other apparatus. The feedee is said to enjoy the feeling of being dominated and the feeder experiences pleasure from controlling the feedee. When force-feeding occurs, it is usually done with liquid that is made up of mostly fat and is easy to consume. Some feeders advocate litres of melted ice-cream with syrup or jam mixed in, or as Ruben's Fat and Feeding Page suggests:

---

[59] www.fantasyfeeder.com.

> If you want to get fat quick, and love stretchmarks on your tummy, then you gotta take pure fat—that can be butter or oil. I know of some feedees that love to drink several quarts of liquid butter every day. And these women gain with incredible speed.

The same website details how to create a tube-feeding device and describes how the writer went about tube-feeding his partner (with her full consent). The website does caution that care is required as "the stomach really can burst!"

There are any number of websites and chat rooms that facilitate role-play of feeder or feedee so people who are interested in the concept of feeding (as opposed to the activity itself) can live out this fantasy. Fat admiration has even crept into the mainstream, with episodes of the sitcoms *Malcolm in the Middle* and *Family Guy* running story lines in which the husbands go to various lengths to fatten up their wives, including shovelling sugar into the orange juice and plying them with cakes.

Related Interests

Fat admiration, body inflation, domination and submission, giantess fantasy.

Jargon and Search Terms

Body inflation—self feeding to gain weight.
Body builder—a person who deliberately overfeeds themselves to gain maximum weight.
Encouragers—homosexual version of the feeder.
FA—fat admirer.
Fat feeder (FF)—a man who gets pleasure from encouraging a woman to eat or by feeding her.
Feedee—a woman who gets pleasure from eating or being fed.
Feeder porn—watching women gorging themselves on food.

Force feeding—when the feedee is tied down and force-fed.
Gainers—generally (but not always) homosexual men, the male equivalent of a feedee.

Body Inflation

Body inflation in this context refers to body parts that magically inflate to monstrous cartoon-like sizes. By its nature, this interest can only be realised through fantasy, cartoons or video special effects. The most exciting aspect for a body inflationist is watching the transformation of the body part, and he would feel cheated if simply presented with images of an inflated chest or monstrous lips. The Internet has made it possible for body inflationists to access clips, video and art centred on the theme of inflation. These can be anything from cartoon narratives that end with a body part inflating, the morphing of a flat-chested woman into a barely recognisable body holding two breasts, turning a normal woman into a type of superhero, people finding they are wearing enchanted clothing that inflates them, to the tried-and-true magic potion that somehow inflates a body part or whole body. A cult movie for body inflationists is *Willy Wonka's Chocolate Factory*, for the scene in which a girl who gobbles some experimental bubblegum, turning into a purple ball with only hands, feet and head sticking out.

As it is difficult to replicate this fantasy in real-life play, various ruses such as stuffing balloons or soft toys into clothing may be used, or partners may choose to view images of inflation or inflation art together or even use inflation dirty talk—whispering key words such as "swelling", "growing", "gigantic" or "blow up" into each other's ears. Body inflationists may have an interest in balloon fetishism, fat admiration or breast fetishism, because of the expansion aspect shared by these other interests.

Related Interests

Balloons, fat admiration, breasts, giantess fantasy.

Pregnancy

> There is something so wrong in my mind about having sex with someone who is pregnant; I just feel I shouldn't be doing it, so because of that it feels even more sexy.
>
> —Male, early twenties

Maieusiophilia: maieutikos (to bring forth children) and philia (love of) is a sexual attraction to women who are pregnant or appear pregnant. In a benign fashion, some men simply love and enjoy being with, or looking at, a pregnant woman and worship her for her fertile and luscious form. In its darker form a pregnancy fetish also includes finding pregnant women servicing men sexually, and in sexually denigrating positions, to be erotic. There are an extensive number of websites catering to an interest in pregnant women, from those that feature scantily clad pregnant women to those featuring heavily pregnant women in hardcore pornography videos or images. A classic preggers porn scenario is one of a doctor examining a pregnant woman in stirrups. Unlike some other fetishes that focus on a particular object of fantasy, this interest can be attractive because it breaks cultural taboos that imply a would-be mother is not a sexual being and should be respected and venerated for her impeding motherhood. The school of Freudian psychology maintains that some men can develop what is known as a Madonna-Whore complex. When a woman is perceived as a mother (the Madonna figure), then in the mind of the sufferer he cannot have sex with her or view her in any way as sexual, as sexuality is reserved for 'bad' or 'dirty' women—not mothers. For men who think this way, seeing pregnant women in overtly sexual poses or activities is arousing because of this perceived taboo.

Another major attraction to pregnant women can be psychological. If a pregnant woman allows a man to have sex with her, there is a high degree of trust involved in the act as she is sharing herself at a highly vulnerable time; for some men this makes them feel special and protective towards the woman, and therefore good about themselves. Mick is a shy, slightly overweight man in his late twenties. According to him he has only ever had sex with women who were pregnant, starting with a family friend when he was seventeen and she was (he guesses) in her thirties:

> You have to be very careful with pregnant women and I enjoy being careful and tender. Letting me make love to her is like she is giving me a gift—the gift of her trust that I won't hurt her or hurt the baby. I am a single guy, so I have to be a bit careful about trying to date the pregnant ones, but I like that special feeling so much that I do go looking for them.

As cultural taboos about sexual acts during pregnancy are universally quite strong, any level of attraction to a pregnant woman may be perceived as fetishist, even when the attraction is simply erotic, as is common for many expectant fathers.

For some men an interest in pregnancy can extend to an interest in the birthing process. In 2002 a New Zealand *60 Minutes* television documentary featured a pregnant woman who planned to be filmed giving birth for a pornographic movie. There was a huge furore surrounding this as many felt the purity and sanctity of the birthing space should not be compromised by being moved to a place that was explicitly sexual.[60]

Related Interests

Body inflation, lactation.

Height

Nanophilia: nano (dwarf) and philia (love of) is a strong attraction to short or small people by someone of normal height. A tall or normal-height woman may be attracted to a very short man, or vice versa. Dwarfism is a genetic condition characterised by adult stature under 4 feet 10 inches.[61] There are specific dating sites for people who suffer Dwarfism[62] and who are seeking like partners; but this is not considered to be nanophilia.

Anasteemaphilia: anasteema (height) and philia (love of) refers to people who are attracted to someone because of their difference in height. Unlike Nanophilia, which is specifically about being attracted to small or very short partners, a height fixation can be for either a short or a tall partner. It is common to see short, wealthy or successful men with taller woman (both in the media and in real life). This is probably because it allows them to flaunt the convention that women prefer men to be taller than themselves, drawing attention to their power to go against the laws of nature; being attractive to tall women may also boost their self-esteem. Women who seek out unusually tall partners may be looking for the manifestation of a powerful protector figure or even have a tendency to infantilism.

---

[60]Longhurst (2006).
[61]Little People of America website at http://www.lpaonline.org/.
[62]Such as www.dwarfdate.com.

Jargon and Search Terms

AP—average-statured person or average-sized person, opposite to little person.
Inter-spacial—adjective for a mixed couple when one is tiny or tall and the other is of average height.
Short-statured person, LP, little person—acceptable terms for a person with Dwarfism.

Age Difference

The general term chronophilia: chronos (time) and philia (love of) describes sexual arousal from being with a partner of a different age group, either older or younger. This is further divided into the categories of gerontophilia: geron (aged) which is a sexual attraction to an elderly or older person by a younger person (colloquially often referred to as granny grabbing); pedophilia: pedos (child), which describes an adult person who is attracted to a pre-pubertal child, and ephebo-philia: ephebos (post-pubertal), referring to a sexual attraction by an older person to a newly pubescent or adolescent person of the same sex.

While the younger woman/older man combination is the most socially acceptable, women are no strangers to having a younger partner. Replying to a question on how she felt about the age difference of 32 years between herself and husband number five, the actress Joan Collins said, "if he dies, he dies". American actress Demi Moore is another well-known older wife, with her actor husband 16 years her junior. A recent BBC America program, *Sugar Mummies*, examined older women/younger men partnerships. The age differences in the partnerships were radical, with one woman aged 38 and the 'man' 17; while another woman was 67 and her partner 32. *Sugar Mummies* reported that these types of couples tended to live isolated lives; the couples spoke about how difficult it was for them to make friends with other couples and how they felt censured for living together.

Reasons for an attraction to an older male or female partner include a desire to be with someone who is socially or financially more secure, pleasure in experiencing or being introduced to a different phase of life, or simply finding an older person sexually alluring. The comedy show *Little Britain* (2007) ran a segment over a number of series in which a young man was hopelessly attracted to a friend's granny, finding it very sexy when she drooled or he caught sight of her stockinged ankles. While this show was satirical, there is a market for pornography, erotica and stories about mature-aged women, and search terms such as 'horny granny porn', 'easy elders' and 'outrageous grannies' will quickly locate some of the hundreds of websites catering to this interest.

Jargon and Search Terms

Chickenhawk—used to describe an older gay man who sexually pursues younger males.

Cougar—a sexy, older woman, usually in her early 30s or 40s who pursues younger men.

GILF—acronym for 'grannies I'd like to fuck'.

Lolita—a sexually precocious young girl who is the object of desire of a significantly older man. Taken from the novel *Lolita* by Vladimir Nabokov.

MILF—acronym for 'moms I'd like to fuck' referring to mothers who attract the sexual attention of high-school boys; a relatively recent term.

Tadpoling—refers to a relationship between a younger man and an older woman.

Further Search Terms: mature babes, hot grannies.

Heightened Senses

Smell

> When I think about my first husband I remember
> the smell of peppermint toothpaste from our first
> kiss—and I was only 15! And even though I can no
> longer picture his face, when I think about this guy
> I had a hot 6 month affair with something like 10
> years ago, I still remember him as smelling of fresh
> peaches.
>
> —Married woman, 42

Olfactophilia:[63]olfacto (to smell) and philia (love of) is an erotic arousal from smells. As a fetish it is mostly focused on smells and odours emanating from the sexual areas of the body, so a common attraction for many men is the smell of a sweaty or unwashed vagina or buttock crevice. The highly popular TV series *Sex and the City*[64] aired an episode in which one of the key characters discussed her dilemma in responding to her boyfriend's attempts to lick her post-run butt crack as she found it both embarrassing and weirdly erotic.

Olfactophiles don't just find certain smells pleasant and attractive; they seek them out, as they are essential for erotic arousal. To those who enjoy erotic play with feet or shoes, the smell that arouses them will come from that specific body part or article of clothing; the smell of a male armpit is nominated as highly erotic, as this woman writes on her Facebook page:

> Men's body odour is incredible, it is like some
> fabulous, perfect expensive perfume. The hor-
> mones and pheromones, make it the most perfect

---

[63]Also sometimes known as osphresiolagnia.
[64]Episode 'Baby, Talk is Cheap', *Sex and the City*, HBO.

and natural scent, it's alluring and will always
send a shiver to the right places. Providing the
man is not unhealthy and showers regularly the
BO is dynamite!

Some people who have an attraction to smokers will experience a sexual response to the smell of exhaled cigarette
smoke, reporting they find the smell of the smoke "different"
or more feminine if a woman exhales it. Interestingly, a
number of women have written to discussion forums about
enjoying the smell of their own vaginal juices, describing how
they will touch their own genitals then sniff their fingers, as
they find the smell of their own vaginas sexually arousing.
This may be done prior to masturbating or used as a form of
perfume prior to a sexual encounter or date, as it is dabbed
where one might a fragrance. As an actual scent it is not really
distinguishable unless the woman has not bathed recently or
has a particularly strong smelling discharge, but it is said to
work very successfully as a subtle flirtation device.

All humans (either consciously or subconsciously) are
attracted by the pheromones secreted by those of the opposite
sex (or for non-heterosexuals, of the same sex), and it has been
known for thousands of years that the sense of smell can
stimulate a sexual response in human beings and other living
creatures. Pheromones, the chemical molecules secreted by
living beings, are interpreted in the olfactory receptor sites at
locations in the nasal canal. The job of these receptors is to
send signals to the brain. If they are of the 'right type' for the
receptors, these signals usually cause a sexual stimulatory
response in the opposite sex and attraction occurs.[65] American
researchers have recently claimed that if men eat more celery
(as it contains a naturally occurring steroid), this will increase

---

[65]Hays and Warren (2003); Wyatt and Tristram (2003).

their pheromone levels, thus making their sweat more attractive to women.[66]

Smell is also known as the strongest sense in terms of memory and association, with a whiff of something like freshly cut grass allowing someone to re-experience the memory of a childhood back garden or even an early sexual awakening:

> One of my earliest memories is of talking the kid next door into getting under the bed with me and then we took turns smelling each other's fingers after rubbing them in our butt-cracks. I have no idea how a 7 or 8 year old little girl even stumbled onto this practice, but smell has remained with me as a strong trigger for all my life. (Female 55, in personal exchange)

The love of a specific smell may also be complicated by being part of a larger fetish. For example, a person who loves the smell of urine may well be into all things urine and in fact be a urophile, with a love of this smell simply a by-product of that interest.

Related Interests

Domination and submission, soiled personal garments, flatulence.

---

[66]Anderson, Gaman and Gaman (2010).

Sound

Voulez-vouz avec moi – cest soir?

Acousticophilia acoustico (sound) and philia (love of) describes arousal from specific sounds. Sexual arousal can be
triggered by music, verbal abuse and foreign languages, or by
screaming, moaning, heavy-breathing or the sounds people
make during sex. In *The Addams Family* TV series, Gomez
Addams always goes crazy when his wife Morticia speaks
French, and in the movie *A Fish Called Wanda* (1988), Jamie Lee
Curtis in the character Wanda becomes sexually excited each
time Kevin Kline as Otto speaks Italian or John Cleese as
Archie speaks Russian. Sound can be so crucial that high-end
sex dolls are now made with audio chips.

Ecouteurism: from the French ecoute (to listen) also refers
to experiencing arousal from sound, but it is specifically about
listening to others having sex or speaking about sex, and is
arousing because it is non-consensual. Because of this, some
ecouteurists may also be voyeurs. Their partners in crime are
the agrexophiliacs, who become aroused by knowing that
others can hear them having sex, so they practise group sex or
sex in public places. Many people who enjoy this are also
involved in the practice of what is called dogging, as in "I am
just taking the dog out for a walk dear", a well-known practice
in the Western world and particularly popular in England.
Dogging involves driving to known parks and having sex in
the car, often with the lights on; or watching and listening to
others. With the advent of the Internet the dogging community
has become well organised, with text messaging and the web
being used to publicise dogging sites and events.

Narratophilia: narrato (to narrate) and philia (love of) refers to arousal from telling sexual stories or jokes or from
reading sexual material aloud to a sex partner. Phone sex, on
the other hand, is arousal from discussing sex on the phone

and implies a consensual dialogue, while non-consensual phone sex is referred to as an obscene phone call.

Related Interests

Voyeurism, dogging.

Touch/Taste

> As long as it's wet and it came out of a woman, its nectar to me...

Hygrophilia: hygro (wet) and philia (love of) is sexual arousal from contact with bodily fluids. Hygrophiliacs are said to enjoy a wide range of secretions without necessarily favouring one—this includes nasal mucus, tears, urine, blood, saliva, semen, faeces or vaginal secretions.

Both men and women say sharing vaginal juices and sperm between partners as well as tasting their own is enjoyable:

> I often taste my own sex. If I feel really horny I lick my fingers after I have had them in my vagina. I find it mostly tastes quite sweet. I don't think its bad to do it, after-all, I have often sucked my partner's penis after it has been inside me. (Anonymous post on female101.com)

So-called 'snowball kisses' are a popular way of enjoying this interest. In this practice the couple practice oral sex and the women then passes the ejaculated semen back to the partner by kissing him. Otherwise the couple have sex and the man then sucks up his own ejaculate mixed with the juices of the partner and then French kisses the woman. A variation on this (which some women refer to as wet kissing or pussy sauce), is the man filling his mouth with vaginal juices after oral sex and transferring it while kissing his partner:

> My husband will suck his come from my pussy and then we swap a wet cum/pussy kiss. I consider myself very lucky to have a husband who loves to have me feeding him our love juices. It makes our sex life great, even after all these years. (Couple married 24 years)

The term felching is sometimes also used to describe this method of exchanging bodily fluids, but strictly speaking that is a sexual practice involving the licking or sucking of semen that has been ejaculated into the rectum during anal sex.

When they cannot touch the actual secretion, hygrophili-acs enjoy finding it on articles of clothing, and in this hy-grophilia has a lot in common with mysophilia (an attraction to soiled personal garments).

Related Interests

Soiled personal garments, tears, urine, blood.

Jargon and Search Terms

Snowballing—sexual play in which one partner passes semen into the mouth of another.

Tickling

> My favourite sort of tickling is blowing a raspberry on her tummy, and fingering her navel, while I love being tickled by her toes anywhere on my body.
>
> —Male, anonymous

Titilagnia: titil (to tickle) and lagnia (lust), is arousal from tickling. A person may experience a sexual thrill from either tickling a sex partner or being subjected to tickling, usually to the point of helpless laughter

Common tickling spots are the feet, underarms (as might be expected), the navel, neck, legs and back of knees and what is used for tickling can vary from fingers, feathers and fur to soft-bristled brushes. Where a person is tickled depends on personal preference, so foot fetishists may be drawn to tickling feet or having their own feet tickled.

People who enjoy being tickled love the rush it causes. This rush is described as both horrible and wonderful—or as one woman puts it, "like being punished and given a present at the same time". Tickling as a fetish often deals with control issues. Ticklers enjoy the feelings of control when tickling someone to distraction and the receivers enjoy giving up all control to the helpless laughter tickling causes, as this woman relates:

> I finally worked out why I like being tickled. I was brought up in a strict Catholic family, so anything related to sex was pretty much no-go. I had a partner once who tickled me so much I had to beg for mercy, and to make him stop I had to agree to some sex acts I usually feel shy about. It took away my reason for saying no and allowed me to try something without guilt, because I had to do it to stop the tickling…does that make sense?

Initial tickling is erotic and playful, but continued tickling loses these features. Tickling by its very nature involves submission. Often the victim submits willingly at first and may even encourage the tickling; however, after it begins a victim may become helpless with uncontrollable laughter. Frantic struggles ensue to escape the tickling, and the humiliation of not being able to stop laughing or avoid the treatment may be become intense.

While it is often enjoyed purely for the tickling pleasure, it may also be done as part of BDSM play and include some form of restraint to prevent escape or to avoid accidental hurt from the person being tickled flailing their arms or legs. Besides being actively involved as the tickler or receiver, tickling lovers may also become excited by watching others being tickled.

Related Interests

BDSM, feet.

Pain

Come on, just a little slap, please?

Algolagnia: algos (pain) and lagnia (lust) is a love of pain, most specifically pain that is experienced on erogenous zones. There is often confusion between algolagnia and masochism. A person with algolagnia enjoys the physical pain (though they often wish they didn't), while a masochist has a psychological desire for pain (and usually humiliation) that results in sexual arousal, but does not physically crave it as the algolnagist does. Jenna is a divorced mother in her early thirties and by her own admission fits the algolagnia profile:

> I have asked boyfriends over the years to be rougher with me, (like a bit of a whack or something), but most of them have trouble getting around the "you don't ever hit a girl" business they were taught as kids. I understand the difference between fun and aggression and domestic violence isn't what I am after. What I want, and really I guess you could say I need, is a good hard

slap. The rush of adrenaline that this creates equals good sex for me, but try explaining that and anyone actually getting it!

Studies into algolagnia began in the early 1900s and continue today. Most current research suggests the 'pleasure from pain' experience has a biological basis as it has been proven that pain, just like other sensory pleasures such as sexual contact or sweet foods, causes the release of endorphins, the chemicals that induce pleasure. However, some neurologists and neuropsychologists argue there is a further aspect to consider, which is that the brains of those with algolagnia may interpret nerve input differently and for these individuals it is necessary to experience pain in order to experience pleasure. Neurophysiologist James Prescott links this to the experience of some newborns, children and adolescents who have been subjected to what he terms ritual genital mutilation such as circumcision.

Prescott (1989) believes that when the area of the human brain designed to experience pleasure and the expression of sexual love is first encoded with what he terms "extraordinary and excruciating pain"[67], the long-term outcome is that all subsequent acts or experiences of genital pleasure are experienced against a background of genital pain that has been deeply buried in the subconscious or unconscious brain. According to his thesis, early experiences of genital pain contribute to the subconscious encoding of the brain's pleasure-seeking receptors to seek out sado-masochistic experiences, making it completely out of the individual's control.

The similar sounding word, algophobia, means the opposite: an obsessive or excessive fear of pain.

---

[67]Prescott (1989, p.14).

Jargon and Search Terms

Pain sluts—women who enjoy pain during sex.
Painogasm—an orgasm facilitated by pain.

You Dirty, Dirty Boy...

The one who can defile others, whether clean himself or not, is the boss.

—Enzensberger, 1972

Body fluids and emissions are considered to be highly
personal in Western society, and for most people contact with
the sweat, menstrual blood or fluids of another person is
considered a form of defilement. However for some people the
opposite is true and they find it sexually exciting to have
contact with dirt or body waste.

Defilement/Soiling

Salirophilia: saliro (to soil) and philia (love of) refers to
erotic pleasure from deliberate soiling or dishevelling. It is
enjoyed by the perpetrator who soils someone who is considered sexually attractive and/or by the person who has their
appearance spoiled. The act of tearing or damaging their
clothing, covering them in garbage, filth or sexual emissions or
simply roughing up their hair or makeup can be so arousing
that it results in orgasm. In more extreme forms it can also
include arousal from making a partner vomit or vomiting on
them or spitting on a partner as a form of humiliation (see
Emetophilia). The fetish does not as a rule involve physically
harming or injuring the subject—only their appearance. One
twenty-something gay man describes how he and his lover
play with garbage:

> We know this one particular restaurant that leaves
> the garbage out back, we don't visit often, as we
> don't want to caught. We make a date of it and
> dress up for occasion—my favourite outfit for him

to wear when we do this is a thin PVC catsuit and high heels. I don't get dirty, but I like to supervise him rolling around. What we play with varies according to what we find, so desserts, vegetable scraps, chicken, rice, whatever they throw out, including cigarette butts and the refuse from the bathrooms—once we even found used condoms!!

Trashbag play is by natural extension a part of this play. One person will climb into a very large trash bag and the other goes around house emptying various containers of trash from the kitchen or bathroom onto the one in the bag. The bag is then tied up and the person is left with the garbage. Trashbag play satisfies an interest in bondage or encasement as well as dirt, and for some a further attraction is having contact with the plastic material of the bag in the same way that people enjoy the feeling of latex, rubber or PVC.

This type of play can also be a subconscious metaphor for demonstrating how the partner is sexually dirty, by using outwardly visible symbols of socially unacceptable dirt such as garbage or body waste. In an exploration of what they term "the power of dirt", researchers Clark and Davis (1989) noted that it is extremely important to a person's identity to be considered a socialised member of society. If a person is confronted by practices, objects or activities they consider unclean, such as physical contact with sexual fluids, urine, sweat, blood or dirt, they can become distressed or feel defiled. The worst terms of insult are constructed around sex and elimination—"shithead", "arsehole", "prick"—and are in a way a verbal method of soiling another person. When these behaviours are included in sex play, the enjoyment comes from doing something that upsets the socially accepted norms, or from having the power to deface, debase or otherwise make another person 'dirty'.

Because my man is so domesticated on the outside (nobody can believe how lucky I am—he irons, does his share of cooking, opens car doors for me), it makes me feel even hotter when he dirties me up a little. By this I mean when he rips my clothes, snags my stockings and then comes on my body, I cannot tell you how hot I feel when I'm his dirty little bitch. It goes without saying that I dress for these occasions, it would just feel weird if we did this when I'm lounging around the house in my PJs.

The majority of submissive men enjoy humiliation and will seek (and often pay for) name-calling as well as choosing to perform ass worship or act as a human toilet for a Mistress. Couples who enjoy cuckolding may include clean-up duty for the husband after the wife has had sex with another man, which involve him orally cleaning up the other man's ejaculate (see Cuckolding).

A love of dirt or filth is not limited to men as evidenced by the heroine in the German novel *Wetlands* who describes her love affair with toilet seats:

> I enjoy plopping myself down on any dirty toilet seat anywhere. I rub the entire seat with my pussy before I sit down, going once around with a graceful gyration of my hips. When I press my pussy onto the seat it makes a smacking noise and then it sucks up all the public hairs, droplets, and puddles of various shades and consistencies. I've been doing this on every sort of toilet seat for four years now. My favourites are the ones at highway rest stops where there's just one toilet shared by men and women. (Roche, 2009)

While most available research on dirt focuses on middle class heterosexual men and women, the practice is well known in the gay male and lesbian communities and across a broad range of social classes. This fetish may sometimes manifest itself in the defacing of statues or pictures of attractive people (especially celebrities) and is always done with sexual rather than vandalistic intentions. Clips of attractive women destroying their clothing, including items such as shoes, jeans or leotards, can be purchased at clips4sale.com. An 18 minute clip of a woman cutting holes in a pink silk dress and then throwing it onto a burning fireplace sells for US $15.99; while $US5.99 will buy a short clip of a pair of silver women's boots being set on fire.

Related Interests

Soiled personal garments (mysophilia), urine, faeces, vomit, BDSM, wet and messy play.

Jargon and Search Terms

Facials—ejaculating on a woman's face.

Salty Body Fluids

Salophilia: salino (salt) and philia (love of) is frequently confused with salirophilia (an obsession with soiling or dishevelling). Salophilia describes people who are aroused by the taste of salty body fluids such as perspiration or tears. Typically they indulge their interest by licking areas of the body that collect perspiration, such as underarms, feet or butt cracks, and this is further influenced by a personal preference for that body part—so not surprisingly the foot fetishist will worship a sweaty foot that has been in a dirty sneaker all day long. In the Middle Ages, perspiration was thought to have magical qualities and was often used in love spells. The romantic image of a man drinking champagne from a woman's high heel comes from the ancient belief that it was an antidote to a love spell cast by a woman. Unlike the romantic images popular in media of a man drinking from a woman's elegant high-heeled slipper, the man drank wine from one of his own shoes, as it contained his sweat and thereby created an antidote.[68]

Related Interests

Underarm hair, feet, shoes, tears, ass worship.

Soiled Personal Items

> It makes perfect sense, when some people can't get a share of the sweeties, well—they just make do with the bag.

Mysophilia: mysos (defilement) and philia (love of), is the term for sexual arousal from contact with soiled personal garments or items. Mysophilists particularly enjoy smelling, touching or tasting dirty or soiled personal articles such as panties bras, socks or pantyhose. Men who have a fetish for feet are more likely to be attracted to dirty socks stockings or pantyhose as well as well-worn old sneakers. One married middle-aged man said he thought it was hardly unusual behaviour for men to sniff women's underwear, maintaining that virtually every man on the planet had done it at some time in his life, even those who lived with partners and did not need underwear as a sex substitute:

---

[68]Love (1992, p.240).

Let's say its my turn to do laundry. I'm sorting
(lights from darks, as you do), and there will be her
panties. Sometimes I just can't help it and I'll put
that pair right to my nose; would she like to hear
me saying this...probably not.

A desire to be close to an absent partner may also manifest in smelling a loved one's underwear, with women also
enjoying the smell of clothing such as shirts or T-shirts worn
by someone who is the object of their lust or affection.

However, not all contact with used personal articles is
motivated by a desire for closeness, with some men simply
enjoying contact with any woman's worn underwear from
whatever laundry basket comes their way. Online discussion
forums on this topic are plentiful, with specific websites
existing purely for the enjoyment of panty sniffers. The
conversations include descriptions of smelling underwear
from sex partners as well as relatives, friends and visitors to
the house with no apparent link to the wearer, as the intimate
smell of the woman (regardless of who she is) considered
sufficient.

A number of websites advertise worn panties, bras and
pantyhose for sale, easily found with the search string 'worn
panties'. Many of these sites purport to belong to ordinary
women such as housewives, university students and mothers.
Panties are by far the most popular item, with prices starting
at around US$20 a pair. The buyer can specify whether they
want a thong (g-string), bikini or full brief, and choose a
particular colour. It is common practice on worn panty sites to
offer 'extra staining' at a premium price. This means the
panties have been worn for either 24 or 48 hours, worn during
a menstrual period or worn for masturbation. Buyers are
assured the article will be zip-locked in plastic and in most
cases they are advertised as vacuum sealed to ensure the
smells remain intact. Some sellers are happy to work directly

with the purchaser to create a specific product in terms of how they want the panties presented, and whether the buyer requires photographic proof of them being worn.

Some of the specialist sites such as Ebanned.net offer other intimate items for auction such used tampons, used sex toys, 'pussy pops', which are actual lollypops which have been used for masturbation, pubic hair clippings, toenail clippings, pedicure shavings and even saliva. The clippings, shavings and saliva are used as garnishes and consumed (they may be sold already mixed in with other food stuffs such as biscuits or cookies), or the saliva is used as masturbation lubricant.

Money Mistresses[69] often sell personal articles to their money slaves, with a sample price list from Mistress Michelle below:

> Toiletries - I get many requests for the contents of my bathroom trash bin. Depending on how nasty the item, the more it will cost you.
>
> - Q-tip - $10
> - Napkin - $10
> - TP (#1) $15, (#2) $30
> - Razor - Legs - $10, Arm - $15, Pubic shave - $25
> - Cigarette butts (5) - $15.[70]

While pornographic magazines in the West have long contained advertisements for used women's underwear (mostly panties), this fetish became very popular in Japan some years ago. Known as Buru Sera, it centres specifically on the purchase of panties worn by schoolgirls. Although this has now been outlawed, a black market trade still flourishes. The

---

[69]A BDSM practice. Money Mistresses are online mistresses who allow men to become their financial slaves for a negotiated price.
[70]www.drainyourwallet.com.

girls sell their underwear to an adult store which on-sells them to fetishists. Attaching the girl's photo and a biographical note (e.g. "my name is Mikito, I am a high school student") further increases the value of the article.

The American actress Marilyn Monroe was comfortable with bodily emissions and dirt, bathing infrequently, choosing not to change the bed linen after sex and refusing to wear sanitary pads during her period. She also chose to spend most of her time in her dirty bed, eating meals there and dropping food, crumbs and even chop bones amongst her bedding, while making it a habit to wipe her dirty hands on the bed sheets. Household staff understandably found this behaviour problematic. Martin Luther (founder of the Lutheran church) was said to have a penchant for not changing the linen on the matrimonial bed for up to one year, preferring it to become saturated with bodily emissions.

Some early research[71] suggests that the distaste people express for body emissions is related to a perception that the emissions signal decay of the body and hence contact with germs and illness. As is the case with salirophilia (soiling another), unwanted contact with body emissions is associated with defilement or pollution and also destabilises a person's identity as a socialised member of society, as opposed to animals who are unconcerned with dirt.

Related Interests

Defilement (salirophilia), urine, faeces, vomit, feet, Femdom.

---

[71]Clark and Davis (1989).

Vomit/Spitting

Let me hold your hair back dear....

Emetophilia: emeto (vomit) and philia (love of) is a sexual fetish based on arousal from vomit. This can include being vomited on, observing others vomit or creating a fantasy around vomiting. It can be incorporated in either foreplay or the sex act. Emetophiles enjoy the feeling of vomit on their bodies, the look of vomit or the smell of vomit, and they can also have a fascination with the expulsion aspect of vomiting. The enjoyment factor arises from humiliating a partner by vomiting on them or from feelings of power when making the partner vomit, or vice-versa, being the one who is subjected to vomit. It is an interest that is largely indulged in online and there are a number of websites selling with pay-per-view videos that cater to the predominantly male fan-base, such as this man in his fifties:

> I can't tell you why I find this so erotically charged. I personally couldn't vomit before, dur- ing or after sex—or ever vomit on demand. But seeing a man vomit on a woman straight after coming and seeing the look of horror on the girl's face, it is so shocking and at the same time sexy and powerful. I would never ask my girlfriend to be involved in this and nor would I even let her know I watch this sort of thing, but I do and I can't get enough of it.

Internet pornography related to the theme of vomit can be easily found, and ranges from stills or videos of semi-naked or naked women vomiting or being vomited on, to more hard- core scenes which feature women giving oral sex or having sex and then being vomited on during or after the act. On the tamer end of the scale, pay-per-view of female performers known as 'barf girls' whose routines are simply vomiting without sex are also popular. It is possible to purchase actual vomit from the girls performing on some of these websites, which the seller handily vacuum packs to ensure freshness of the product.

To force a partner to vomit, a man performs deep or rough oral sex which causes the gagging reflex and then vomiting. People who are not able to vomit on demand, or who find actual vomit off-putting (while still enjoying the concept of vomit-play); simulate vomit with various foodstuffs like porridge, which they spit out as if vomiting. People who are fascinated with vomit share candid or amateur photos of women vomiting because they are ill, bulimic or drunk, as well as sharing sightings of vomiting in mainstream movies or television shows.

Spitting on a partner or being spat on is also aligned to this interest. Submissive men like Marc who unbeknownst to his wife pays professional Dommes to humiliate him verbally or physically find it particularly arousing:

> I like it because it's really degrading and demean-
> ing. It's something people very rarely do to each
> other and it's powerful because it's gross and in-
> sulting. When they spit in my mouth or on my face
> it really makes me feel like they see me as a piece
> of shit, someone to totally disrespect and abuse
> without consequences.

When being spat on in person is not practical, websites such as Ebanned.net advertise vials of spit produced by attractive models. Buyers may use it as a lubricant or mix it with food.

Related Interests

Defilement, faeces, urine, Femdom.

Jargon and Search Terms

Barf girls—women who vomit as a performance.
Roman shower—one person vomiting on another.
Vominatrix—a dominatrix who specialises in vomiting on her clients.
Vomitiquous—used to describe a strong smell of vomit which is arousing.

Tears

> The about to cry state is fine—but if I see actual tears it's a victory and makes me want to immediately have sex.
> —Celesta, Crying Appreciation Forum

Becoming sexually aroused from tears is known as dacryphilia: dacryo (tears) and philia (love of). Dacryphiliacs become aroused when they see other people crying or with tears in their eyes, whether in a sexual situation or not. Enjoying tears is most commonly thought of in relation to BDSM play when crying has been caused from receiving physical pain or humiliation. When it is enjoyed in the BDSM dynamic the submissive (sub) partner is humiliated, smacked or hurt to the point of tears and the dominant partner finds this arousing. Tears may also be a part of what is known as after-care, when a submissive partner may often cry after experiencing an intense BDSM session. The sub is then comforted by the dominant partner, and this often becomes a source of arousal for both.

Outside the BDSM dynamic some men and women (this interest appears to be fairly equal gender-wise), become excited or aroused from seeing a person they find attractive crying—this may be from sorrow, emotional pain or even happiness. Men nominate aspects such as streaked mascara, pouting and quivering lips or the glistening of a woman's wet eyes as highly attractive, while women speak about the allure of a man's tears showing he is unafraid to expose his weaker, emotional side to a woman. Both men and women prize the intimacy of watching a partner cry and it is universal that people drawn to a crying partner or even to sightings of crying celebrities or strangers, are fascinated with the weeping person's vulnerability. They speak about valuing the honesty and even strength it can take for a person to lay themselves bare and show their emotions in such a raw and open way. As the tears flow they enjoy comforting the weeping partner and especially enjoy offering emotional support and nurturing. Showing weakness in this way is seen as a strength, particularly when men cry, given that it goes against the grain of 'how men are supposed to act'.

Canadian 'Wounded Puppy' is married and in her thirties, and loves being with a weeping man as it gives her the opportunity to show him how much he is loved for sharing the intimacy of such a private act. For most lovers of tears, the emotional vulnerability of the crying, or about to cry partner, has become sexualised or erotic in some sense:

> The right kind of gasp, wobble in the voice or help-less expression behind the eyes could do as much or more for me as seeing an actual tear fall. And if crying is like sex, then the quivering voice is probably part of the foreplay, and the tears are like the climax.

Descriptions of tears and crying tend to be quite poetic, describing the beauty of brimming eyes, wet lashes and teardrops like pearls, with full-on hysterical crying that may include snot, redness and a swollen nose having no real part to play in this interest. Anecdotally people who enjoy tears are generally not aroused by crying themselves, preferring a crying partner. However that being said, a few members of the Crying Appreciation Forum say that they would find their own crying erotic if it was in response to the crying of a partner. 'Tearhunter' has been married for many years and considers his wife's tears a unique gift. He recalls his wedding night when they finally sank into bed together after their celebrations and he glimpsed his wife's silent tears of joy and emotion sliding down her cheeks as being the perfect end to a perfect day:

> I can get turned on when I am crying with a crying woman—its a very intimate bond—and as well as seeing a woman cry, which is always beautiful, this bond (of crying together) is very special.

Wounded Puppy also enjoys crying when the circumstances are right, which for her is when she is comforting a crying male:

> I think my own crying would simply mean that I was extremely moved and therefore experiencing intimacy with him, and intimacy is the HUGE turn-on.

Celesta is a member of the Crying Appreciation Forum and loves tears so much that she has taught herself to weep and enjoys watching herself crying in a mirror. However she would not cry in front of strangers as she considers being seen with tears in her eyes as highly private:

> Crying is like laughing with a benefit—the tears that flood down the face feel great—like the gentle touch of a lover. Don't wipe them away, let them fall freely. Be proud of the tears in your eyes and

on your face—they mean you are human enough to allow yourself to feel, and that you have a heart so full it's overflowing.

Mark, married and in his forties, enjoys his own tears but he is not turned on by women crying. He is drawn to being comforted by a woman and likens crying in front of a woman as the emotional version of one of his other interests, CFNM (clothed female, naked male), as the tears make him emotionally naked in front of the woman. He describes himself as very in charge and controlled in his day-to-day life and readily admits that these interests are based on being able to let go:

> I have a huge fantasy about being the only man in a room full of women—and then, for whatever reason, starting to cry. This is powerful to me in two ways. First, it would mean I would get comforted by several women at once. But it would also totally unman me. All those women would see me cry, and I wouldn't be able to take back the tears. That loss of control would be both scary and exhilarating.

For those who like their tears and orgasm mixed together, there is the 'crygasm', showcased in a website called (what else?) crygasm.com, which sells pay-per-view videos of women either crying in sadness, their tears changing to tears of joy as they climax, or women becoming so overwhelmed by the sheer intensity of their orgasms that they begin crying.

Related Interests

Domination/submission, salty bodily fluids.

Urine

> Look it's pretty harmless; I think many couples play around with this at some stage. What my partner likes to do is sometimes sneak into the shower while I am in there say washing my hair and then take a wizz on me, waiting to see how long it takes before I realise it isn't the warm water. He finds it even more exciting if I don't realise and we usually end up having sex in the shower.
>
> —personal exchange, woman, early twenties

Urophilia[72] ouron (urine) and philia (love of) is a sexual fixation with urine. The urophile can be aroused by seeing, smelling, touching or tasting urine, and these folk often incorporate being urinated on, or urinating on the partner into sex play. Many pee lovers experience pleasure from the physical sensation of warm urine on their bodies or enjoy the sexual thrill that comes from a sense of defiling the partner or being defiled themselves. Others enjoy urination play because they value the intimacy of sharing what is usually a highly personal practice, and the trust and closeness they believe this brings. Some women who enjoy this fetish believe that their orgasm is more intense if they have a full bladder and they intentionally combine urination with climax as this thirty-something woman describes:

> Pissing and climaxing is such a weird but sexy thing to do. My current boyfriend turned me onto it, I didn't realise it could be part of sex. Because it's messy, we don't do it in the bedroom. Luckily for us, we have a large spa. He lights candles in the bathroom and puts down some old towels, other-wise it is too cold and uncomfortable. It is actually

---

[72]Can be also known as urolagnia.

the only time we also have anal sex, not that the two go together, but it's just how it has worked out. I lie on my side and he masturbates me, then when I can't take it anymore he eases himself into my tush. Once we are comfortable he starts to seriously masturbate me and gets his hand right up there. He knows how to press on my bladder and really goes for it. Of course I'll have had a couple of wines knowing we are going to do this, so it doesn't take much. The first time was a shock, but now—wow—it is just incredibly liberating. The pressure from both openings being filled blows my mind and then him whispering in my ear telling me to piss all over his hand...well...I freakin' love it!!

Some people like to make a game of this, reverting to child-like behaviour such as peeing in their pants or watching the partner do so, while others keep it for the shower or set up their bedding with plastic sheeting. Eboni is a single 21 year old African-American cross-dresser who enjoys seeing girls engaged in pee play as well as watching himself peeing while dressed as a woman. He regularly posts online photos of himself peeing at different locations, including in public and while dressed in women's underwear. He also has a foot fetish, so seeing urine on feet or toes is a further turn-on:

I remember one time I had on this sexy thong, heel, and my toes were painted red. I took a mirror walked a few feet down the road hiked up my dress pulled my panties aside and a golden flow just shot out of me. Pee was everywhere on my thighs, legs and on my feet. It felt so warm on my toes and I loved that could see myself doing it with a mirror. When I finished peeing I took off my

heels and splashed in my fresh pee for a couple of
minutes then I went back home and masturbated.

For others pee play is just another aspect of BDSM play,
making it more about the power to belittle or defile that the
dominant partner takes when urinating on the submissive
partner. In this respect domination games include commanding the submissive partner to urinate on demand, hold urine in
the mouth or swallow it (known as toilet play), or deliberately
stopping the submissive from being allowed to urinate. These
are all services that can be purchased in professional fetish
establishments. For people who prefer not to play with real
urine, yellow liquids such as apple juice or sports drinks are
used as a substitute. When the game playing involves wearing
nappies or diapers, then urine play becomes a part of diaper
fetishism or infantilism.

Related Interests

BDSM, defilement/soiling.

Jargon and Search Terms

Accident prone—used in personal ads as code to describe
someone who likes to defecate or urinate while clothed.
Flooding the cave/golden douche—urinating into a partner's
vagina.
Golden showers—one person urinating on another.
Golden nectar—urine.
Water sports—urine play in sex.

Safety

Medical practitioners warn that any form of play in which
another person's bodily fluids are ingested carries inherent
health risks in the form of communicable diseases such as HIV
or Hepatitis.

Faeces

> Our fun thing is for the GF to have a poo without
> wiping and then we jump into the shower together
> and I wash the shit off her. We both get really ex-
> cited by seeing the water change colour to brown
> as I get to lovingly shampoo her butt. Not sure
> how it happened, but we both love it and it's be-
> come our thing.
>
> —Male, early thirties

Coprophilia: copro (dung) and (philia) love of, is a sexual
response to human faeces. Coprophiliacs are attracted to the
smell, taste or sight of the faeces of another person (generally
someone for whom they have a sexual attraction) although
some folk report enjoying interaction with their own faeces
and may use them for lubrication during masturbation.

People vary in how they prefer contact with faeces. For
some people it is enough to merely think of human excrement
when engaged in sex, or to look at pictures, visit websites or
read stories that involve shit, while others, such as this 22 year
old woman, require a more 'hands on' approach:

> While I know this sounds really gross, my boy-
> friend likes us to have sex after I have been to the
> toilet (as in no.2). He prefers it if I haven't had a
> really good wipe and then when he goes down on
> me he likes to lick that area. I have trouble ac-
> knowledging this happens, so I just pretend it was
> accidental.

This type of play can include one partner defecating directly onto the body of the other, or both playing with
excrement as one might play with clay or dirt, smearing it onto
each other's bodies or sandwiching it between them as they

have sex. Another popular practice is for one partner to lie under a glass table while the other partner squats and defecates above, giving the watching partner a view of proceedings without actually coming into contact with the faeces.

Despite the fact that there are serious health risks associated with ingesting human excrement such as contracting Viral Hepatitis or Giardia, some people enjoy playing a game known as 'human toilet', when one defecates directly on the face or into the other's open mouth. This may be between couples or as a service that is provided by a professional Domme. It is done by the woman sitting on either a custom designed toilet box or an invalid toilet chair and the man lying with his head underneath the opening. Contributors to discussion forums advise that having another person's shit in your mouth takes some getting used to, and there is plenty of advice on what a person might eat to make the taste more palatable and easier to swallow, including recommendations for eating sweet fruits such as pears, apples and grapes. Eating saccharine-based sweeteners and cutting out red meat is also said to make the taste more palatable. First-timers are advised by the old hands that holding their breath or breathing through the mouth is a good trick, because if the smell is bad, it is what is more likely to trigger an urge to vomit.

However Prodommes who provide this service as a deliberate form of humiliation delight in their faeces smelling and usually accompany their bowel movement with verbal insults to ensure the experience is as degrading as possible.

Those who prefer the fantasy version of shit play use foods such as chocolate to mimic faeces. Mini Mars Bars and Snickers are nominated as favourites because of their size and colour. These chocolates are also used as 'training' for eating human faeces. Either way, the chocolates are stuffed up the partner's anus (forum contributors advise that freezing prevents breaking or melting), the partner pushes them out and the other person consumes them.

For some people the desire to interact with faeces as part of sex play may be enhanced by the psychological high that comes from having a partner do something 'forbidden' for them or to them:

> This is how we do poo play. It has to be in the bathroom, because of the mess. He sits on a small stool, that is close to the ground and then calls me in and says I've been a bad girl and that I have to bend over his lap. Because the stool is low I can balance on my knees and elbows as well. He gives me a couple of bottom slaps and then reaches under and starts rubbing lube into my pussy lips. That completely gets me started. With his other hand he tippy toes his fingers into my butt crack. It takes nothing for him to slip them right in because I am just so hot. He finger fucks me but only briefly because I come too quickly when we do this and I can't climax twice. Then he reaches those long, strong fingers up until he hooks into some poo, and works out it of me…it is the weirdest feeling. The first time he did it I was just so embarrassed that he had felt my shit – I didn't know he was actually searching for it! Anyway, soon as he starts fingering it out I just lose it and climax. That's it. We don't do it often and when we play this game I never face him, I never talk and we never kiss or embrace—it isn't that sort of game.
> (Personal disclosure, female, late forties)

A number of websites specialise in human excrement. Coprophiliac porn consists of attractive women having bowel movements, men or women having bowel movements on each other, women giving oral sex with faeces smeared on their faces, women holding faeces in their mouths or women masturbating with faeces. There are also websites specialising in pictures of people's excrement that have been sent in with information on what was eaten to achieve a particular texture or colour.

Some women who willingly defecate on their partners say they enjoy the experience of taking a dominant role and defiling the willing partner. Both men and women who enjoy this practice report a deep pleasure in witnessing a partner demonstrating complete worship and acceptance by the act of eating, touching or otherwise interacting with their faeces.

The practice of BDSM often involves scenarios in which water sports (urophilia) and coprophilia are performed on a submissive partner. While this is consensual when performed in a master–slave or Dominant/submissive context, faeces and urine are always used as tools of punishment, domination or humiliation and so are more to do with the pleasure of domination and defilement[73] than with sexual arousal from the acts themselves.

Both Adolf Hitler and Martin Luther, founder of the Lutheran Church, are documented as having had an interest in coprophilia, and in gay leather culture wearing a brown bandana denotes an interest in coprophilia.

The term coprophilia is easily confused with the word coprolalia, which is used to describe involuntary swearing which is an occasional characteristic of Tourette's Syndrome sufferers.

Safety

Medical practitioners warn that any form of play in which another person's bodily fluids or waste are ingested carries inherent health risks in the form of communicable diseases such as HIV or Hepatitis. Swallowing human faeces puts a person at risk of contracting Viral Hepatitis or Giardia.

---

[73]Clark and Davis (1989).

Related Interests

Flatulence, defilement, urine, BDSM.

Jargon and Search Terms

Brown showers—when one partner defecates onto another's body.
Caviar—faeces.
Cleveland steamer—one partner defecates on the other partner's chest, then spreads the faeces around with his or her buttocks.
Hot lunch—defecating into a partner's mouth.
Recycle—slang for eating faeces.
Scat play—playing with faeces.

Flatulence

> A fart it is a pleasant thing,
> It gives the belly ease,
> It warms the bed in winter,
> And suffocates the fleas.
> —anon

Flatuphilia: flatu (flatulence) and philia (love of) describes erotic arousal from the expelled intestinal gas of another person, otherwise known as farts. Many websites cater to this interest, allowing those who share this passion to read and share stories about flatulence, watch video clips of women passing gas and listen to sound-bites of women farting.

Discussion forums contain topic threads relating to what to eat in order to generate particular types of smells and sounds, with the obvious ones of beans and cabbage mentioned frequently. An Australian forum contributor shares the advice that taking peppermint oil capsules (designed for symptoms of Irritable Bowel Syndrome) has the unexpected side effect of adding a whiff of peppermint to intestinal gas and recommends it as a 'fun surprise' for partners. The ultimate in this practice is when a person passes gas directly onto the face of the other, as one lover of flatulence describes it:

> I would love to find a girl/girls that would sit on my face wearing tight jeans and fart right into my nostrils for long periods of time until I can barely breath. PLEASE girls, let me be your fart sniffing-slave!!!! (Online singles advertisement)

Those with an interest in flatuphilia are often also interested in coprophilia, as intestinal gas is closely aligned with human excrement. For them, having a partner fart can be an exciting precursor to a bowel movement. To ensure it is enjoyed as an all-round form of humiliation, professional Mistresses who are engaged to defecate on a client routinely fart on their submissive clients as a lead up, while verbally castigating them and describing the smells.

Related Interests

Defilement, smell, faeces, urine, Femdom.

Jargon and Search Terms

Gassy erotica — all things fart related.
Sniffy slave — person who wants to be farted on.
Stinky links — websites related to farting.

Blood

> I'll just have a Bloody Mary—oh, and hold the celery stick…

Haematophilia: haema (blood) and philia (love of) is an erotic attraction to blood. It includes the vampire fetish and an attraction to menstrual blood. As it can be difficult to obtain the blood of other people, many blood lovers cut themselves and then enjoy looking at, touching or smelling the blood. Some blood lovers also use blood (their own or others), in place of a lubricant for masturbation or are simply enamoured with blood in any form:

> If I have my period I like to sit on the toilet and watch the blood float into the water. Sometimes it just hangs in the water and kind of has the effect of a lava lamp which looks really cool.

In the world of BDSM, the term blood sports is used to describe any activity in which skin is broken, bitten, scarred, abraded, burned or scratched; and it doesn't focus specifically on blood.

Safety

There are health risks associated with physical contact with any type of blood, as it carries inherent risks such as contracting HIV or Hepatitis.

Vampirism

> Fangs for the memories...

Vampirism[74] is a love of drinking blood. While this may involve biting a person's neck as seen in classic vampire movies, it is more commonly done by making a cut in the skin and then licking or sucking the blood, or by using a hypodermic needle to collect blood. Vampirists are not interested in their own blood as they do not consider it to have any life-giving energy (as has the blood from another person); and for the same reason, menstrual blood is of little interest as it is considered 'dead blood'.

Menstrual Blood

> To my mind washing her blood off my genitals and pubic hair the next morning means that I have been as close to her as is possible for a man to be close to his mate, and that really means something to me.

Menophilia: meno (menses) and philia (love of) is a fetish for menstrual blood. Men who are attracted to menstrual blood enjoy sex with a menstruating woman (often as a preference), or choose to perform oral sex when the woman is bleeding. What men enjoy about it varies. Where one man may enjoy the look of a menstruating vagina, or the way blood looks on his penis, for another the attraction may be in the tastes and smells that blood adds to the sexual mix. A sublimi-

---

[74]A vampire is a mythical creature which sustains itself by drinking the blood of living beings.

nal attraction may also occur, as a woman has increased hormone and pheromone levels during menstruation.[75]

The slang term for a menstrual fetish is red wings and a man is considered to have earned his red wings once he has had oral sex with a menstruating woman—the term alludes to the wings awarded to qualifying pilots. For some men, erotic blood play extends to looking at, touching or fantasizing about used menstrual pads or tampons, which may also be used for masturbation. There are a number of websites specialising in images of menstruating women, and used tampons or menstrual pads can easily be purchased online.

Women also enjoy menstrual blood during sex, and some women prefer sex at this time because they experience a higher level of genital arousal; as an added bonus, some women say it relieves cramps. Others find it empowering or highly complimentary to see their partner enjoying their menstrual blood or simply enjoy the breaking of social taboos:

> Going down on me when I'm bleeding is a bit of a test, how keen is he? How much does he really like me? When he's finished and looks up at me with my juices and blood smeared all over his face and he's not instantly reaching for a tissue or looking like he wants to gag, then I know he is a keeper.

Related Interests

Mysophilia.

---

[75]In fact in ancient witchcraft a spell to make a man fall in love with a woman was often concocted with her menstrual blood, and this is based on the similar idea of bringing her essence or spirit to his attention.

Jargon and Search Terms

Red wings—signifying a man has had given oral sex to a menstruating woman.

Red wing warriors—men who swallow the menstrual blood.

Ride the cotton pony/swim the red river—to have sex with a menstruating woman.

Strawberry tip—penis with blood on it after sex.

Handicap Access Only...

I live pretty much as a paraplegic at home, I go out pretending a few times a month, and yes, there are many days when I wake up and just WISH my legs would stop working, that my spine would break but it isn't going to happen so I make do by pretending.

—contributor to the Yahoo group, Devotee of
Women on Wheels

Disability

Disability fetish[76] is a sexualised interest in the appearance, sensation or experience of disability. It has been described and written about since the 18th century. In this culture people who feign a disability are known as pretenders, while those who wish to actually acquire a disability, even to the extent of engaging in self harm, are known as wannabes. People who are sexually attracted to others who are disabled without having a disability themselves are known as devotees. Many of the online disability communities emanate from Europe (in particular Germany and the Netherlands), where this interest is highly popular.

Trudi is a 48 year old Australian woman with slight birth defect in her left foot. This has made it smaller and weaker and as a result she finds it tricky to wear heels. While Trudi has always loved high-heels and beautiful footwear, she was unable to find these types of shoes with any sort of attached support for her leg, so stuck to flats. 10 years ago she met Paul who was an engineer but not trained in orthotics. As he has

---

[76]This has more recently also been referred to as Factitious Disability Disorder, see Bruno (1997).

long been a lover of women in elegant footwear he bought her some high heels and then modified them with a leg brace. Trudi was delighted and as a result is now able to wear all the heels and high fashion she desires. Trudi and Paul made some YouTube videos of their shoe and brace creations and were surprised at the attention they received from disability models and wannabes to cross-dressers. She has now created a brand for her product[77] and sells it solely through social media contacts made on YouTube and Facebook, to a client base of fetish models, disability lovers, cross-dressers and ordinary women who buy them to indulge their partner's interests. While the fetish aspect is of no personal interest to her or her partner and she hides her cottage industry from our adult children, she is amazed by the high-level of interest people show in creating the appearance of disability and can see it has commercial possibilities. Three of the most common types of disability fetish are discussed below. These are the cast fetish, which involves the wearing of plaster casts and orthotics such as neck braces; acrotomophilia, an attraction to amputations; and apotemnophilia, the desire to be an amputee.

Amputee (Self)

Please, save my mind ...sacrifice my leg.

Apotemnophilia: apo (away) temnein (to cut) and philia (love of) otherwise known as amputee or amputation fetish, is the overwhelming desire to amputate one or more healthy limbs. This relatively new term was coined by American psychologist John Money[78] after he treated patients who

---

[77] Search for TUUS on Facebook or Yumbubble on YouTube.

[78] The first time this term appeared in print was in a chapter by John Money entitled 'Paraphilias', in *The Handbook of Sexology*, Money and Musaph (eds) (1977).

persistently fantasized about experiencing sex as amputees. In later research it was found that many of these people believed they were unable to experience genuine sexual fulfilment as able-bodied individuals.[79]

While apotemnophilia remains the term by which the condition is known, recent and ongoing research is moving towards replacing this term with Body Integrity Identity Disorder (BIID)[80] or Amputee Identity Disorder, as the identification of this disorder as a paraphilia is increasingly believed to be incorrect. Researchers into BIID believe it may be a neuro-psychological condition associated with an anomaly in the cerebral cortex relating to the limbs, and they downplay the element of sexual fetishism that Money originally focused on. They suggest that although it is certainly a fetish in some sufferers, the theory cannot be generalised to all apotemnophiles. Current researchers believe the question of sexual pleasure may be implicated, but only in terms of sexual identity being a part of the person's overall identity; so if a person does not feel 'whole' with his limbs intact, this will affect how he views himself holistically.[81] The majority of BIID sufferers are believed to be middle-aged and male.[82]

Until their desire for amputation is realised, people with true apotemnophilia can be chronically unsatisfied with sexual relationships or even be sexually dysfunctional due to the persistent feeling that they should not have a particular limb. Which limb they consider surplus varies according to the individual, so it might be an arm or a leg, with further specification of a left or right-sided limb. Some individuals can become fixated on obtaining an amputation in a hospital,

---

[79]Money, Jobaris, and Furth (1977).

[80] Although it most commonly refers to people who wish to amputate limbs, the term BIID also applies to those who wish to alter their bodily integrity in general.

[81]Bridy (2004).

[82]Ellison (2008).

although very few surgeons will treat apotemnophilic patients by giving them what they want. The well-known exception is Dr. Robert Smith, a surgeon from Scotland who successfully amputated the healthy limbs of two men before being forbidden by the British Medical Council from performing any more non-medical patient mandated amputations.[83] The exclusion to the rule is male circumcision, which remains one of the few legitimate ways an apotemnophile can indulge his needs to chop off a body part without having an actual medical condition.[84]

Because there are so few ways of having a healthy limb legally amputated, some sufferers may engineer accidents that will amputate one of their limbs.[85] Discussion forums for people with BIID or apotemnophilia, such as Ampulove Forum and Body Modification Ezine[86] offer an opportunity for them to talk about their experiences of obtaining a self-administered or legal amputation as well as sharing the anguish of living with what they feel is an extra limb. Toe amputation is one of the most common self-amputations, given its relative ease (compared to cutting off say, an arm or leg) and these forums are used to garner advice on how to go about it, such as this post to the Ampulove Forum:

> I would like to know how to get rid of my big left toe, is there a lot of blood when you cut this off?

---

[83]Beckford-Ball (2000).

[84]A 2008 episode of the popular American TV series *Grey's Anatomy* also featured a story around a man arriving in the ER upset and demanding surgeons cut off his foot which he maintained did not belong to him.

[85]There is still debate in America as to whether there are any legal caveats that would stop a doctor from performing this type of surgery on a willing patient, with most medicos refusing to do so because of their allegiance to the Hippocratic oath of 'do no harm'. See also Dotinga (2000).

[86]www.bmezine.com.

Can someone advise me please. I don't wanna die,
I just wanna be an amputee. A toe is the perfect
start for me.

YouTube's adult content section contains videos of amputated toes along with discussions on the procedure, while a full interview with a man who has amputated multiple toes can be found at Body Modification Ezine's website.

Given how difficult it is to obtain any type of amputation of a healthy limb, many apotemnophiles make do with pretending to have had an amputation: while out in public, in private, as a prequel to, or as part of sex. A popular way of simulating an arm amputation is to create or purchase a prosthetic arm, which is attached to a shoulder cup or sling. The real arm is hidden under clothing, and the prosthetic is attached directly to the wearer. To make a hand appear cut off, a stump is created large enough for the wearer's actual hand to fit inside, and the shirt sleeve lengthened to disguise the slight extra length. A way of simulating a leg amputation is to tie the ankle to the back of the thigh and then use crutches or a wheelchair. A wheelchair can be modified so that the real legs are enclosed in a false area under the seat, and this gives the appearance of the person in the chair having no legs. A less convincing method is to kneel with calves and feet folded under the seat.

Some folk pretending to have had an amputation say they enjoy the way they are made to feel special by other people. This can include being given handicapped parking, being helped with wheelchairs, or being spoken to with sympathy and kindness. For others it simply engenders a feeling of normality and being anatomically correct—a state they find impossible with all their normal limbs. This feeling of wholeness and normality is a welcome respite, even when it is only temporary, and for some is the only time they feel good enough about themselves to have sex.[87]

> I pretend that my underarm was amputated at the elbow. I regularly bend the left arm to the extreme and stick it into a wide coat arm. Like that my hand and forearm are completely hidden and I appear as an amputee and it means that for a few hours I can be me. The relief these brief periods of time gives me is immense. (Interview with a male pretender in Money, Jobaris & Furth, 1977)

Amputee (Others)

Acrotomophilia: akron (extremity) tome (cutting) and philia (love of) describes an erotic attraction to amputees of the opposite or preferred sex. People with this interest are colloquially known as devotees, with the vast majority of acrotomophiles having an attraction to female amputees. However, while there may be lots of women willing to have their toes licked or their bottoms spanked, women with an amputation are generally not as interested in being pursued for their disability or having a man fondle or ogle their stump. As a result, many devotees have never actually met an amputee and their interest remains in the realm of fantasy.

Websites that cater to amputee fetishes are fairly tame in comparison to what some might consider conventional erotica, as scantily clad or nude amputee models are the exception rather than the norm. This is because the focus of attention is the amputation, and seeing the amputee going about her day-to-day-life is attractive enough for a lot of devotees. Amputation erotica extends to images such as a female amputee with an above-the-knee amputation showcasing her lack of a limb

---

[87]Bruno (1997).

by wearing a short skirt while posing on crutches. While acrotomophilia websites and chat rooms cater more for male admirers, there are also Internet sites such as Ampulove[88] which cater to men and women seeking to meet others with amputations or who wish to share amputation fantasies and amputation play, or discuss their obsession.

Like most people, amputees may not enjoy having one part of their body sexualised, and so are not necessarily grateful for the attention that comes from devotees. Instead they are more likely to be suspicious of the strong allure an amputated stump holds for admirers, with posts by several women to online forums expressing concern that devotees see them as "just stumps" and not as complete people. Added to that, for people who have lost limbs being an amputee has mostly been a source of pain, trauma and loss. The sexualisation of that experience by devotees is as a result far from flattering, as amputees find the attention misplaced at best and insulting, inappropriate or trivialising their disability at worst. Male amputees in particular have great difficulty in accepting acrotomophilia when pursued by able-bodied women.[89]

Devotees generally have preferences for the type of limb amputation they find sexually attractive, often specifying a leg or arm amputation. When it is not possible to meet or date an amputee, activities for devotees vary from simple sexual fantasy about being with a partner with a missing limb, to viewing images or videos of amputees, to getting a partner to role-play being an amputee.[90] In terms of attraction to an amputation, contributors to online so-called 'amp' forums describe how the look or feel of an amputated area is a sexual turn-on, while others write about how the sight of a woman

---

[88]www.ampulove.com.

[89]Gregson (2002).

[90]It is possible to purchase prosthetic limbs on the eBay website, and I would imagine this would not be for the benefit of people who have lost a limb through accident or trauma.

with an amputation brings out feelings of nurturing and compassion which are then linked to sexual feelings. With the permission of their female partner, some male amputees may use their stump as an extension of the penis.

With a storyline of a doctor who cuts off his girlfriend's legs and then her arms in order to satisfy his Venus de Milo obsession with the perfect woman, the controversial 1993 movie *Boxing Helena* starring Sherilyn Fenn is a devotee favourite.

Related Interests

Cast fetish, apotemnophilia.

Jargon and Search Terms

AK—above the knee amputation.[91]
Amp—short for amputee.
BK—below the knee amputation.
Congens—short for congenital, refers to those born with a missing limb.
Devotee—a person who loves amputees but is not one himself.
ES—electronic surgery, in which pictures are digitally re-mastered to show a person as missing limbs.
Pretender— a person who pretends to be an amputee by binding limbs or disguising them with loose clothing.
Wannabe—someone who actually wants to become disabled, sometimes going to extraordinary lengths to have a limb amputated.
Wheelie—someone pretending to need a wheelchair.

---

[91] A full glossary can be found at www.overground.be, a website devoted to all things amputee.

Casts

> I don't mind who is being plastered—basically the
> more plaster the better!
>
> —Male casting enthusiast

A cast fetish is an erotic attraction to limbs in a plaster or
fibreglass cast, with casting the term used for carrying out the
practice. While more men than women enjoy casting, both
men and women enjoy wearing casts, applying casts, having a
partner in a cast or looking at someone in a cast.

Castz is in his late twenties and single. His interest in casting began one summer when he was around 8, after a teenage
cousin broke her leg water-skiing. He remembers being
fascinated by her painted toenails peeking out of the cast, and
loved the feeling of her plastered limb when he was allowed to
sit near her. As a result, he spent a lot of time fetching and
carrying or helping her hobble around, and his interest in casts
has remained:

> I like to wear casts myself, but going out with a
> woman with a cast on (preferably leg cast and
> crutches) would be the icing on the cake, but as yet
> has only been something I can dream about. I try
> to bring it up with new partners, but you can soon
> tell if they might be open to this or not. Maybe one
> of these days I will get lucky.

Serious casters apply a cast to a non-broken limb for recreational purposes. The erotic pleasure comes from applying
the cast, wearing it, or being with a partner who has been
casted. As there is a market for non-medical casting, a number
of online shopping sites provide everything necessary for
putting on a home-made plaster or fibreglass cast. While most
casts can be applied in around 30 minutes, Plaster of Paris

casts can take up to 24 hours to set, so when people want to cast and can't afford to disappear from their everyday lives, they use fibreglass as it sets in about 20 minutes. If time doesn't allow, a cast can also be reused by being applied with tape and bandage to save having to reset a new cast. Fibreglass is generally preferred because the user can order it in many different colours. The art aspect of a cast decorated with slogans, pictures and designs is nominated by many casters as one of the attractions of casting.

Most casters like to wear their cast for a few days if not longer, so there are some practical aspects to consider. As one cast forum contributor pointed out, if a person wants to cast it is something that has to be planned ahead of time and perhaps done on a weekend away. That way the caster avoids any suspicion from neighbours or friends who may see the caster hobbling around the neighbourhood over the weekend with a supposedly broken limb, and then two days later see him walking normally minus a cast.

Aussicast is a 30 year old Australian who did his first cast at 20, after thinking about it for as long as he can remember. He prefers traditional Plaster of Paris for its authentic look and feel. He has always tried introducing new girlfriends to his interest and many, to his surprise, have been willing to give it a go. He has now settled with a woman who willingly shares his love of casting. When they want to cast they either book into motel or stay at home for the weekend, telling people they are going away so that they don't get any unexpected visitors. They lay down plastic as it can get messy, and then take turns putting casts on each other. Aussiecast says he puts more casts on himself than on his girlfriend, because while he could happily do it every day, he knows she is not as interested in casting as he is, and he doesn't want her to become sick of it. The culmination of casting is to have sex with his girlfriend while she has the cast on because:

I just really like the feeling of the plaster rubbing
on my skin and I like nothing better than holding
onto a silky, cool, plastered arm while we make
love.

Some of the reasons casters offer for their enjoyment are
the feeling of confinement they experience when wearing a
cast, the feeling of having to struggle to accomplish day-to-day
tasks, and how the body looks when only some of it is
exposed—for instance, when the foot is in a cast and the toes
are on show. For others, the attraction is in how the cast
creates a 'sculpture' of the limb. Most casters take a great deal
of care with how the cast looks. DC is in his forties and has
been casting most of his adult life. He has a long-term
girlfriend who casts with him. He is very particular about the
aesthetics of the cast, and while he enjoys the process of
casting, this can all be ruined if the cast "looks like garbage":

The main thing I love about casts is the art-work
and quality of workmanship. If the cast is poorly
made or looks like it has just been slapped on in a
hurry, it is an absolute turn off no matter who it is
on, because it's hard for me to get sexually excited
if the cast looks like garbage. Casting is about the
whole experience, not just the fact that there is a
cast. To me it is the difference between admiring a
beautiful painting or walking past graffiti.

Another attraction for casters lies in being and feeling
vulnerable when casted. This reflects the experiences of
amputee wannabes, who also report enjoying the attention
they get from being in a wheelchair or using crutches. When a
partner is casted, he or she is hampered and immobilised and
reliant on the un-casted partner. Again there are similarities to
amputee devotees, who report getting enjoyment from their
role of protector or helper.

Having one partner casted can also set up a dominant and submissive dynamic, as the casted partner wears a form of bondage mandated by the dominant partner. The person who is casted is also vulnerable to having sexual moves made on him or her, as mobility may be limited; and this is part of the sexual thrill for cast enthusiasts. DC says that his girlfriend is always up for some casting because she knows that being casted ensures sexual attention and because she enjoys its bondage aspect. Excitement builds between them as the casted partner wonders "when will I allowed to take it off?", "how long do I have to wear it?" or "when will my partner take advantage of me in my vulnerable state?" Not surprisingly, some casting couples report enjoying bondage activities with ropes, chains and leather for the same reasons. While he and his girlfriend are not into any painful activities, DC believes there is a strong link between what a person experiences in bondage and what they feel in casting; and that casting is simply a type of complementary activity:

> Casting has a much stronger "mental" component (than normal bondage), with the castee being able to feel the cast harden, the limb being frozen and unable to move. With normal bonds like say rope or chains they can untie it or locate the key, but with a cast it is much harder to remove without them possibly cutting themselves. The casted person is at the mercy of the partner, particularly if they are casted in a way that leaves them vulnerable to being played with.

For those who don't actually cast, the interest remains a fantasy that can be indulged by looking at videos or images of women who are wearing casts, or by enjoying films or stories about a woman falling or having an accident and then having to wear a cast. Despite the fact that both men and women enjoy casting, the online market caters mainly to men, with cast websites and videos available that range from clothed women wearing casts to nude or semi-nude women with plaster casts on a foot, leg, arm or wrist. A popular online activity is sharing sightings on mainstream television shows of injuries that include x-rays or plaster casts. Some online casting sites also offer 'candid camera' style images of ordinary people in wheelchairs or on crutches as a result of legitimate injured or broken limbs.[92]

As well as sharing videos and images online, discussion forums and casting websites provide a venue for the thriving market of used casts, which are on-sold to enthusiasts. Used casts sell from between US$24 to $100 on the Internet and people purchase them for much the same reason someone acquires any other collectible; and these items become something they display, caress or spend time admiring. As many casts are decorated, some collectors treat them as a type of art. One caster said that used leg casts are popular because they are a pleasing reminder not only of the outline of the leg, but of the casting experience itself. Some websites offer purchasers the option of 'bespoke casts', allowing buyers to specify the female model to be casted, the type of cast (fibreglass, artwork applied, etc) and the specific limb to be casted. After the model has worn the cast for a designated time it is mailed to the purchaser. Proof of legitimacy is provided in the form of a picture of the model wearing the cast, or the model appearing on the website or video cam while in the cast.

Related Interests

Bondage, amputees.

---

[92]While these sightings of real-life injuries and casts are very popular, they are unauthorised images, so most people are shown with a blackout over their eyes to avoid identification.

Jargon and Search Terms

Caster—anyone involved in casting.
SA—short arm cast.
LAFS—long arm and fingers cast.
LLC—long leg cast.
L2—two legs in plaster.

Blind Play

> For those with an interest in the simulation of
> blindness through the use of visual occlusion de-
> vices such as eye patches and sleep masks.
> —Introduction to Yahoo's Blindsim group[93]

Amaurophilia: amaurosis (dark/darkening) and philia
(love of), describes a preference for sex with partners who are
either genuinely blind or blindfolded, and is also used to
describe a preference for pretending to be blind. Blind play is
known as blindsimming or blindsim, short-hand for the words
'blind simulation'. Simulation of blindness is achieved by
wearing sleeping masks, eye patches or vision-restricting
opaque contact lenses; or simply by having sex in complete
darkness. Websites catering to this interest mostly feature
women in blindfolds, which can be any type of fabric that can
be tied or fastened over the eyes to block sight, such as sleep
masks, ties or scarves. Some blindsimmers choose to extend
this type of play into real life by going out in public with dark
glasses and a white cane, learning to read Braille or 'going
blind' in the safety of their homes.

Enjoyment comes from seeing the partner helpless while
in a form of sensory bondage, or from the visual stimulation of
gazing at the partner's face without looking into the eyes. For
the partner who is sight deprived, the excitement comes from

---

[93] A restricted site requiring signup.

not knowing what will happen next and the heightening of other senses such as touch and smell. The 1980s cult movie 9½ *Weeks*, for example, had a memorable and erotic scene in which actress Kim Basinger sits blindfolded at the refrigerator door while being fed morsels of food.

Discussions on web forums show that many people who enjoy experiencing a level of blindness find it important that the casual observer believes them to be genuinely visually impaired. In this respect the blind fetish has much in common with pretending to have a broken limb. Amy Casseaux is a prolific writer of blindsim fantasy and what follows is excerpt from one of her short stories, *Saturday at the Bloodbank* as it appears on a glasses over contacts website:

> I decide to get into character early. All the lights in my apartment go out, and I put on eye patches. I take a shower and wash my hair, imagining scenarios where someone breaks in and I can't see them. Frightening, but arousing so long as it remains a fantasy. I have no desire to be raped, so I keep my apartment locked up tightly.
>
> I dry off and do my hair up in a towel. I'm kind of snacky hungry, so I make my way to the kitchen for some ice cream. In the past, I have made a blind banana split, exulting both in the flavors and in the sensations of having it drip down my face and onto my bare breasts. Messy, but erotic, which is kind of what blindsimming is for me. (Bobby's GOC website[94])

For dedicated blindsimmers, a simple blindfold may not be sufficient. In the interests of authenticity they may purchase specialist opaque contact lenses or sight distortion glasses (see

---

[94]http://bobbygoc.sweb.cz/amy/amyframe.htm.

Glasses Fetish) sold by specialist retailers as well as practising moving and behaving as a truly blind person would.

Related Interests

Bondage, amputee fetish, cast fetish, glasses fetish.

Jargon and Search Terms

Blindsim—simulating/pretending to be blind.
Visual occlusion devices—masks, eye patches, contact lenses.
OPs—ocular prostheses, such as contact lenses or very heavy glasses.

Wear It

Rubber

> By the time I was three I was a full-blown rubber
> fetishist. No raincoat, bathing cap or pair of baby
> panties was (or is) safe from me.
> —Dennis Dailey, *The Sexually Unusual*

People who are sexually aroused by seeing, touching or wearing rubber-like fabrics are known as Rubberists. Rubber in this sense is an umbrella term covering not only rubber but also PVC, lycra, spandex, latex, neoprene and silicone. One of the peak bodies in this community is The International Association of Rubberists (IAR), a global organisation providing help, information and community to rubber fetishists world-wide.[95] The welcome page of their website includes the following statement of purpose, which neatly sums up their intentions:

> Help Rubberists overcome loneliness and isolation
> by nurturing comradeship between like-minded
> people on an international scale. If you have a fet-
> ish for rubber, latex or PVC, *you are NOT alone!* We
> understand you!

Ataxaria[96] is the founder and head of IAR, and he was kind enough to spend many months discussing the Rubberist lifestyle with me. He is in his early sixties, has been married to the same woman for many years and has adult children.

---

[95]http://www.rubberist.net.

[96]The name means a state of tranquility free from anxiety and emotional disturbance.

Ataxaria is open with family members about his love of rubber, and while they don't pretend to understand it, they are tolerant and allow him to pursue his interests with a minimum of fuss. According to Rubberist.net statistics (correct as at early 2009), the IAR site gets about 1,500 unique visitors daily and has over 8,000 email-verified, registered members. IAR's member base is overwhelmingly male, with female membership of approximately 8%. The largest Rubberist[97] community exists in the UK, followed by other mainly English-speaking countries like USA and Australia.[98]

Data kept by the IAR shows that Rubberists are generally middle class, older (40 plus) and with a good level of education. Many Rubberists are in normal monogamous relationships, sharing their fetish with wives and partners who, while they may not be interested in rubber themselves (known as NRP, non rubber partner), accept the Rubberist dressing up (rubbering up), or will dress up for them or with them.

Rubberists enjoy wearing a variety of clothing made from materials in the rubber family, including body cat-suits, skirts, singlets, jeans and underpants, full zippered hoods and gas masks. These clothes are commonly made from latex, as it is a fine, malleable material that can easily be sewn into various articles of clothing. Depending on the type of outfit chosen, rubber fetish clothing and mainstream fashion can intersect, given that wearing tight, shiny clothing is seen as both acceptable and desirable for women and the young in most Western societies. *Harper's Bazaar* fashion magazine graced its October 2007 issue with model Jennifer Hawkins on the cover wearing a custom-made rubber cat-suit from *Reactor Rubber*, Australia's premier rubber shopping emporium and in May 2010 the English singer Rihanna caused some controversy by

---

[97]The community always capitalises the term Rubberist in the form of a proper noun, as they consider it the name of their 'tribe'.
[98] The largest number of Australian Rubberists can be found in Perth, Western Australia.

wearing a skimpy PVC outfit on stage. However, the problem that heterosexual Rubberists face when going out in public is that any form of rubber clothing (say tight shiny pants or anything in PVC) is not considered 'acceptable' street-wear except on the young or homosexuals. This results in most Rubberists confining themselves to wearing their rubber clothing within a circle of accepting family and friends, at specific rubber events or just in the privacy of their own homes or bedrooms. Rubberist activities include:

- Having just the female partner dressed up in rubber.

- Wearing rubber clothing under normal clothes (e.g. shorts, singlets, underwear) or wearing latex outer clothing that can pass as street-wear, such as a long-sleeved latex cycling top.

- Wearing rubber 'dress up' clothing such as cat-suits, full body suits or masks only for special occasions, such as in the company of other Rubberists or when engaged in sexual acts.

- Wearing rubber when masturbating.

- Wearing rubber as part of a rest and relaxation regime (e.g. listening to a CD or having a glass of wine at home alone).

I asked what motivated Ataxaria to wear rubber clothing and he responded with his own question:

> Why do women wear high heels and skin tight skirts when going to a disco? We both know the answer to that—they like how they look and how they feel in terms of their sexuality. While this may sound simplistic, Rubberists aren't much different—we also enjoy how rubber makes us look and how it looks on others—and it is as plain as that.

Rubberists always enjoy rubber for how it looks or feels on their bodies, but some equally important aspects include handling it, inhaling the smell, and even listening to the sound the material makes. All Rubberists enjoy touching or stroking rubber—whether a rubber-clad body or simply a garment—and this can extend to enjoying the ritual of maintaining the rubber and spending many pleasurable hours shining and admiring it. The smell of rubber is probably a little-known aspect of this fetish, but to some Rubberists the smell of different types of rubber is a type of aphrodisiac in itself. Rubberists report a number of distinct smells that rubber can give off, depending on whether it is cold or warm, or what type of rubber it is. Some even claim that different colours of rubber give off different scents (in a similar way that balloon enthusiasts maintain that different coloured balloons have different smells).

The taste of rubber can also be attractive to Rubberists. While rubber is an organic material and not digestible, some Rubberists find what they describe as the strong, "vivid tang" of rubber to be erotic, and enjoy licking or sucking it—for example, nibbling on a rubber-clad penis or toes. As well, Rubberists find the sound of rubber enticing or sexy. As we know from balloons, rubber makes loud, squeaking noises when rubbed. A Rubberist recognises the more subtle sounds of rubber, such as rubber clothing being prepared for wear or being pulled onto the body, a rubber sheet being ruffled or a slap on a rubber-clad rump.

Wearing latex or rubber is not always just for sexual reasons, and the theme of 'enclosure' is frequently mentioned in relation to the fetishisation of rubber. Some Rubberists describe dressing in latex or rubber as comforting, and de-stressing, and as providing a 'womb like' place for the wearer. A number of Casters (those who wear plaster casts for enjoyment or enjoy watching others in casts) make similar reference to the feeling of enclosure that casting gives them.

Many Rubberists say they realised from early childhood that they had an attraction to rubber, tight clothing or the feeling of enclosure. Writing about this aspect, one forum contributor described it as a visceral impulse which was present in his memory before he was 10 years old. Another Rubberist suggested that people who like the feeling of something tight, stretchy and rubbery on their skin might even have started out accidently enjoying the feeling of something ordinary like a glove. Rubber or latex gloves of the type used to wash dishes are a common item of interest for young Rubberists, especially as they are easy to obtain. Many forum contributors to Rubberist.net report their initial attraction to rubber occurring around puberty:

> I noticed my fetish when I was around 13 years old. At my parents' house we had a bright yellow rubber raincoat hanging in the hall. I used to wear it when playing in the garden. I became fascinated by the smooth rubber texture, the pleasant smell and the warm hugging feeling it gave me when I put it on. It was at the same time when I discovered the pleasures of masturbation. So I often masturbated, while touching the yellow rain clothing.

Whilst Rubberists recount memories of feeling some type of sexual excitement when smelling or touching rubber clothing or items at an early age, it is not possible to know if this is because of the rubber, or because the experience is simply linked to a period of time associated with recognising sexual feelings. However it begins, once the association is made, Rubberists generally continue their interest into adulthood as this poster to the Rubberist.net forum explains:

> I saved up and bought my first rubber wetsuit at 10. I'm 50 now and still have a tiny square of it,

which I pull out occasionally to stroke. I've always liked bodysuits and straps, for as long as I can remember. When I was 2 I climbed out of everything so mom strapped me in to my crib with a belt with tethers on both sides and a crotch strap. I probably cried myself to sleep writhing on it for comfort.

One school of thought suggests that rubber fetishists are likely to have been bed-wetters as children, and the sexual connection they maintain with latex is tied to the combination of genitalia and rubber pants or rubber sheets used to protect the bed. Therapist Dennis Dailey (who admits to rubber fetish himself) surveyed over 200 rubber fetishists and reported that for some of them the rubber fetish began when their sheets were removed, leaving the bed-wetter in direct contact with a rubber sheet. After getting pleasure from stroking it or rubbing themselves on it, some of them deliberately wet the bed so that the rubber sheeting would remain on the mattress.[99]

The founder of Rubberist.net estimates that, based on records kept by his organisation, well over 50% of Rubberists seem also to have some interest in cross-dressing and costume play (maids, nuns, nurses and schoolgirls), however the cross dressing does not necessarily have to involve rubber, but can be simply clothing made from ordinary fabrics. The profiles section of Rubber.net also indicates a preference for BDSM and a poll conducted by them shows that approximately 50% of members enjoy BDSM activities, with bondage high on the list.

Related Interests

BDSM, cross-dressing, transvestism, masks.

---

[99]*The Sexually Unusual* (1989).

Jargon and Search Terms

Body bag/total enclosure—fully enclosed rubber bag into which a person is sealed. Used in restriction or mummification games.

NRP—non-Rubberist partner.

Rubbered up/Rubbertime—dressing in rubber.

Rubber holiday—when a person can wear their latex or rubber as much as they wish.

Rubber doll—wearing rubber outfits e.g. cone breasts, masks or high heels, to take on a female form.

Rubber slut—a person who will stop at nothing to get in touch with rubber, to the point of obsession.

24/7—wearing the rubber clothing 24 hours a day, including in sleep.

Shining—polishing the rubber using a shining or polishing agent which can be either latex shiner or silicon oil.

Squeak—the action of rubbing on someone who wears rubber.

Vanilla—all those who are not into a fetish, in this instance rubber.

Zentai—a term for skin-tight garments that cover the entire body, e.g. a rubber catsuit.

Fur, Leather and Fabric

Doraphilia: dora (skin) and philia (love of) is the love of animal fur or leather (or both). Some fur fetishists simply enjoy looking at images of women dressed in furs or skins as a prelude to sex, while others satisfy their need by amassing a collection of fur or leather which is worn, smelled, viewed or handled as foreplay or during sex. The activities carried out with fur vary, and include massaging the body during or before sex with fur, having sex on top of a fur garment, masturbating while holding fur or holding it close to the face so it can seen or inhaled. Deana discovered her carnal attraction to fur when she was in her early twenties:

> I have this old silver fox fur cape that I got for an absolute bargain in a weekend market, probably 10 years ago. It has big boxy shoulders and I would never wear it out. But I like nothing better than laying it on my naked body with a sleeve between my legs, which I use to masturbate with. Depending on the boyfriend, I sometimes get to make love lying on it, but nobody has really worked out yet how much I love (in the literal sense), my fur.

People can also be particular about what form the fur takes, from keeping a little square or piece of fur to sniff and hold, to having a pronounced interest in fur cuffs, boots, gloves, throws, capes, jackets or hoods. As a rule, fur fetishists are particularly opposed to fake or fun fur. People can be similarly attached to favourite types of fabric—for example satin—and their behaviours are similar as this 18 year old girl describes:

> From when I was tiny I loved satin and couldn't sleep unless I had a satin pillow, scrap of satin, or article of satin clothing in my hands. My parents thought it was a cute and girly thing to do until they realised I wasn't growing out of it and the idea became embarrassing. They would have been more embarrassed had they known I masturbated with it and still do it now. Really, the only thing that's changed is that I can buy all the satin I want!

Writing on the Rubberist.net forum, this man describes how a love of satin made way for his love of spandex and rubber:

As a child, long before I hit puberty, I discovered my fetish for satin. I don't know where it came from. I was bored and in a fabric store with my mom one day when I ran my hand through a bolt on the shelf. I think my worldview shifted a bit. I instantly imagined that it was like a liquid that I could wrap myself up in, and I wanted that very badly. As I got older and became aware of spandex and the slinky way that it follows the contours of the body, it appealed to me in the same way.

There are a number of Internet communities that focus on fur and the sharing of images and discussion around fur. While the images tend to be of women wearing furs, the over-riding focus of these communities is less concerned with sex or pornography and more about sharing photos and discussing the various fur articles of clothing that the women wear.

There are some interesting theories about why people fe-tishise fur. Freud maintained that there was "no doubt" that women wore fur because it reminded them of pubic hair (whether their own or that of others was not made clear), while another early psychoanalytic theory maintains that a fur fetish is developed when a baby comes into contact with the mother's pubic hair during birth, hence the practice of shaving women prior to childbirth.[100]

An attraction to leather spans the gay, lesbian and hetero-sexual community, and also describes a lifestyle that involves BDSM. This is most prevalent in gay communities and is recognised as subculture simply called 'leather' and its followers known as leathermen. For them, leather is a part of their sexuality and a way of distinguishing themselves from mainstream culture. Leather has a long history of masculinity and male bonding going back to the bomber pilots in WW I

---

[100]Malin and Saleh (2007).

and II and the motor cycle clubs of the 1940s which became a type of template for the early gay leather bars. When homosexuality was still banned (in Europe and America), men would wear leather to specific bars as a type of code for their sexuality.[101]

For others (regardless of sexuality), leather is arousing in similar ways to rubber, as they enjoy the sight, smell, fell, creak and taste of the material as well as the aura of sexuality that comes from wearing it. Leather is often found on chastity devices and restraints and of course on whips and floggers. As the *Gay Leather Fetish History* website says:

> Leather (the material) arouses people in very different ways. But really explaining why leather is arousing is almost impossible. You either understand, or you don't.

Jargon and Search Terms

Fur massage—rubbing the body (particularly the sex organs) with fur.
Fur sluts—women who wear furs during sex.
Furvert—men who love women in furs.
Leathermen—homosexual men who enjoy the leather subculture.

---

[101]See The Gay Leather Fetish History site for more comprehensive information on this topic: http://www.cuirmale.nl/index.htm.

Masks

Many Rubberists and people in the BDSM scene enjoy the use of masks, including full bondage hoods and gas masks. However, a mask fetish can be a 'standalone' interest, with fetishists enjoying either wearing the mask themselves or watching someone wearing or taking off a mask, without any further interest in either rubber or BDSM.

Followers of the Jung school of psychoanalysis link the preference for masks to a way of playing out the shadow aspect of the personality; in this theory, wearing a mask hides the public persona and allows a person's 'dark side' to surface.[102] Festivals such Mardi Gras and Halloween and the Brazilian Carnevale are said to be popular because they offer people a socially acceptable way of revealing another side of their personality when wearing a mask. Regardless of the reason, people enjoy various types of masks: gas masks, scarves, Halloween, ninja or surgical masks, and rubber, leather or bondage hoods. Perennially popular styles are the cat mask, the bat mask and the bandit mask (think Zorro), with leather the most favoured mask material.

Some people who are of an age to remember World War II may have a gas-mask fetish, developed at the time they had to wear a mask during air raids, when the mix of anxiety and the strong smell of rubber in the mask had a long-lasting effect on their psyches. Gas masks are so popular that replicas can be purchased at specialty outlets. For those who enjoy a medical fetish, the oxygen mask and the surgical mask remain firm favourites.

Related Interests

BDSM, rubber, blind play.

---

[102]Richo (1999).

Glasses

> Alice (Candy, Mandy or Gina), through the Look-
> ing Glass...

A glasses fetishist is attracted to people wearing prescription glasses or is someone who himself wears glasses for
pleasure. People who enjoy wearing eye-glasses refer to
themselves as 'optic obsessive,' while people attracted to
others wearing glasses refer to themselves as 'myope lovers' if
they are attracted to short-sighted people, and 'hyperope
lovers' if they prefer long-sighted people.

There are many chat and websites that cater exclusively
for this fetish, ranging from pornographic to G-rated. Those
without any sexual material provide a community forum for
friendship and discussion of this interest, which includes
frequent technical references to prescriptions and strengths as
it is common for those interested in the eye scene (as this
interest is commonly known), to have a high level of technical
ophthalmological knowledge; discussions are peppered with
references to the wearer's prescription details such as "My
glasses are now -18D for my left lens and -19.5D for the right
lens."

This group likes to talk about trying on glasses, wearing
glasses, buying glasses, frame styles and visual problems.
They also enjoy looking at pictures of clothed or nude models
and people wearing or holding glasses, celebrity sightings and
stories that revolve around the characters wearing glasses. The
largest English-speaking online community can be found at
the Eye Scene discussion forum, with members from across
Europe and America.

There are distinct preferences for either short-sighted
(near-sighted) or long-sighted wearers. Glasses lovers can tell
at a glance what type of lenses someone is using, because

those who are short-sighted wear lenses with minus diopters[103] which make their eyes look smaller, while those who are long-sighted wear plus diopter lens, which make their eyes look bigger. Some men refer to short-sighted girls as having a "come hither" style as these type of lens make the eyes look smaller and what they term "more curious". As plus lenses magnify the eyes and make them appear large and accented, wearers are referred to as 'Bambis', and are preferred by approximately 25% of the glasses community.

If a glasses lover wants to wear prescription glasses but has no optical impairment, a common trick is to wear contact lenses that distort sight and then wear eye-glasses to correct that distortion. This is known as GOC, glasses over contacts. Doing this allows a person to wear glasses of any power they want, as they first insert contact lenses of an opposite power which alters their vision and means they need glasses. By employing these techniques a girl with excellent eyesight can wear 'coke bottle' glasses, take them off and be genuinely stumbling around short-sightedly because her contacts are distorting her ability to see. This sort of play would be considered highly erotic to a glasses lover.

Fantasies and scenes for those interested in this practice extend to watching women cleaning their glasses, appearing naked but for glasses, playing with or otherwise handling the glasses, or struggling and squinting because they are groping for their glasses. While a simple attraction to people wearing glasses would not be considered a paraphilia, extreme forms of this attraction include only dating women with glasses, having a preference for the partner to be wearing glasses during sex, or preferring pornography or sexual images to include the wearing of glasses.

---

[103]The unit of measurement used to describe the power of corrective lenses, so a minus setting makes thing smaller, a plus setting larger.

Bobby is a 50 year old man who runs the website Bobby's Site About Glasses which receives between 200-300 visitors daily. He has been a lover of glasses (both as a wearer and on women), since he was around 5 and wears glasses over contacts on a daily basis:

> Yes, I am an eye-glasses fetishist. I like girls and women who wear glasses, especially those who need to wear very strong minus glasses. I like plus glasses too, however I really prefer thick minus lenses. Frames and lenses have always drawn my attention. There is nothing like looking at a nice woman with spectacles sitting on her nose and seeing her small eyes hidden behind the thick lenses.

Bobby is now divorced, but says his ex-wife would happily wear glasses for him, as have other girlfriends. While he enjoys being with women who wear glasses, he does not make it a mandatory requirement for dating.

A good glasses story generally contains some technical details about the strength of the glasses or the severity the short-sightedness, such as this small excerpt from *Talk on Train*, from Bobby's website:

> Only two people were sitting in the compartment of the train. A dark-haired lady reading a magazine and a young man, who was trying to concentrate on a textbook. Both of them were wearing glasses. The glasses of the man were quite modern with thin lenses of a low power. It was difficult to say if he really needed them to read. Probably they were more a fashion item than an optical aid, as the lenses were really thin. On the contrary, the glasses the lady was wearing were of a strikingly high power. Although the lenses were rather tinted, nothing could hide the huge optical power

of those two pieces of glass. The edges of the lenses were thicker than the fashionable plastic frame. The rear held a small bowl ground into the material making the eyes of the woman look small and sunken. The front surface was ground, too. It went inwards, it curved towards the lady's eyes providing the lenses with extra diopters.

Opinions offered by glasses enthusiasts on why they prefer a woman wearing glasses range around her perceived air of vulnerability to the belief that it adds an element of class to the sexual act or fantasy. Those who find the vulnerability aspect attractive enjoy how a woman with glasses brings out their protective instinct, describing how nice it is to help shield her from the world in which she is helpless without her glasses. Other men perceive a woman with glasses as scholarly, so are attracted to the intellectual aspect, while for some the attraction comes from seeing a woman who is social powerful, let's say a glasses-wearing teacher or corporate manager, in the act of getting naked or having sex—while keeping on her glasses.[104]

The glasses lover is sexually aroused by the act of a woman taking off her glasses, referred to as 'the Christmas package,' as taking off her glasses or taking them off her, is symbolic of unwrapping a gift. Once she removes her eyewear he is then privy to a different, more private side of the woman. The media trades on this concept quite heavily with advertisements and films frequently featuring the instantaneous transformation of what is (usually) the so-called ugly duckling in glasses and what happens when she whips these off and shakes out her mane of hair to suddenly become a ravishing beauty. For others the simple act of a woman handling and playing with her glasses is fascinating in itself.

---

[104]Powerful women involved in sex acts are colloquially referred to as power sluts.

An opinion offered by enthusiasts is that a glasses fetish stems from a fascination for how the actual glasses lens modifies the look of the eye, believing glasses give eyes a mysterious look, in the same way a veil might—with the term 'glass veil' often used when referring to women wearing glasses.

Jargon and Search Terms

Bambis—magnifying lenses.

High myopic girls—women who need to wear strong glasses.

Hyperope lovers—people attracted to those who are long-sighted.

Glass-glaze—When the man ejaculates onto the lenses of a woman wearing glasses, this becomes a glass glaze.

GOC—the abbreviation for a technique called glasses over contacts.

GWG—girls with glasses

Myope—a person who needs to wear short-sighted glasses, taken from the term Myopia, the description for short sighted-ness.

Myope lovers—people attracted to those who are short-sighted.

Wannabe myope—someone pretending they need glasses.

Diapers

> Baby Mikey vewy tired. Going to get my diaper changed, take some NyQuil, and hitting the sack.

The diaper lover (DL) likes to wear diapers (also known as nappies) for non-medical purposes. The DL is generally a man, although women also enjoy wearing diapers. Preferences range from cloth diapers to disposables made for adult incontinence, with or without plastic or rubber pants, and under normal clothing or only for special occasions. There are numerous websites selling adult-sized cloth nappies, plastic pants, rubber pants and disposables, making the process of purchasing these items a discreet and straightforward experience.

The range of interest varies, from full-time or night-time to occasional wear. For some people the simple experience of wearing a diaper (either in day-to-day activities or at specific times) is pleasure enough, while others get their enjoyment from masturbating in them or from wetting or soiling their diapers (see also urine and faeces).

Some diaper lovers are unable to become sexually aroused unless they are wearing a diaper or viewing images of people wearing diapers, while for others a diaper is an occasional treat for a special occasion. As well as finding it erotic, many DLs describe diaper wear as emotionally satisfying and simply a way of relaxing. I placed a survey question on the Diaper Talk Facebook page asking if diaper wear was for sexual or emotional reasons and the responses came out at fifty-fifty, with most of the people who chose sexual also clicking on emotional.

The stories of most DLs is remarkably similar in that they report a fascination with diapers from as long back as they can remember. For a number it is also associated with a traumatic experience, such as being ridiculed by other children or being punished for wetting themselves. Transsexual Bree, for example, is now in her fifties and while she enjoys diapers now, was made to wear them by a foster mother as punishment for bedwetting when she was 11 years old. Ray is a 26 year old Canadian in a blue collar job and while he didn't have any bad early memories, his interest started early:

> I remember as a kid having a diaper on one of these larger stuffed dolls and taking it off the doll and putting it on top of my regular clothes. I was

always fascinated by them as a kid and when going to a store I loved to go to the diaper isle and
touching the bags of diapers. I would tell my
friends at school that I wanted diapers and stuff
but back then I didn't realise it was taboo, I didn't
understand. I remember being with a friend and
her telling me as we walked around the diaper isle,
"we are not getting diapers." It wasn't until I was
16 or so until I discovered adult-diapers that I
gained a full interest in them.

Baby Mikey is 36, a single father of one and works in the
entertainment industry. He remembers being 4 years old and
getting into trouble with his father over bedwetting. To avoid
punishment he stole diapers from his baby-sitter's house to
wear at night and then just continued to wear them:

I started buying diapers from my allowance, yard-
work and paper route money. At about 11 years of
age I had to switch to small adult diapers, as I'd
outgrown the toddler size ones by that time. I have
been pretty much wearing diapers every night of
my life.

Baby Mikey had a sexual experience when he was 15 with
another female diaper lover. He only realised later in life how
unusual it was to have connected with a female DL so early in
life. He married and had a child and his wife accepted the
diaper wearing, particularly as it was predicated on night-time
bed wetting. He says it was not the major reason for their later
divorce. While he must wear them now for medical reasons,
he says he would continue to do it by choice as it has become a
way of life. He finds them an emotional comfort rather than
sexual, although he readily admits they were a turn-on earlier
in his life. Aside from masturbation in diapers, DLs particu-

larly enjoy the act of diapering or being diapered as Baby Mikey describes:

> Something so simple as a diaper change is such an intimate act to me. You put so much trust and level of intimacy into the person who is doing this. I still remember my first girlfriend and how she powdered and fastened my diaper like a pro!

Ray also relies on wearing diapers in times of stress and for emotional comfort, particularly when he feels his romantic life isn't going well. Conversely, if a relationship is going well he tends to have no need for diapers:

> A great deal of my confidence comes and goes with how well my relationship with a girl is going. When I put a diaper on a lot of my stress and worries just seem to fade away. I think that wearing the diaper brings me back to a time when I was younger when I didn't have to worry about these things. I can put my problems aside and just focus on wearing my diaper, coloring in a book.

The Daily Diaper[105] bills itself as the largest online community for diaper fetishists and adult babies, while Facebook also has a number of groups for diaper lovers such as Diaper Lovers Talk, with 1150 members on at time of writing of which approximately 25% say they are women. While there is opportunity to meet a female DL partner in these type of community forums, a common problem men face is not knowing if the online person is actually a woman. Baby Mikey believes there are a reasonably high number of female DLs, but they tend not to make themselves public online. On the

---

[105] www.thedailydiaper.com.

question of sharing their interest with a woman, none of the men I spoke with said this was mandatory; but considered finding a like-minded partner would be a bonus. The youngest of my respondents (at 21 years of age) is marrying shortly and has never told his fiancée about his interest. He intends to give it up completely after marriage because in his words, he "doesn't think she should be subjected to this". In contrast, 'J' is in his mid-fifties and continues to insist on wear them when he feels like it—despite his wife's objections.

When a diaper lover also likes to regress and role-play an infant or small child, the interest crosses over to infantilism or adult baby play, known as AB (see Adult Baby for more information).

Related Interests

Adult baby, urine, faeces.

Jargon and Search Terms

DL—diaper lover.
AB—adult baby.

Play Acting

Adult Baby

> Available online now! Soft and feminine baby-grows in all colours to suit most AB sizes up to XXL. The 'funny bunny' growsuit comes with a gorgeous appliquéd bunny-rabbit on the front and it is 100% cotton with easy open neck and studs. Ask your mummy or daddy to buy you one today!
> —Advertisement on Dailydiapers.com

Infantilism or infant play is an attraction to acting as a young child or baby, and is most commonly known as adult baby or AB for short. It should not be confused with pedophilia, a sexual attraction to pre-pubescent children. There is also confusion between a diaper fetish and infantilism. People who have a diaper (nappy) fetish wear diapers but may not always dress or behave as babies, whereas adult babies almost always wear diapers while behaving as babies, see also Diaper Fetish. Those with a strong interest in adult baby as well as diapers are known as ABDLs, short for adult baby diaper lovers.

Along with wearing diapers, adult babies enjoy all manner of babyish things and behaviours. These may include sleeping in a baby's room or in an adult-sized crib, playing with children's toys such as rattles or stuffed bears, sucking on a pacifier, or dressing in baby or toddler-style clothes such as romper suits, plastic pants, frilled diaper covers or baby-style playsuits. Some men choose the role of sissy baby, so all clothing and behaviour must be female. A search on Ebay for 'sissy baby' yields pages of items such as frilly socks, bibs, rubber pants, panties and pacifiers, all in adult sizes. For those with an account at Ebanned.net, an auction and selling site for items that Ebay refuses to sell or has banned, used diapers are for sale, so the AB can purchase one that has already been broken in.[106]

Adult babies may drink milk or juice from a sippy cup or baby bottle, or eat baby food. For some this can extend to adult nursing, though drinking breast milk in this case is a part of being a realistic baby as opposed to indicating a breast milk fetish. When the woman is the baby, she may pretend that her partner's penis is the baby bottle.

If the adult baby is lucky enough to have a nanny, aunt, mommy or daddy, then staged role-plays such as 'naughty baby', 'baby bath-time' or 'reading baby a bed-time story' are common scenarios. Some babies require medical intervention from their carers, such as being given an enema or having their temperature taken with an anal thermometer. The parental figure will also feed and dress the baby, change its nappy when it is wet, and perhaps punish the baby with a spanking when he or she has soiled the diaper. A very enjoyable activity for most babies and their partners is the cleaning, powdering and dressing of the baby after a wet diaper, with much caring attention lavished on washing the baby's genitals, drying them and rubbing them with lotion or baby talc. It is fairly common to read advertisements such as these on adult baby sites:

> I'd like to meet a nice but strict mommy or babysit-
> ter. One who will change me when I wet my dia-
> pers and punish me when I do so, because I'm a
> big boy and should know how to use the potty by
> now.

When it is not practical to do these things in real life, adult babies join online groups which allow them to express themselves as their baby persona, posting comments such as "need a mommy to change my wet diaper" or "baby feeling

---

[106] Ebanned also sells such diverse items as a sissy baby blanket, a blanket made out of used tissues.

sick, needs his juice and a goodnight story". I was able to speak with one non-professional mommy, Emma, a 30 year old English academic, who is also kind enough to chat online with the many ABs looking for a parent figure. She comments on how they look in their sissy baby outfits (posting pictures of themselves wearing diapers is common), writes punishments for them such as "you must sit in the naughty chair," or praises them when she considers they have been good babies. They in turn thank her and refer to her as Miss Emma.

She and her boyfriend, who has a highly stressful job, use baby play as a way for him to relax. They play mummy and baby games four to five evenings a week and sometimes on the weekend too. She does all the traditional mothering tasks, which means putting on his nappies and dressing him in baby clothes as well as bottle feeding, bathing and playing games with him. He's allowed to wet his diaper but not soil it and sometimes she lets him use a potty. There is no sex when he's being a baby. While it is a common assumption that these games are played with the AB's pleasure in mind, Emma says she very much enjoys being the one in control and having her partner completely surrendering to her.

Emma and her partner are the exception rather than the norm, as most AB men have difficulty finding a partner to act out the role of caretaker, or hide their interest from partners; so when they use baby items like pacifiers, sippy cups and diapers, they must do this covertly or alone. The men I interviewed were from a wide range of ages, Dave—at 18— was the youngest. He attends a prestigious American university and does all the things an all-American college boy would do, including running track and cross-country, working out in the gym and playing golf and racquetball on the weekends. The only difference is that when he goes to bed he wears a pull-up and takes a pacifier with him. His interest started early and he remembers desperately wanting a pacifier when he was 9 years old. Having a younger sister in the house he was able to make use of hers as well as borrowing her pull-up diapers and he continues to use both today. As he shares a room with his older brother he has confided in him, but believes nobody else in his family is any the wiser.

While the sexual aspect is nominated as highly enjoyable, many ABs say they enjoy the emotional aspects of the role-play just as much; their interest is based on the nurturing experience as opposed to sexual pleasure, as they enjoy being taken care of in the same way as a baby or toddler. ABs such as Baby Danny, a successful business man in his early fifties with adult children, say they are attracted to this practice because it is such a complete way to let go of the cares of the world. Every couple of months Baby Danny treats himself to a baby session from a professional mommy, and has done so for most of the twenty-five years he has been married. He spends an afternoon in baby clothes sucking on a bottle and then has his nappy changed, after which he is allowed to masturbate. In between these visits he chats to other ABs online. To him, being a baby means he is not expected to do anything or be anyone, and adult responsibilities are temporarily suspended. Baby Danny feels this is one of the few times he can relax completely, as he is allowed to demand nurturing and attention without the burden of returning it, making it a guilt-free 'all about me' experience.

Many of those active in the adult baby communities are men, although one of the leading diaper community websites suggests that females taking a baby role may be as high as 40%—however this is difficult to confirm as anecdotally women prefer to keep the practice private. As this community is well catered for online[107], men who are in their forties and fifties finally have somewhere to connect with other ABs, after

---

[107]One of the largest is www.dailydiapers.com, a site catering to both adult babies and diaper lovers. It features thousands of photos of diapered men and women as well as stories, diaper reviews, advice columns, personal ads, message boards and more.

spending years believing they were isolated in their interest. Many sites enable babies and caretakers to make contact, get information, buy goods such as adult-sized baby clothes, nappies or baby furniture and bedding, share stories or simply talk about their interest without ever meeting. If their interest is not shared by an understanding partner, or if they are not in a position to have baby trappings such as a cot, toys, or clothing in their homes, there are weekend retreats where, for a fee, they can spend the time completely in character being cared for as a baby; or they attend group meetings where they can get together dressed in nappies and baby clothes. There are also many women advertising online as professional mommies, nannies or aunts, who provide personal services or pay-by-the-minute chat or email that appeals to adult babies.

Related Interests

Diapers, cross-dressing.

Jargon and Search Terms

AB—adult baby, adults who enjoying dressing and behaving like babies.

Age play—a common variant of role play where one partner acts as a parent (e.g. dad or mother) and the other takes the role of a child.

Caretaker, nursemaid, nanny—an enabling adult who role-plays the mummy, daddy or other parent role.

Sissy baby—a male adult who enjoys pretending to be a girl baby.

Human Cows

We are a couple seeking human cows for milking
and live lactation training and play here in Hawaii.
Have barn and lots of quiet acres.
—advertisement, ALT.com

The term human cows refers to women who consent to
being treated as farm cows and having their breasts, or udders
as this group likes to call them, milked—either manually or
with farm milking equipment. Despite the focus on breast
milk, this interest has little to do with adult nursing relationships, as the milk is rarely consumed and the woman is
playing the role of an animal, not a nurturer. The person who
milks the woman is known as the farmer or the owner and his
role is to milk and/or breed (have sex) with the so-called cow.

A typical role-play scenario or fantasy involves the woman being milked in a barn or an outdoor area set up as a barn.
The erotic elements include the 'cow' stripping out of her
clothes, getting down on all fours, having a head or neck
harness put on, and then being led by the farmer into a
milking stall, where the cups from a milking machine are
attached to her nipples and switched on. For the sake of
authenticity a butt plug 'tail' may also be inserted into the
woman's anus. Depending on the couple, they may have sex
while the machinery runs or choose to do so afterwards. Some
couples like to introduce a third person, who breeds the cow
while the farmer supervises. Many of the men on human cow
discussion forums say they are actual farmers involved with
cows or goats, and advertise themselves as having the correct
equipment to milk a woman.

While the practice is cow and not goat milking, goat
milking equipment is mostly used as it is more suited to the
breast size of an adult woman. For those who do not have

access to a farm or appropriate milking equipment, the electric breast pump is considered the next best thing.

> I am looking for a real man or woman that really has experience with milking and currently has milking cows. I have been lactating for six months since the birth of my baby and I want to grow into a milking lifestyle. I love milking, lactating, pumping, nursing...if it has to do with my milk, I love it. (Online personals advertisement, ALT.com)

Judging by online advertisements, there appear to be equal numbers of men and women interested in human cow play. As is the case for women who enjoy adult nursing relationships, regular daily pumping can induce lactation; and an enjoyable side benefit is said to be a heightened sensitivity of nipples and breasts, particularly when equipment rather than manual milking is employed. Some women have work done on their nipples, known as conditioning, in which a tiny needle is placed into each milk duct to open them out and make milk flow more readily.

Related Interests

Breast fetishism, BDSM.

Jargon and Search Terms

Breed—have sex.
Farmer—man who treats a woman as a human cow.
Milking—in terms of BDSM relationships, this term is used specifically to describe the practice of commanding a submissive woman to express milk for her dominant partner or others of his choosing.
Udders—breasts.

Cannibal Fantasy

When the term 'dinner date' takes on a whole new meaning...

Cannibalism, also known by the Greek term Anthropo-phagy[108] is the act of eating members of the same species: e.g. human eating human. However, cannibal fantasy as a form of erotic play has no link to the actual consumption of human beings. Ask any cannibal fantasist about real-life cannibalism and he will quickly point out that there is nothing erotic or sensual about watching someone suffer horribly as they boil to death in a pot of water, or in seeing someone's skin peel off as they are basted on a rotisserie. Cannibal fantasists also go to great pains to distance themselves from the activities of men such as Armin Meiwes, the real-life cannibal who in 2001 killed a man and then ate him. While the case horrified the world, it was even more mystifying (as well as causing legal problems about culpability) as the victim was a willing accomplice who had answered an online advertisement looking for someone to be eaten.

Many languages use metaphors of consumption for affec-tion—for example, an attractive person is often described as "a dish", "luscious", or "tasty". And while the actual consump-tion of human flesh is neither legal nor safe, many people still manage to enjoy the fantasy version.

Cannibal play hinges on preparing a woman to be eaten, so includes themes such as the archetypal girl in the cooking pot surrounded by natives on an island. Sometimes the woman is prepared as if she were actual food: she may be basted with oil or honey, have an apple stuffed in her mouth or be trussed up like a turkey or piglet. Play can also be as

---

[108] As well as by the little-known term gynophagia, literally, woman-eating.

simple as the woman presenting herself with an array of food on her naked body—an image that is not unfamiliar in mainstream media.

A common assumption about cannibal fantasy enthusiasts is that they are acting out misogynistic feelings towards women. While this may be the case for some men, those I interviewed went to great lengths to explain that pain, domination or torture have no part in their fantasies. Instead they spoke about their pleasure in the fantasy of enjoying a woman on a highly intimate level by metaphorically consuming her and in the words of Joe, a long-term cannibal fantasy enthusiast, "making her a part of you". This links to the ancient tribal belief that eating another's flesh gives access to that person's spirit. Both men and women who enjoy cannibal play also find the aspect of abandoning civilised modes of behaviour and indulging in an activity which is essentially 'forbidden fruit' in most cultures to be highly erotic.

People who enjoy cannibal fantasy generally describe it as harmless, and the men who have partners willing to go along with this fantasy all describe themselves as very lucky (if not blessed) to be accepted and indulged. For those men who do not have a partner willing to pop an apple in her mouth and hope on a plate, the alternative is sourcing cannibal fantasy videos, stories and images. Muki's Kitchen[109] is one of the very few who are in the business of fulfilling the cannibal fantasy in a way that is both playful and a safe expression of what can be a dark fantasy. Nik, the co-owner (with his wife Jo), believes that the reason some women find this play erotic can attributed to both the symbolism of becoming food for their lovers and being an object of worship or adoration. Women often nominate the preparation aspect, such as being oiled for 'baking' or being stuffed with vegetables and fruits before

---

[109]www.mukiskitchen.com.

'cooking', to be a fun form of sexual play, as this woman who has been married for twenty three years describes:

> We have recently renovated and the centre piece of what was a spare room (kids have moved out), is the homemade rotisserie put together by my husband. It even has an electric fireplace that crackles rather realistically. It still makes me laugh when he says I am good enough to eat and being lovingly massaged with oil before he 'eats' me is not the worst thing that can happen to a girl! Setting up this space just for us has really given our sex-life a second wind.

While younger people enjoy this interest, businesses that sell cannibal fantasy material such as Muki's Kitchen, report that their customer base appears to be more in the 30 to 40 year old bracket. Aside from having the income to buy images and videos, this could also be attributed to the fact (as is the case with most kink), that they have had more time to accept their interest and are therefore more comfortable admitting to it. Muki's Kitchen also report that while their customer base is overwhelmingly male, they receive a high number of emails from women and couples who take the time to thank them for being the bridge that allowed their partner to share the fantasy in a safe way.

Some well-known movies which explore the theme of eating another human are *The Silence of the Lambs*, *Delicatessen* and *The Cook, The Thief, His Wife and Her Lover*.

Jargon and Search Terms

Longpig—slang for the human body.
Meatgirl—a woman who actively participates in cannibal fantasy to fulfil her own erotic needs.

WE—women eaters' community, another term for those who enjoy the fantasy of cannibalism.

Vorarephilia

> Though it was dark, I could not see,
> I felt the throat agape
> And in a second I dropped in
> to where I could never escape.
> —poetry by Duamutef, a Vorarephile

Vorarephilia: vorare (to swallow) or devour and philia (love of) includes an interest in cannibalism (or fantasy cannibalism) but is not limited to the eating of humans. Most Vorarephiles use the short-hand term 'vore' to describe themselves. Vorarephilia is the fantasy of devouring or ingesting a variety of beings. While it includes animals and people, fantasy creatures such as dragons, monsters or anime beasts are by far the most popular.

As devouring a dragon or other monster is not something you can pop out and do on a quiet Saturday night, the only way vore fans can enjoy their interest is to join online communities, where they meet up with other vores to share stories, discussions and artwork related to the vore theme.

There is a large element of menace in this fantasy, as a person role-plays consumption and capture as either predator or prey, and of course what is found to be erotic or sexually titillating depends on the individual involved. For some it can be as simple as watching the Discovery Channel and observing underwater amoebas being swallowed by fish, or seeing a lion tear its prey apart; for others it involves complex stories and role-play focused on monsters, dragons and other strange fantasy creatures swallowing people or animals alive. As people use fantasy characters, names and personas for themselves, true gender is masked, though it is believed the vore community contains only slightly more men than women.

An interesting aspect of the vore community is that it is not skewed to 'men doing things to women' (one of the most popular vore websites is run by two women), and in most vore fantasy there is little preoccupation with gender, given that characters change gender and role-play gender frequently. Instead it is a community in which male characters eat female characters, female characters eat male characters and everybody eats...well, everything in between. There are various types of vore play, with a major distinction between what is termed 'soft' and 'hard' vore. Hard vore (often short-handed to gore) involves violent scenarios which involve ripping, cutting, biting or tearing as well as blood. Soft vore describes stories or images that do not rely on dismemberment or injury and are centred on the prey being swallowed or consumed live; but these creatures are not harmed as they live in the stomach or come out again in some way. Some vorarephiles speak about wanting to go back to the womb (literally) and view conventional intercourse as a form of consumption by their partner.

There are a number of creative ways that a person can be consumed other than through the mouth. Breast vore, for example, involves the prey being drawn into the predator's body through a nipple. Genital vore is, as the name implies, consumption through the predator's genitals. When the female genitalia are the consumers, this is referred to as vaginal vore or un-birthing, as the victim is sucked up through the vagina and back into the womb. When the victim is ingested via the male urethra, this is known as cock vore, with the victim considered to be captive in the scrotum. Depending on the story teller, ingested victims may be transformed into other beings, digested or expelled as some type of bodily fluid: so in cock vore, they might be expelled as semen. Vore stories and fantasy always involve ingestion in some way, along with erotic or sexual descriptions of the process.

Given that vore play is not an activity that you can role-play in real life with any authenticity (aside from perhaps rubbing your stomach and saying "yum-yum" with gusto), it is mostly carried out online, which means that vore practitioners are able to keep their interest private. Given the fantasy nature of vorarephilia, and the lack of person-to-person contact, most partners of vores consider it a benign activity along the lines of comic-book fantasy, and either tolerate or simply ignore it.

Related Interests

Cannibal fantasy.

Jargon and Search Terms

Gore—hard vore.
Pred—Predator.
RP—role-play.
Vore—vorarephilia.

Somnophilia

> For the first time in sixteen years, I will sleep well tonight.
> —Walt Disney's Sleeping Beauty

Somnophilia: somnus (to sleep) and philia (love of) also known as sleeping beauty syndrome, or by the slang term 'sleepy sex', refers to the practice of having sex with a partner who is sleeping or pretending to sleep.

Those who enjoy it say that this fantasy attracts a large number of women because of the perceived romantic aspects of seduction, vulnerability and trust in the partner. It also gives the women licence to enjoy sexual acts that they might otherwise find embarrassing when awake as well as allowing them to have a sort of selfish sex, as being asleep means they do not need to reciprocate any sexual favours. Of course the reverse is also true, because when the awake partner is the man he takes a dominant role, having the freedom to move and position the body to suit himself, dictate the sexual activities and be in theory excused from having to worry about the partner's needs. When faking sleep is not enough, some women use sleeping pills or alcohol to achieve deliberate unconsciousness.

So-called 'sleeploitation' is very different: it refers to the non-consensual sexual exploitation of women who are asleep—usually because they are drunk or have unknowingly taken a date rape drug such as Rohypnol. There are a number of Internet sites that cater to an interest in sleepy sex and they largely focus on erotic or pornographic images of sleeping girls/girls with their eyes closed, being fondled or having sex.

There is speculation that for some people an interest in this practice comes about as a result of childhood experience of covert sex with a cousin, sibling or friend who was either asleep or pretending to be asleep to avoid being involved in the act. Having begun their sexual lives this way, they become conditioned to having a 'sleeping' partner and the practice becomes necessary for sexual arousal. For some folks this is a form of necrophilic fantasy, in which a person pretends to have sex with a dead person (see Necrophilia below).

Amaurophilia (blindness fetish) is a similar interest, with amaurophiles enjoying sex when the partner cannot see them; however they do not require the partner to be feigning or actually be asleep.

Related Interests

Necrophilia/pseudonecrophilia, blindness.

Jargon and Search Terms

Sleeploitation—have sex with a person who has been rendered unconscious without their consent.
Sleepy sex—having sex with a partner who is sleeping or appears to be asleep.
SPS—sleeping princess syndrome: those aroused by a partner who is sleeping or appears to be asleep.

Necrophilia/Pseudonecrophilia

Necrophilia: nekros (corpse) and philia (love of) is an erotic attraction to human corpses. While well known in a sensationalist sort of way, it is relatively rare in terms of the numbers who actually practise it.[110] Far more people enjoy a necrophilic fantasy, which is known as pseudonecrophilia. In this fantasy the one partner pretends to be dead, so is required to keep his or her eyes closed and not move during sex. Given that sleeping and pretending to be dead are similar, it has much in common with somnophilia.

Related Interests

Somnophilia.

Giantess Fantasy

I am woman, hear me roar!
— Apologies to Helen Reddy

Enjoying a giantess fantasy is known as macrophilia: macro (large) and philia (love of). A macrophile enjoys role-play, images and stories related to fantasies about interacting with

---

[110]Love (1992).

gigantic women. Large in this context isn't about a normal woman's girth or weight, but about the fantasy that the woman is an actual giant and of unrealistically large proportions. The giant woman is never grotesque, but has a traditionally attractive body—just much larger in proportion to the environment or to normal-sized humans. The macrophile (macro for short) enjoys the thought of being the much smaller and powerless one in this relationship. While giantess fans enjoy either the fantasy of an evil giantess who terrorizes or hurts men, or the gentle giantess who toys and plays with them; the dominating, evil Giantess is anecdotally more popular. All macros enjoy being at the whim or mercy of the giantess, and most enjoy some type of violence and domination, so Giantesses are often portrayed as goddesses or warrior women who, if displeased with their subjects or underlings, will crush them with their body weight, step on them or consume them. Sexually exciting images for a macro might be a giant woman poised with her foot ready to stamp on a man, crushing a man between giant breasts, or forcing the human male to sexually pleasure her before crushing or trampling him. To most fans Giantesses are not expected to be nurturing or comforting, as the thrill is related to how threatening and menacing the gigantic woman appears:

> In my fantasies I become a beautiful giantess' playtoy. She finds me cowering and shaking in corner, then she traps me under her leather boot and crushes me flat as a pancake and I die—but with a smile on my face.

Given that humans are unable to expand to giant size, most macros indulge their passion through computer-manipulated images or movies. For example, a digitally altered image of a woman in sexy stockings bending over a bridge full of cars, or with her gigantic foot poised over the roof of a house would get a macro very excited. Some macros bring their fantasies to life by having their lovers play with miniature cities or cars made from Lego-type sets or with small dolls, while others may get their partners to walk on them or sit on them while pretending to be giants. However most men say they don't have much luck doing real-life role-playing as it either lacks realism or the woman gets bored with it. One man described how he can't look at a girl without thinking what it would be like to be tiny and picked up in her hands, but he knows she won't be looking back at him thinking "wow I wish I could shrink him." As well, for those who are not in a relationship, it is bothersome to explain the interest to new girlfriends in the hope they will go along with it, so most men are happy to turn to online content.

A smaller number of men prefer the gentle giantess, someone who will be playful and mischievous, but not specifically violent and destructive. She might dip the man in some type of food such as cream and lick it off him, pick him up and play with him, blow on him and knock him down, or use him as a sex toy. It could be said that the macro male's affinity for giantesses is a positive role reversal with the man taking the 'helpless damsel in distress' role. For this reason (and the fact that this is the closest they get to interacting with a physically more powerful woman), giantess fans may also be interested in Lift and Carry, which is an erotic interest in being lifted and/or carried by a woman.

Related Interests

Trampling, facesitting/smothering, vorarephilia, feet, crush fetish, fat admiration, lift and carry, Femdom.

Jargon and Search Terms

Giantessophiles—men who worship giantesses.
GTS—giantess fantasy.

Palm Size Women

> I've gotten into the shrinking woman thing quite a
> bit myself thru my own fetish fascination with
> cannibalism and vorarephilia (eating someone
> alive), due to the fact that...er...well...it's easier to
> imagine swallowing or eating someone alive if
> they're shrunken right?
>
> —Online, anonymous

The microphile: micro (small) and philia (love of), enjoys
role-play, images, stories and fantasies about adult women
who have been shrunken to miniature size. This is a community in which both men and women participate fairly equally:
men as the lovers of shrunken women and women who
fantasise about being shrunken. People who enjoy the
shrunken fantasy more commonly refer to themselves as the
SW (shrinking women) community. In terms of shrunken, this
fetish has nothing to do with Dwarfism (little people) or those
who are simply small humans. It is most commonly about
fantasising that a woman is doll sized like a Barbie doll,
though some people prefer even smaller, think fairytale
characters Thumbelina or Tinkerbell, so that the SW can fit
into the palm of a human hand.

As is the case with the giantess fantasy, practicality means
that there is a heavy reliance on computer-enhanced pictures
or photos and the use of story-telling. Unsurprisingly, the SW
community is widely represented on the Internet, with many
sites catering to discussion forums and the exchange of
images. The explanations in the stories, fantasy and art for
how the woman becomes shrunken include the use of shrink
rays, magic spells or potions, science experiments, alien
abduction or anything else that an author can dream up. There
are variations on how SW fans prefer to experience their

fantasy, ranging from the woman shrinking while her clothing remains the same size, to those who prefer both the woman and her clothing to become smaller until she is a miniature doll. The fantasies are fairly standard in that they involve a woman being made small by some method (Sci-Fi gamma ray, potion, etc) and then being captured by a normal-sized man. Depending on the story, the man may be violent towards the woman, sexually abuse her, romance her or simply care for her in a 'gentle giant' type of way.

For real-life role-play, participants may wear oversized clothing or build furniture on a gigantic scale for use as props.

Related Interests

Vorarephilia, domination and submission.

Jargon and Search Terms

Collage—an image created through computer manipulation of a woman next to giant-sized objects, clothing or people.
Doll-sized—the size of the average Barbie doll.
Hand-held—any picture or image of a tiny woman being held in the palm of a human (giant) hand.
Hand-sized—a woman as tall as the length of a hand.
Thumb-sized—a woman about the size of a thumb.
Shrink ray—any imaginary beam or ray that causes its targets to shrink.
Shrinkable—in reference to a woman whom someone thinks would look good shrunk.

Pony Play

> For 25 years, My Little Pony has given little girls a
> world of surprises and spontaneity, sunshine and
> silliness.
>
> —the My Little Pony Official website[111]

Adult pony play always requires two players, one who
pretends to be a pony and the other who acts as either the
trainer or rider. Pony play encompasses all the things that a
horse owner and his pony would participate in, such as riding
the pony, grooming it, feeding it and sometimes training the
pony to prance, canter or pull a cart. Aside from wearing a
saddle, harness, and head-dress the person who is the pony is
generally naked, while the trainer wears riding uniform or
western attire. Depending on how seriously the couple are
about this fantasy, the pony may also wear a full leather hood
with small ears attached, blinkers, face harness and mouth bit,
and be fitted with a fake tail. While some people purchase
these things from horse suppliers, there are a number of online
retailers catering to the pony market with equipment that has
been modified for the use of humans.

The pony generally stays in one role (for example show
pony or cart pony) and does not switch to a different type of
pony. Show ponies are popular, and given they are for
showing, form and grooming, this type of pony is expected to
prance and parade gracefully, so must undergo a lot of
training. Other pony roles are cart pony and riding pony; but
as most of the ponies are women (although some submissive
men will take the role of riding pony), there are strength and
weight issues related to carrying a rider or pulling a cart, so
these activities are not as popular. However, the women who

---

[111]www.hasbro.com/mylittlepony/.

can manage it pull a cart modified for human use, or a chariot attached to the shoulders:

> When I'm being the pony, that is a sexual thing it-self. I am no longer me, I am the horse and I get my erotic charge from being treated, handled and groomed by my master. We don't have sex when I am being a pony, as that would be wrong, we have sex later, when I am a human again. (Female ponygirl)

The riding pony is ridden either on all fours or upright, in piggyback style, and both of these positions need to take the man's or woman's strength and abilities into account. A discussion forum on one of the specialist pony play websites[112] advises that when riding ponies on all fours the pony needs to be equipped with pair of pads (like those used by carpet installers) to ensure the knees are not damaged. There are also front and back 'hooves' (think a boot with a hoof on the end) available online; and for those ponies who carry their rider piggyback style but still want look like a four-legged pony, there are front leg extensions which are worn on the hands—think stilts but for arms.

It is expected that the pony communicates appropriately by whinnying, stomping a foot or snorting instead of speak-ing. The pony is rewarded by being offered carrots or other horse-type treats, and may also be expected to eat from a muzzle bag.

---

[112]See for example the pony play community at Equus Eroticus: http://equuseroticus.com/.

Safety

Those who enjoy this play recommend protecting knees with knee pads and that riders be aware of the dangers of weight bearing play.

Related Interests

BDSM, lift and carry.

Jargon and Search Terms

Groom—the person who handles and helps a pony, but does not train, ride or own it.
Pony boy or pony girl—a person who play-acts being a pony.
Trainer—the person responsible for training the pony and who usually owns it.

Puppy Play

Sit... sit... I said SIT! Who's a good boy then...?

As the name implies, puppy play (also called dog or doggy play) is when one person acts as a dog and the other as the owner or trainer. While both men and women enjoy taking the role of the puppy, anecdotally it appears to be more common for men to take the puppy role and women to act as the owners. Puppy play is a common role-play in the BDSM community (with the submissive partner acting as the puppy), but couples who enjoy puppy play are not necessarily into the BDSM lifestyle.

In the puppy play community, biological dogs are referred to as canines and human role-players are known as a pup, dog or 'alpha'. While the trainer remains clothed, the human dog is usually naked but may wear a simulated dog tail, mittens and knee pads. Aside from giving the impression of having paws, the mittens are considered vital as they cushion the impact on the 'pup's' knuckles and avert damage to the hands. The mittens may be boxing gloves or any other type of leather or rubber fist mittens. Knee pads are also considered a necessity,[113] given that the pup will spend a lot of time on all fours.

When in puppy mode, the pup cannot speak and must communicate as a dog. This includes barking, growling, whining or yelping, as well as using canine body postures such as head down when being chastised or sitting on the haunches and begging if treats are on offer. A gag or hood available from specialist outlets (often with small ears attached) may be worn to stop the dog from talking. Given that a biological dog does not use a toilet, the puppy may also be required to toilet either on newspaper or outside. The puppy may be banned from climbing onto furniture, and be required to sleep on the floor or on a dog bed or blanket.

Toys and equipment used in this play are the same as for a biological household dog, and include a collar, lead, feeding bowl, dog bed, dog treats, doggie toys, grooming brushes and perhaps even a kennel or cage. The collar is the most symbolic item used in puppy play (this may be an ordinary canine collar or one found in a fetish shop), with the very act of putting on a collar causing an immediate switch into puppy mode for many practitioners. A dog tag with the pup's name and perhaps its owner's name is said to make a pup feel special. For the sake of authenticity, most pups eat out of a dog bowl when role-playing. The type of food will depend on whether the person acting as the dog prefers human treats or actual dog biscuits, and to what degree the owner wishes to assert his or her authority in dictating what the pup should eat.

---

[113] Any type of sports knee pad as used for volleyball or rollerblading is considered to work well.

Common scenarios in this type of play include feeding the dog, house training it, teaching the dog obedience commands such as sit, stay and heel, getting the dog to fetch, taking it for a walk on the lead and having it perform oral sex on the trainer. The attraction to pet play varies across couples, but the simple act of worshipping (the owners enjoying their pup licking their hands and sitting docilely at their feet, the pups enjoying the feeling of being able to openly adore the mistress or master) is often nominated as a highly attractive part of the practice. This male puppy explains:

> When I am being her puppy it is just a more re-laxed space for me. I don't have to talk, I can just be loving—say rub my cheek against her boots without asking, kneel on the floor at her feet and feel her massage my ears or head. It is just sweet and tender. While I am humble and loving as a good dog should be, she is loving and caring, just like a good owner should be.

Other puppies relish being naughty, say by getting up on the furniture or urinating in the house, and then being punished. Punishment for wrongdoing may be a spanking with a rolled-up newspaper or banishment to a kennel or cage.

For some people puppy play is not so much about literal puppy play as what is called playing a 'human pet'. The human pet is simply the human acting and being treated as a beloved pet. They describe it as taking a different perspective on each other, with the 'person as pet' viewing the lover as a larger-than-life figure on whom they rely emotionally. They retain the activities that encourage a larger-than-life perspec-tive (such as sitting at the feet, stroking and hand-feeding), but don't participate in barking, fetching or training activities.

Doctors and Nurses

Medical Fetish

Medical fetish, also known as medical play, includes dressing up and role-playing a doctor, nurse, or patient confined to bed and aactivities such as performing or submitting to 'medical procedures' such as enemas, genital examination, rectal temperature taking, supervised urination, sponge bathing or body shaving. Some people go so far as to use real or pseudo-medical equipment such as rectal proctoscopes, sounds, dipsticks (stainless steel anal or vaginal insertables) or the Wartenberg Wheel, a neurological tool used to test the skin's nerve reactions and used in sex play on sensitive parts of the body such as the nipples or penis. All of these items, as well as IV stands, latex gloves, instrument trays and scrubs are readily available from online specialist retailers. Medical play can also involve more dangerous activities such as Catheter Play or 'vacuum pumping', which are detailed below.

A Singaporean nightclub called *The Clinic* (believed to be the only one of its kind in the world) caters specifically to people with an interest in medical play. The club's décor and the ambience resemble a hospital environment. Entrance is through the 'emergency admission room' complete with a red cross on the door, into a space that is typically hospital in look and feel, with stainless steel fittings, green lounges, sixties chairs and round 'aspirin' plastic tables. Instead of conventional dinnerware, syringes, drips, test tubes and other medical paraphernalia are used to serve food and drinks; and patrons are invited to lie on hospital-style beds to take their drinks from a test tube beaker. Dinner is served at stainless steel operating-type tables with gold wheelchairs to sit in; and the ceiling of the dance area is spot-lit with pharmacology codes for drugs, such as DZP for Diazepam and MOR for Morphine Sulfate.

Medical fetishism has a long history in Europe and Asia, but is not as popular in North America; however, it is well catered for online. Anecdotally some of the people who enjoy this have a history of spending time as children in and out of hospital, and have grown to eroticise medical procedures.

Urethral Play

This is any play involving the urethra, the tube that carries urine from the bladder to the outside of the body (and semen for men only). For men it emerges at the end of the penis and in women just inside the vagina. In urethral play, medical instruments such as catheters and sounds (see below) or other household items are introduced into the urethra either for sexual stimulation, as a way of dominating a person, or as a stretching mechanism prior to genital piercing.

Some men with a fingernail fetish enjoy having a long fingernail inserted into the urethra. When they do not have a long-nailed or willing partner they will purchase stick-on nails and insert these themselves.

The sound is another item inserted into the urethra; it is a metal probe which when used in a medical context increases the diameter of the urethra or locates obstructions within it. Sounds are smooth, stainless steel rods in graduated sizes, which can be straight or slightly curved at the ends. The type known as the Sim Sound was designed for medical personnel to measure the depth of the uterus during pregnancy. In medical play the sound is inserted into the man's or woman's urethra (more commonly the man's). The erotic element for men is associated with stimulation of the prostate gland and resulting internal orgasms. As in the case of catheter play, the psychological stimulation of controlling, or being controlled by, a partner forms a large part of the attraction.

In early writings on the subject, English sexologist Havelock-Ellis reported that more than 90% of the foreign bodies found in the female bladder or urethra were placed there during masturbation; hairpins were the most common article to be removed. In 1862 a German surgeon found the problem so common that he invented a special instrument for extracting hair-pins from the female bladder.

Safety

There are very high risks involved with this type of play, as anything inserted into the urethra further than a few millimetres must be sterile, or infections (including HIV) may be contracted. When a person without medical training inserts objects or uses excessive force there is potential for serious damage to occur to the urethra, including permanent injury or scarring.

Catheter Play

> I'm just an ordinary guy. If you'd mentioned catheters as being sexy a year ago, I would have laughed at you. But I needed some surgery and long story short, they put me on a catheter. Every time one of the nurses adjusted it, checked it or even looked at it, it turned me on, but I found it deeply embarrassing. I don't tell anyone about this, and I just make do with catheter play sites online.

Catheterophilia: catheter and philia (love of) is a sexual interest in catheters. The catheter is a flexible tube inserted into a bodily orifice to allow drainage, and this is usually performed by trained medical professional—an example might be inserting a Foley Catheter for bladder drainage. In medical play, a catheter is for no other purpose than pleasure, and is always inserted into the urethra.[114] It is also more likely to be the man who is catheterised, as women's urethras are shorter and more difficult to work with, as well as being more susceptible to bacterial infections.

Erotic pleasure is experienced from the sensation of inserting the catheter into the urethra, from watching a catheter being inserted, or from taking the role of inserting the catheter. One of the biggest draw-cards of this practice (reportedly enjoyed by both dominant and submissive partners) is the element of control. A catheterised person has no control over urinary function and instead relies on the partner. If the catheter tube is left open, a person's bladder will drain until it is empty, and continue to drain as additional urine is produced. However, if the tube is clamped shut, the person will not be able to urinate even if he feels a need to. As controlling a partner is a cornerstone of BDSM, catheter play may be included even if the submissive partner does not find it physically pleasurable. Some diaper lovers and adult babies are interested in catheterisation because it simulates being a baby who has no control over its bladder.

Safety

Inserting anything into the urethra is dangerous when not performed by a medical professional; see **Urethral Safety** section above.

Speculum Play

Another popular medical device used by both men and women in the medical scene is the speculum. The speculum is

---

[114] In the female the urethra lies between the vagina and the clitoris, while in a male it opens at the tip of the penis (in case anyone was wondering!).

designed for use by medical professionals when examining the rectum or vagina. It is a device made of steel, similar in shape to a hinged duck-bill, with the two 'bills' opening once the device is in place givinge the user a clear view into the vagina or rectum. While both partners may enjoy the erotic aspect of one person sharing such an intimate view, people who enjoy having the speculum inserted nominate the physical sensation of stretching as pleasurable, while those who enjoy administering the device are often drawn to the 'power play' aspect.

Safety

As is the case with **urethral play** above, there are high risks of disease, injury or scarring when medical instruments such as specula are used by people who are not qualified medical professionals.

Vacuum Pumping

Vacuum pumping is another medical procedure performed by a role-playing doctor or nurse. It is done with a specifically designed device consisting of a cylinder attached to a pumping mechanism. When applied to the penis, breast, labia or clitoris it exerts a vacuum pressure. The technology behind the vacuum pump is based on the cupping devices used in Oriental medicine to draw toxicity to the skin surface; and these types of pumps are readily available from specialty stores.

Some people report that an enjoyable side effect of using these devices is that they produce pleasurable sensations similar to oral sex, while others are attracted to the physical changes that the pumps produce, as using a pump will induce temporary swelling and colouration to the area. According to some suppliers, regular use will eventually increase the size of the area, as the process stretches and enlarges the organs; the promise is a longer penis for men, and for women a larger, puffier vulva. The term 'camel toe' is often used to describe the 'cleavage' made by the fullness of the outer labia when they are squashed into tight fitting panties, shorts or jeans.

Jargon and Search Terms

Camel toe—vaginal cleavage.

Prostate Massage

Prostate Massage is included in medical play as part of a medical examination. In an erotic context, prostate massage is for the pleasure of a very intense orgasm that does not require ejaculation or any manipulation of the penis; however, semen will leak from the penis and when this occurs it is known as milking.

Prostate massage is done by massaging a man's prostate gland directly through the anal cavity (although some people will use sounds inserted into the urethra for the same reason). The prostate gland is located about two inches (5 cms) inside the rectum on the front wall, close to the penis. The gland itself is about the size of a walnut, and aficionados say it is generally fairly easy to find. The massage can either be done manually by the partner inserting a finger into the anus of the male, locating the prostate gland and massaging gently; or with the aid of a commercially available prostate massager which looks similar to a dildo with a handle at the end.

Enthusiasts describe prostate massage as similar to the manipulation of the female G-spot. It was originally performed by medical practitioners as a way to promote prostate health, and to relieve and manage a variety of prostate problems by removing what was deemed to be excess fluid from the prostate.

In a BDSM context, this is known as prostate or sissy milking as the dominant partner 'milks' a submissive male partner of his semen. It can also be a part of chastity play, where a man remains chaste but is forced to ejaculate as part of a controlled orgasm scenario.

Related Interests

BDSM, prostate milking, forced feminisation, chastity play, sounding.

Deliberate Clitoral Enhancement

Making the clitoris bigger is achieved by taking oral steroids, rubbing steroidal creams into the clitoral area or using a vacuum pump known as a pussy pump, which draws blood into the area and gives a temporary swollen look to the genitals (see also Vacuum Pumping above). The reason steroids work in this manner is because the clitoris is of similar tissue to the male penis, so it is sensitive to testosterone. If exposed to increased levels of testosterone, the clitoris will become larger and can take on the shape and look of an uncircumcised male penis, including pronounced erections when stimulated. The use of a pussy pump gives the most immediate result in terms of plumped-up vaginal lips and clitoral area, and some women who employ the pump report it is a highly pleasurable way of masturbating, as the pump mimics the sucking rhythm of oral sex.

Women who deliberately pump up their clitoral size do so for a variety of reasons, aside from enjoying how it feels to pump it up, including that they or their partner prefer its look, or that they enjoy the feeling of power that comes from the illusion of having a penis. Women with enlarged clitorises are said to have a 'clit-wiener', slang for a penis-like clitoris. The large clitoris is a niche area of pornography with its own online fan base.

Enemas

Darling, why are you holding that hose....?

Klismaphilia: klisma (enema) and philia (love of) refers to the practice of giving or taking enemas for sexual purposes. It was identified as a sexual fetish as recently as 1976.[115] The use of enemas for health and well-being dates back to the ancient Egyptians and was widely popular in Europe from the 17th to 19th centuries. French physicians administered them up to four times daily as they believed they added vigour to one's constitution or cured impotence.[116] During this time various types of enemas, including herbal and tobacco varieties, were administered in pharmacies. Tobacco enemas were very popular, with the pharmacist himself blowing the smoke into the patient's rectum; however this caused tobacco addiction as well as posing real health risks as too much air in the rectum may cause a fatal embolism.[117]

A love of enemas is often discovered at an early age, particularly for those who grew up prior to the 1970s (when giving an enema was something most parents did as a matter of course) and is enjoyed by both women and men. Today, enemas continue to be used as a means of cleansing as well as for sexual enjoyment. It is reported that the sexual thrill comes from both the sensation of the flow of water into the body and the stimulation of the anal area. For this reason there are arguments that the use of enemas for cleansing is simply a form of legitimate masturbation, as it allows individuals to fulfil their need for anal eroticism without acknowledging any desire for anal sex. Psychologists describe this type of klisma-

---

[115]See the work of Dr. Joanne Denko (1973).

[116]Agnew (1982).

[117]People who have nasal problems but enjoy cocaine will have it blown up their rectums in the same way rather than snorting it through the nasal passages.

philia as a masked anal activity, which may be necessary when a person feels guilty or ashamed about a desire for anal sex but can justify the activity when the enema is for medical or health reasons;[118] as this woman in her thirties describes:

> I have always wanted to be restrained and blind-folded while given an enema, but up to now this is all just fantasy until I meet the right man. I usually make do with home enemas when I daydream about it and sometimes I spoil myself and have one done at a professional colon care establishment. Once your eyes are closed it doesn't matter who is giving it really.

Inserting the enema nozzle stimulates the sphincter and the muscles surrounding the rectum, while the use of an enema solution also stimulates the receptors along the colon walls. Women who enjoy enemas say that this type of stimulus can provide the same sort of pleasure as regular vaginal sex, as the pressure caused by filling the rectum with various enema solutions mimics conventional intercourse. Men report experiencing similar pleasure, as filling the rectum with an enema solution places pressure on the prostate area.

An enema is administered with an enema bag, a rubber bag with a long tube and a nozzle on the end. The nozzle is inserted into the rectum and the water flows into the body when the rubber bag is pumped. Erotic pleasure comes from the feeling of the fluid flowing in and then having to hold the water in. Some people masturbate on expelling the fluid, while somee report managing to have sex while the enema is taking place or is being expelled. While water is the most common liquid used, it is not the only one: many 'recipes' can be found

---

[118]Caprio in Agnew (1982, p.560).

online, including enemas made from lemon juice, aloe vera, milk, coffee and garlic juice.

Enema play is fairly popular with Rubberists, as the enema equipment is often made of rubber, appealing to their fondness for the material. Enemas may also be used in BDSM play, when a submissive person is forced to hold the liquid and must beg the dominant partner for permission to go to the toilet. People who prefer the fantasy rather than the actual practice of enema play can join online discussion forums or easily locate videos, movies or stories on the topic. The milk enema, combined with anal milk squirting, is highly popular online. These videos follow the basic plot line of a woman having a quantity of milk pumped into her anus, which she then squeezes out in a stream onto the face of another person, who then drinks (or simulates drinking) it.

Safety

All literature related to the use of enemas cautions that enemas can cause damage if not performed by a trained professional. There are health risks when playing with enemas, including the possibility of pumping in too much water, using water that is too hot or mixing up solutions that are dangerous or in the wrong proportions. Because hoses and nozzles come into contact with human waste, it is essential that they be sterilised with measures sufficient to destroy any viral or bacterial matter, or that sterile disposables be used.

Related Interests

BDSM, rubber.

Jargon and Search Terms

Golden enemas—when a man urinates into a partner's anus.

Fun and Games

Inflatables

A love of inflatable items is known as inflatophilia: inflato (inflation) and philia (love of). Inflatables can be balloons, beach balls, vinyl swim beds or flotation devices for the pool such as fish, whales, horses or small-sized blow-up children's toys. The shape of the object is not as important as the material and its malleability, so for this reason an inflation fetishist may also have a rubber, PVC or vinyl fetish.

Looking at images of inflated objects and touching or handling them are the most popular activities, while chat forums discuss a variety of topics such as "have you ever made love on an airbed?", the best place to buy a jumping castle and brands of vinyl pools. From my searching it seems the largest online population of inflatable lovers come from the Eastern Europe. People who enjoy inflatables can fall into one of these groups:

- Poppers get their primary enjoyment from puncturing their inflatables (this is mostly balloons, see below).

- Inflators become sexually aroused from lying or sitting on the inflatable while it is blown-up under them. They may also enjoy watching someone inflate a balloon.

- Deflators are most aroused by deflating their inflatables while sitting on them, holding them or masturbating with them.

The inflatable water wing commonly used by young children in the swimming pool is a popular masturbation tool. The wing is inflated about 80% so that it becomes soft but not tight and some lubricant is applied to the inside of the wing, then the penis is then slid into the arm-hole. There are many video clips for sale online catering to an interest in inflatables, with an advertisement for one reading:

> Debby adds the finishing touches to this purple in-flatable shark by tightly inflating his fins. Once he's full, she climbs on top of him, and gives him a hell of a ride, giddy up! ($24.95).

While some videos and pictures may include nudity or lewdness, inflation porn does not necessarily rely on it; instead the primary focus is on the inflatable object and how the person interacts with it.

Related Interests

Balloons, rubber.

Jargon and Search Terms

Ping—unlike the term used in IRC chatrooms (Internet relay chat), pinging is the act of flicking a finger on an inflated object such as a pool-toy to make a 'ping' noise.

Balloons

> Come to the bright coloured dark side...give in to the balloon.

A subset of inflatophilia (see above), a balloon fetish is a sexual interest in traditional blow-up balloons, including looking at, playing with or otherwise touching a balloon.. While the balloon is a toy that children play with, the balloon lover has no interest in seeing children with balloons and this practice is in no way associated with Pedophilia. An interest in balloons runs the gamut of touching, smelling, blowing up or otherwise playing with balloons. Balloon lovers are known as looners and describe being stimulated by the colour, clarity, smell, tactile sense, sound, or movement of the balloon. Members of the balloon community span across a wide range of ages and socio-economic groups and while it is popular with both men and women, more men than women enjoy balloons. Jenny is in her twenties and has always loved balloons. She describes herself as a 'stuffer', someone who enjoys blowing up balloons inside her baggy clothing as she finds this the best way to maximize the tactile sensation of a balloon that she craves:

> Why do I love balloons...gosh, where to start, well they are pliable, huggable, soft and yielding and I love pressing my body on them. As well, feeling the balloon expand in my clothing gives me the sense of being overcome by it, which I just adore. The smell of a balloon is also something very special—blue smells best to me as it just reminds of my youth and makes me happy..

Balloon lovers are divided into two groups, poppers and non-poppers. For non-poppers, pleasure comes from seeing the shape and size of balloons as they expand, enjoying the physical stimulation of touching a balloon or rubbing it on the body, or from the process of blowing up the balloon. With this group, the fun stops if the balloon pops, and many non-poppers are scared of the popping noise. Non-poppers tend to humanise their balloons, putting them away and re-using them and treating them as a favourite toy or friend they play with. Non-poppers don't like poppers, believing that popping is akin to torturing, bullying or abusing the balloon.

For poppers, on the other hand, the whole purpose of balloon play is engineering the balloon to pop. They get a sexual thrill from the building suspense during the lead-up to a balloon's popping and from the ultimate bursting of the balloon. The pop is so revered that some people develop a knack in timing the balloon pop with their own climax. Popping is done by various means such as by over-inflating the balloon, bouncing on it, touching it with a lit cigarette (in this respect, the balloon fetish is often teamed with a smoking fetish) or crushing the balloon with a stiletto heel, which may appeal to the shoe or foot fetishist as well. Popping with a pin is considered the least exciting, as the surprise element of when the balloon is to pop is the point of the experience.

When balloons are used during sex, partners may watch one another inflate and play with balloons, rub or press balloons against each other's bodies, and pop balloons according to their tastes. Balloons may be placed between or underneath the partners, or under oneself if there is no partner. A man may also put his penis into the rubber nozzle of the balloon and use this to masturbate. While people like Jenny enjoy stuffing inflated balloons inside the clothes they are wearing, a balloon is not put inside the body, as this is not considered fun and is also dangerous.

Erotic balloon videos generally involve scenarios of attractive women and men posing or playing with balloons. These range from fully clothed women posing in a shot with a balloon or many balloons, to naked or pornographic images of women rubbing balloons on their breasts, licking balloons, squeezing them between their thighs in a suggestive manner or having sex surrounded by balloons or while lying on balloons. An ad for a balloon video on one website[119] reads:

> She inflates, rides, double and triple stacks them, will she ever stop…and then uses them to finally bring her satisfaction.

However while balloon lovers are always happy to look at pictures or videos of balloons, most like to handle them. For

---

[119]www.Hoes.com/fetish-balloons.

some people this interest can be linked to breast fetishism given that the shape and size of a balloon can mimic the form of a female breast, and they may make a connection between the similarity of a human nipple and the knotted neck of a balloon.

There are many websites catering to balloon lovers. These advertise balloon parties or events and provide discussion forums and photos of people and balloons. Discussions on balloon forums range from the difference between a teal blue and sky blue balloon, handy hints such as how baking balloons on a low heat will extend their stretchiness, the merits of various balloon manufacturers, debates on particular smells associated with different brands of balloons and the sharing of stories about a good balloon play or popping session. These sites also sell various types of balloons. While balloons are available almost everywhere, most balloon fetishists prefer to buy them online, because going into a stationer or supermarket is as anxiety-provoking as going into an adult shop may be for others. In addition, party balloons may not be strong enough for some looner activities, so heavy duty balloons designed for an adult to handle without easily bursting may be more appropriate.

Related Interests

Inflatables, breasts.

Jargon and Search Terms

99 Luftballoons—Nena's 1984 German protest song is generally acknowledged as the Looner's anthem.
Balloonaut—someone who enjoys jumping into a pile of balloons.
Looners—adults with a fascination with balloons
Stuffers—those who like to stuff balloons into their clothes.

Wet and Messy Play

Honey, get ready for your yummy apple crumble
facial...

For those interested in the wet and messy fetish (WAM
for short), arousal occurs from deliberately getting someone
wet and/or messy, or having it done to them. It is done by
purposely applying so called messy substances to people who
are either naked or clothed. This is different from mysophilia,
as mysophilists seek defilement and dirt, whereas those who
enjoy playing wet and messy tend to use friendlier substance
such as food. Common matter includes whipped cream, baked
beans, custard or chocolate sauce, finger-paint, shaving foam
or sometimes mud. WAM play rarely—if ever—involves
bodily substances such as urine or faeces. There are roughly
four subsets of the wet and messy interest:

- Messy—this includes food, shaving cream and mud. A
  major subdivision of food play involves striking people
  with cream pies much as in silent comedy films. This category also includes wrestling in mud, oil or jelly.

- Wet—completely soaking a person who is fully clothed.
  This can include having a person sit fully clothed in a bath-
  tub of water.

- Quicksand—this is usually enjoyed online in the form of
  drawn or animated images of people sinking in quicksand.

- Underwater—images of people swimming or posing
  underwater. Some subsets of this category are underwater
  fashion (models posing underwater, often while fully
  clothed), scuba, rubber (people in skin-tight rubber wet-
  suits), simulated drowning and underwater sex.

Many wet and messy lovers use the term 'sploshing' to
describe their interest. This is taken from the name of a well
known British magazine called *Splosh!*, which publishes

pictures and stories about women in wet and messy situations. websites and forums catering to this interest give members the opportunity to swap amateur photos or purchase professional images and videos; and there are even modelling agencies that specifically recruit splosh models. Contrary to popular belief, sploshing does not automatically include nudity or pornography because the main attraction is the mess, as this teaser for a brief video clip promises:

> Watch Stacey slowly lower herself on a beautiful pavlova complete with strawberries and loads of thick whipped cream. She smears it all over herself and then tries to cleans it off by taking delicately little mouthfuls of this delicious dessert.

Messy play is popular because it involves all the senses: the sight of someone wearing say only whipped cream, the sound of the food substances as they hit the skin, the smooth, slippery feel of the food on skin as well as undeniably pleasant smells and tastes. The added bonus is that it's a very mainstream kink. Turn on the TV or watch a comedy and there will be jokes or scenes that involve food, making it well-known enough that it's one of the easier things to ask a partner to try.

Plus this is one of the few fetishes where you can buy all the equipment you need at your local supermarket without embarrassing yourself. How the food is played with depends on the partners, but the average splosher enjoys having various substances that they would enjoy eating (e.g. ice-cream, cake, custard) poured on or thrown at them. Some report their play includes sitting in a bowl of something soft like pudding or jelly or even on top of a creamy or gooey cake, after which they may masturbate or have sex. Others enjoy stuffing their underwear with soft foods such as chocolate, cream or porridge and walking around until it leaks out or melts. Some sploshers have sex during or after the mess-making, while for others the sexual release is found in the very act of sploshing. Bill Shipton the editor of *Splosh!* Magazine was interviewed for an online article recently and some of his advice gives an insight into wet and messy play:

> Find things that taste good to the both of you. If it's squishy things you are after, try creams and custards. Things like beans and spaghetti can also work nicely, but the key is not to use them together. I wouldn't put anything together that you wouldn't use together in a meal. You also have to make sure it's something you'll be able to clean up afterwards, so I wouldn't go over the top with a bucket of porridge. I would also stay away from anything with strong artificial colour. There's a famous story over here about a couple who went out and bought a jam with blue food colouring in it, smeared it all over themselves and came out looking like Smurfs. Certain things like batter mixes may seem like a good idea, but when they dry, they form a sort of solid lump. Before you know it, your balls are turned into a piece of unleavened bread.[120]

Many who enjoy this describe it as a form of light-hearted BDSM because it is a form of power exchange, as one person does something to another to make them feel or look foolish or uncomfortable; such as grinding a lemon meringue pie into their hair. However while it may be predicated on humiliation or punishment, it is a far more fun and relaxed form of dominating a partner given there is unavoidable element of comedy involved. It is common for there to be some role-

---

[120]Interview with Bill Shipton at http://www.nerve.com/regulars/ididitforscience/sploshing/interview.asp

playing such as maid or waitress. One theory about the popularity of the wet and messy fetish is that the feeling of wet and messy substances on the skin is a surrogate for the feeling of touching a partners' skin while having sex. Another theory is that seeing another person (or yourself) getting wet or messy is arousing because it is a reminder of the natural moisture the body excretes when sexually aroused.

Related Interests

Defilement (mysophilia), hydrophilia, domination and submission.

Jargon and Search Terms

Sploshing, gunging, WAM, dessert play, messy play—wet and messy play.

Stick Em Up

Robbery

Becoming sexually aroused from robbery is called harpaxophilia: harpax (robber) and philia (love of). This is a stage-managed fantasy between consenting partners. A typical event will involve one person going to bed and the other partner sneaking into the house. The 'victim' usually pretends to be asleep while the burglar sneaks around in the dark and 'steals' things. At some point the sleeping partner will awake and be confronted by the burglar who may tie her up and demand the keys to the safe or the victim's jewellery. The victim will refuse to tell and is then sexually ravished or molested.

Related Interests

Ravishing, weaponry.

Erotic Asphyxiation

> He would put his hand around my throat when we
> were doing it —not too hard—but hard enough for
> me to gasp for air. Not sure why it was so hot, but
> it really, really turned me on.

Erotic asphyxiation is the potentially lethal practice of intentionally withholding a partner's oxygen supply during sex and then withdrawing the pressure at the point of orgasm. When the air returns to the body it is said to enhance the rush of orgasm. Colloquially it is known as erotic strangulation, breath play or scarfing; formally it is hypoxyphilia: hypoxia (oxygen deprivation) and philia (love of) or asphyxiaphilia: asphyxia (without pulse or heartbeat) and philia (love of).

People use various methods to cause asphyxia: the hands-around-the-throat style of strangling; placing a scarf, belt or tie tightly around the neck (hence the term scarfing); suffocation, in which a plastic bag is put over the partner's head; or smothering, when the head is enveloped by a pillow. Less common is compression of the chest, when one lover lies on the other's chest making it impossible or difficult to breathe, or puts the partner into a very tight corset, which also makes breathing difficult. Nose pinching is done by taping or gagging the partner's mouth and then pinching the nose closed with the fingers; this is risky as the taped partner may faint or vomit. See also the Femdom practices of HomSmother, (hand over mouth smothering) and Facesitting. Those who prefer a more hands-off approach while still enjoying breath play may choose to simply tell the partner not to breathe.

Reported attractions to breath play are the enjoyment of experiencing oxygen deprivation, said to create a dreamy state of temporary light-headedness, and the enjoyment of feeling panicky and at-risk whilst in a controlled situation. Erotic asphyxiation appears in the plots of many books, movies, and TV shows; the practice was central to the highly controversial 1976 movie *In the Realm of the Senses* by Japanese director Nagisa Oshima.

While it is a consensual practice that must have safe words or signals in place to stop the act if necessary, this does not take away from the very real danger of encountering risks, ranging from short term memory loss, potential brain damage to accidental death. Enjoying this paraphilia without accidentally overdoing it and killing the partner is a genuine concern, as this middle-aged man's email to an online advice column asks:

> My wife and I are just ordinary people so when
> this happened it just blew me away. Once night
> while making love I had my hand resting at her

throat. She pushed her hand down onto my hand. It didn't take me much to work it out and I pressed on her throat, encircling it with my hands as we continued having sex. She said she had the best orgasm ever. This is all new to us, and it concerns me that I may hurt her or even kill her. We also live the kind of lives where neither of us can go out in public with bruises around our necks, so it is a whole new world for us to come to terms with and any guidance would be appreciated.

Those experienced in breath play caution that there needs to be a high level of discussion around the practice prior to engaging in it, to deal with issues such as what kind of method will be used for the choking partner to signal if there is a problem and he or she is unable to speak. As well, given the real dangers to life surrounding this type of play, they also recommend those involved should have a good idea of the partner's medical history, and a sound working knowledge of both CPR and basic first aid.

When there is no partner involved, this practice is called autoerotic asphyxiation As the person engineers his own breath play (generally while masturbating), the practice becomes even more dangerous. Autoerotic play includes self-suffocation with objects such as pillows, nose pinching, pressure on the trachea, or placing bags over the head. Death in these situations is frequently confused with suicide and may be termed this for the sake of families. Most accidental autoerotic deaths (AAD) result from hanging, with plastic bag asphyxiation the second largest killer.[121]

Since the 1950s there have been an increasing number of autoerotic deaths reported, with the victims predominantly

---

[121]Behrendt Buhl and Seidl (2002).

male. Research[122] has found that autoerotic asphyxia is most often practised by white adolescent males 13–20 years of age, though there are reports of men in their 70s enjoying the practice. It is estimated that between 250 and 1,000 American men die every year while using strangulation to enhance masturbation.[123] While few cases of females dying from this practice are documented, it is possible that women are simply more cautious than their male counterparts, or use methods that allow them to escape their bindings prior to death.[124]

Snuff play and breath control play are often confused. Snuff fantasy is about sex games that involve fantasies or play around the idea of being killed or killing another person, whereas breath play is only about the restriction of oxygen for a period of time with no intention to kill.

Safety

People who enjoy this practice responsibly advise taking a certified CPR and first aid course before embarking on this type of play, and recommend having a good idea of the partner's medical history.

Related Interests

HomSmother, Facesitting/Smothering.

Jargon and Search Terms

Breath play—intentionally withholding oxygen for sexual arousal.
Gasper—a person who enjoys erotic breath play.
Terminal sex, scarfing—breath play sex.

---

[122]Behrendt et al (2002).
[123]Jenkins (2000).
[124]Behrendt et al (2002.

Sexual Arousal From Weaponry

He must have blown her mind...

Sexual arousal from weapons is known as either hoplolagnia: hoplo and lagania (lust) or hoplophilia: hoplo (tool, weaponry or armour) and philia (love of). This type of play uses real or fake guns or knives; and is categorised as edge play, given that it is on the edge of most sexual interactions. Fun with weapons ranges from handling them, to viewing images of attractive women with weapons, to using weapons as an integral part of sex play. Fantasy play involves acting out scenes such as an assault or holdup, where one partner uses a gun or knife to threaten the other. As one married woman explained it:

> Nobody acts shocked or horrified when kids play games in which one points a fake weapon at another and yells "stick 'em up", so why should it be such a travesty when two adults play out a similar but sexier fantasy? My husband surprises me when I least expect it. He sometimes wears a balaclava and other times he blindfolds me. He keeps me guessing as to when and how it will happen and it gives me a licence to let loose. When he says "get on all fours you dirty bitch", well I have to do it if this nasty stranger with a weapon says so, because my life is at stake.

Weapons (real or otherwise) are used to consensually touch or caress the body, or as a penis substitute for oral, vaginal or anal sex. Knives are more commonly used than guns, and this may be because they are more accessible or because they are perceived to be safer, particularly as they can be deliberately blunted for safety, or even fake. Partners are often blindfolded or restrained in some way, which adds to the fun. Lovers of weapons say that a large part of the enjoyment comes from the mental anticipation of what may or may not happen next (particularly when blindfolded), with some saying that the sensations of excitement and fear of the unknown bring a whole new dimension to foreplay as this anonymous female blogger describes:

> The blade feels so smooth, where is it now? Will it remove my skin? What did I get myself into this time? Is this the end for me? Oh no, please don't hurt me....

This is known as the mind-fuck element, common to many games played by the BDSM community. The term mind-fuck describes the illusion, trickery or lying used to deceive a partner into believing that what is about to happen is real. With knives, for example, the partner may be shown a genuinely sharp knife, but when the blade is inserted into the person's body or run over the nipples, something benign like a letter opener or butter knife is substituted without the person knowing a swap has been made.

Internet sites for gun and weapon lovers run the gamut of clothed women with guns, naked women with guns and women involved in pornography with guns. There are thousands of websites that cater to this interest, such as the one described below:

> Gorgeous women looking hot and lethally armed! Watch superhot chicks in tiny bikinis, uniforms and buck naked holding high-powered firearms!

In countries where carrying a gun is legal, there are documented instances of accidental shootings (and even deaths) during sex play involving firearms, so for safety reasons most people choose to play these games with replica weapons, which are readily available.

Safety

It is advisable to play only with imitation weapons.

Related Interests

Ravishment, robbery.

Ravishment/Consensual Rape

Consensual rape is an oxymoron, given that rape is completely non-consensual and involves true aggression, violence and violation. For this reason the preferred term is ravishment, to make a distinction between consensual role-play and non-consensual assault. Ravishment, rape fantasy or forced sex play as it is also known, refers to a consensual act in which partners engage in a forceful sexual exchange which mimics rape. How this occurs depends on what the partners have agreed to, and may involve threat, pain, fear, violence, aggression and forced intercourse. Most rape fantasies involve an attractive dominant male who is overcome by passion and uses mild to moderate force to overpower and penetrate a woman without her consent. Rape role-play generally follows a similar pattern as described by this woman:

> This is one of our hottest activities, as I never know
> when it is going to happen or how. It is usually
> dark and when he first grabs me it gives me the
> biggest fright, but after so many years I know my
> husband, the smell and touch of him, so that's a
> safety net (plus we have signals and safewords).
> Part of what makes it thrilling is the loss of control
> and taking sex away from our marital bed. He

talks to me like I'm a slut (he would never do that in real life) and he becomes very unpredictable. Like last time, he got me outside the garage as I was getting out of my car one night, pushed me up against the wall, ripped down my underwear and said if I moved I would be sorry. I didn't move my face from the wall while he teased and licked me from behind until I thought I would pass out.

For scenes such as this where there is an element of surprise, the 'ravisher' generally uses a start word or other identifying signal to ensure no actual harm will accidentally befall the partner. Unless this ravishment forms part of a couple's agreed consensual non-consensuality,[125] there will be a safe word in place and either participant can stop the scene if required. As the illusion of non-consensuality is important to this fantasy, one or more safe words are usually employed and these are words that would not be uttered during sex, for example elephant or toaster. This way a participant can protest in a traditional sense (for example crying "no, no" or "help"), without mistakenly stopping the scene. Given the taboo nature of rape in most societies, it is also advised that pre-game negotiation should include discussion of possible emotional issues for both partners, especially if there is a history of actual sexual abuse or assault.

Research has found this to be one of the most popular fantasies for women,[126] with 31%–57% of women surveyed having had a rape fantasy and 9%–17% of women reporting that rape fantasies are either a frequent or favourite fantasy. Nancy Friday 1975 compilation of women's sexual fantasies *My Secret Garden*, contains detailed scenarios written by married and

---

[125]Where the partners have agreed ahead of time that one partner gives away all rights to consent or otherwise during the play.
[126]See the work of Salmon and Symons (2003) and Hazen (1983).

single women across a spectrum of ages. Friday says that it is a popular female fantasy because by making the man the assailant she gets him to do what she wants while she is blameless at the mercy of a stronger force. While women's rape fantasies have been the subject of formal studies since the 1940s, they are still not well understood. This may be because researchers and theorists have deliberately avoided any serious study of this area, as drawing attention to the existence of women's rape fantasies may reinforce the myth that women seek out forced sex, which in turn could encourage male sexual aggression.[127] Adding to the taboo around this subject are the writings of Freud and some radical feminists such as Susan Brownmiller, which maintain not only that rape fantasies are masochistic, but that there is something wrong with the women who enjoy them.

Safety

Ensure that safe words are in place to stop play if necessary.

Related Interests

Weaponry, robbery, HOM.

Jargon and Search Terms

Ravishment—consensual rape play.
Fear play—when the game involves some type of implied threat to the sub, e.g. knife way.

---

[127]Bivona and Critelli (2008).

Arousal from Crimes

Hybristophilia: hybridzein (committing an outrage against someone) and philia (love of) is a term used to describe becoming sexually aroused by people who have committed crimes—in particular cruel or outrageous crimes such as murder, rape or torture. This is an interest more popular with women, as can be seen by the high number of death-row or life-term prisoners who are specifically targeted by women wishing for relationships or marriage.

Internet sites such as writeaprisoner.com, prison-penpals.com and cellpals.com exist primarily to facilitate contact between men and women in prison with those on the outside. Anecdotally these relationships have very little chance of success if the offender ever leaves incarceration.

Junk in the Trunk

Anal Play/Eroticism

Variously known as arse play, anal play or anal eroticism, this interest focuses on the anal area. It may include oral sex (known as rimming), inserting objects such as dildos, beads, fists, fingers or various other items into the anus, or having anal sex. While it is a common myth that anal sex is an activity enjoyed mostly by homosexual men, ordinary couples report enjoying it. Many women[128] such as Carla, who is now in her fifties, are very comfortable when discussing their experiences:

> I discovered anal sex in my teens. I come from a very strict Catholic background and it was paramount that I remained a virgin until married — this was an expectation of all the girls at my boarding school. I knew most of the girls had boyfriends from the neighbouring Christian boys' college and they all had sex with them, but so that they could remain virgins it was anal sex. I was horrified when one of the girls told me, but they didn't seem to have a problem with it. When I started going steady with one of the boys he explained how it worked and once I relaxed it was fantastic. We did it missionary style so that my clitoris rubbed up against his pubic bone and I had the best orgasms possible, completely satisfied my boyfriend and remained a virgin. I eventually turned my husband on to it because much as I enjoyed vaginal sex, anal gives me such powerful orgasms.

---

[128] There is even a Facebook page for women to swap advice on the topic.

Women who report enjoying the experience say it adds a completely different aspect to their orgasms, particularly if there is vaginal and clitoral stimulation from the partner's hand or contact with his body, or from a dildo or vibrator. There is also a perception of this act belonging in what one woman describes as a "completely different physical and psychological space". This may be because anal sex still isn't considered mainstream by many heterosexual couples, and there has to be a high degree of trust and care between them:

> When we have anal sex (which is not all the time, we like to keep it special), my husband treats me differently. It takes a bit of coaching, stroking and relaxing to get it in—it makes me a little bit vir- ginal in a way and he gets the deflowering experi- ence every time.

One female sex worker reported that the secret to her per- sonal relationship was that she kept anal sex exclusively for her boyfriend, as this allowed them to have one special activity that nobody else had shared—particularly as he had never tried it with anyone else. As both men and women may worry about the smell, mess and embarrassment of faeces appearing during what is supposed to be an erotic experience, the sex worker shared her advice on cleansing prior to the act:

> I suggest planning for it. Do not do it on a full stomach as I find anal sex just after eating makes me want to empty my bowels and secondly do your best to go to the toilet well ahead of time. I know some people like to buy a bottle of Fleets (a pre-operative cleansing solution) from their phar- macy and take it to clear out their bowels. But whatever you do, you will feel confident and clean if you have an anal douche—no need for a full en-

ema unless you like doing things like that—but a douche[129] will ensure there are no traces of faeces that will end up on the sheets, his penis or under someone's fingernails. I know none of this is sexy information, but it all helps to make the experience better.

However, for some partners the mess itself is part of the turn-on and they take pleasure in seeing the penis adorned with some residue of faeces after sex, as well as enjoying the post coital smell of faeces mixed with sperm.

Experts recommend that those new to anal sex (male or female) should start with a small-sized butt plug, an anal sex toy which is easy to purchase online or at any sex shop, as this can be a way to learn about the practice in a relaxed manner. A butt plug is a penis-shaped device generally not as large as a dildo or strap-on penis, designed for inserting into the anus, where it sits in the rectal canal. Specialty stores also sell what are known as anal dilators, a set of penis-shaped devices graduating in size from 2 to 5 cms, allowing the wearer to become accustomed gradually to the feeling of something large in the anus. They were originally created in the 1800s to help constipation.

Anal beads, also known as climax beads, butt beads or anal poppers, are another type of anal play toy. The beads are in a necklace design made up of a series of balls (usually four to eight or so) made from some type of soft or pliable material; such as silicone. The user covers the beads with lubricant[130]

---

[129]An anal douche flushes out the cavity just inside the rectum area with clean water, using a specially designed rubber bulb and syringe. When the flushing penetrates higher and further into the bowel and colon it is known as an enema.

[130]Experts recommend using only products formulated for surgical and gynecological lubrication and not commercial cooking oils or butter as these can promote infections.

and then inserts them into the rectum one at a time. The beads are generally left in place until the wearer is about to orgasm, when they are pulled out one by one.

Strap-ons are also popular. A strap-on is a dildo attached to a harness device that can be worn by a man or a woman who wishes to have sex anally or vaginally with a partner. Most strap-ons are designed to be used by women, but there are situations where a man may choose to wear one, such as in the case of erectile dysfunction or in a BDSM situation when the dominant female has locked the penis in a chastity device, or when the couple wish to achieve penetration of both anus and vagina at the same time. There are also double-penetration dildos, designed to make it possible for both partners to use the same device simultaneously. Couples who are comfortable in a role reversal where the woman anally penetrates the man say that it can be a very powerful sexual experience for both partners, even if the man is not inclined to be submissive:

> While it is not an experience that the average heterosexual guy can easily access, there really is something to be said for the feeling of being entered by your lover. Talk to your lover and if she is open to it try the strap-on experience. Trust me— the feeling of being impaled by a woman while her free hand squeezes your balls is something so fine that talking about it is never going to do it justice!

For women, the act of penetrating another person can be a liberating and empowering sexual milestone; however, those experienced in this type of role reversal caution that while the woman may feel heady with her new power, she needs to be aware that her partner may be experiencing unaccustomed vulnerability, and these emotions need to be acknowledged by both partners—see the Aftercare section for more on this. The relatively new term 'pegging' is used to describe the practice of a woman penetrating a man with a strap-on dildo. In BDSM scenes when a man is in the submissive role, his mistress may use this as a subjugation technique (see also Forced Feminisation).

Many people report enjoying anal fingering (also known as postillioning), and this may be their own finger during masturbation or their partner's in sex play. When fingers are positioned correctly in the man's rectum, intense sexual pleasure can be achieved by deliberate massage of the prostate gland, a walnut-shaped gland sitting in the rectal canal (see also Prostate Massage). Fisting refers to the insertion into the rectum of either several fingers, the whole hand or for some, even the forearm. If it includes the forearm, there is a possibility of the fingers entering the lower colon, which can be extremely dangerous.

Oral sex in the anal area is colloquially referred to as rimming, as it is around the rim of the anal opening. A major concern with this practice is the transmission of parasites and Hepatitis A, so a dental dam is always recommended. Originally created for use in dental surgery, the dental dam isn't actually worn over the teeth. It is a small piece of thin latex, which can placed over the vagina or anus for oral sex. It should be rinsed first and then held firmly in place over the area while oral sex is performed. A dam should only be used once and discarded, and the side touching the genitals should not come into contact with the mouth.

Related Interests

Forced feminisation, Femdom, ass worship.

Ass Worship

Pygophilia: pyge (buttocks) and philia (love of) is a sexual obsession with the buttocks and anus; including touching, fondling, licking and kissing the area and is colloquially known as ass or booty worship. It is most commonly played out in a Femdom dynamic, with the submissive male kissing and licking the buttocks and/or anus of a female partner. As the woman takes a dominant position the submissive partner may be kneeling, handcuffed, bound or in some type of similar lowly position while he performs this service. It is common for facesitting or smothering to be part of this practice. While the male partner may enjoy it, the intention is humiliation, so the man may not be allowed penetration nor sexual release and is generally forbidden from touching her genitals. He is commonly rebuked and scolded and instructed to cleaning out her anus by using his tongue. Some Dommes will force an act of ass worship onto an unwilling sub as a punishment.

Related Interests

Facesitting, smothering, Femdom.

Safety

Health and safety are paramount in any sex play, but particularly with anal play. Thorough cleaning of the toys before and after anal play is of the highest importance, as well as using and discarding disposable safely products such as condoms, dental dams and latex gloves whenever exposing yourself or a partner to bodily fluids.

Jargon and Search Terms

Chocolate tip—when there is a residue of faeces on the penis after anal sex.
Dental dam—latex used for protection during oral sex.
Fisting/Handballing —several fingers or whole hand inserted into the rectum.
Greek—a code word for anal sexual activities.
Marble peach—slang for a woman with curvy buttocks that are also well-toned from exercise.

Rimming—oral sex on the anal area.
Pegging—a woman penetrating a man with a strap-on dildo.
UAI—unprotected anal intercourse.

Bug Chasers

Breed me, you great big stud!

Bugchasing (also written as bug chasing) describes the practice of actively pursuing an HIV infection (Human Immunodeficiency Virus, which may lead to AIDS) by having unprotected sex with partners who are known to be HIV positive. It is not believed to be a common practice and is limited to a subculture of the gay male community. The HIV negative men are known as bugchasers; the men who are HIV positive and participate in unprotected sex with an un-infected partner are known as giftgivers

HIV positive and negative men may engage in random unprotected sex at events known as bug or conversion parties. Others advertise online for 'poz' or 'neg' partners with the implication that the negative partner wants a positive partner and vice versa. As there are stigmas associated with openly calling oneself a bugchaser, men who enjoy risky sex knowing they may contract HIV simply have a lot of unprotected and anonymous sex, or make their intentions known by advertising for 'raw' sex or 'BB'(bareback)—both slang for unprotected sex—or as being interested in breeding, slang for intentionally contracting HIV.

The term barebacking is often confused with the practice of bugchasing; however, while it may be part of the bugchasing repertoire, it is also a term used in the heterosexual world, describing having sex without a condom (whether vaginally or anally) without any specific intent to acquire a bug. Reasons for choosing to bareback include increased sensation, a greater feeling of closeness to the partner, and a perception that sex is more spontaneous. Backbacking is also more likely to occur inadvertently when someone is high on drugs or alcohol, while some people (such as sex workers in third world countries) either have no choice in the matter or see it as a way to make more money.

In the homosexual community another rationale for having unsafe sex is the belief that HIV infection is inevitable, and rather than feeling like victims waiting for the sword to fall, some men feel empowered by taking control of their fate and trying to get infected on their own terms. As HIV infection has become medically manageable and is no longer the death sentence it once was, the advances in HIV treatment may also have unwittingly contributed to a higher level of complacency about unsafe sex. For others, bugchasing is motivated by the search for the peace of mind some believe will come when, once infected, they no longer have to worry about contracting HIV or AIDS. Daniel Hill, a HIV positive gay man, describes contracting HIV (also known as sero conversion) in an article he wrote in 2000 for *Alternative Magazine*:

> After becoming HIV+ I felt a wonderful euphoric sense of liberation and of letting go—I must confess that my own seroconversion (i.e. becoming HIV+) brought about tremendous grief coupled with a wonderful euphoric sense of liberation, of letting go—a liberation that taught me to love again.

Paradoxically, becoming infected can provide individuals with an opportunity to nurture themselves, as once infected they have a tangible illness that is recognised by society, and this can result in them going on to care for themselves in ways they may not have considered previously.

> I know of many men, including myself, who, when they seroconverted, felt as though they were finally encouraged to take better care of themselves physically, emotionally and spiritually. (Daniel Hill, *Alternative Magazine*)

For others, practicing unsafe sex is tied to the need for a type of deep intimacy with a sex partner, which they maintain is not possible when condoms are used. This can be so important that they are willing to take a risk rather than have safe sex, which is considered second-rate 'pretend sex'. This attitude can be found in both homosexual and heterosexual communities.

For some bugchasers an integral aspect of this practice is the thrill they experience from the act of risk-taking. In that respect, they have much in common with those who enjoy other dangerous activities such as breath play or autoerotic asphyxiation. There is also a line of thought which suggests that some homosexual men experience a great deal of internalised shame and anger in owning and accepting their sexuality,[131] which leads them to indulge in self-injurious behaviour such as drug taking and risky sex. Having sex with somebody who is HIV positive is the ultimate taboo, and for bugchasers the sexual act becomes more eroticised as the sexual charge comes directly from the knowledge that the semen they are receiving may be infected:

> Of course, I make it sound like I barebacked because it was fun. No! I really got off on the risk — big difference. Poz partners were so easy and available where I live. They just seemed so much hotter and I really got off on the risk. I had some fun crazy adventures—took some loads myself (even a poz one). What a rush that was. I fanta-

---

[131]Clinard and Meier (1998).

sized about becoming positive so I could do a little breeding myself. (Anonymous entry on a poz forum)

While the split between the homosexual and heterosexual communities may no longer be so deep, the homosexual community is now experiencing its own divide between those who are HIV positive and those who are HIV negative. In a strange twist of fate, some HIV negative men feel isolated and perceive they are missing the generosity, support and community that is offered to the HIV sufferer. A desire for group solidarity and belonging may influence them to take part in behaviours that will make them members of the 'HIV club'.[132] Some research has also identified a desire to contract AIDS or HIV as being part of a larger plan for some men aspiring to a type of master status within the gay community.[133] One bugchaser's blog describes the moment of what he calls his initiation:

I was so hot and so scared (which is hot itself). Then, the unmistakable—he tenses up and then relaxes. I'm thinking, "did he *really* come in me?", "did I do this?" Is he really poz?" Then I caught sight of his left arm—a biohazard tattoo. The tattoo was so hot and scary—he really was poz. I felt really proud and satisfied.

Such glamorisation, eroticisation, and claims of deeper levels of intimacy are in stark contrast to how some of these men go about having unprotected sex. This includes doing it anonymously, blindfolded, in the dark, in gay saunas and bars or at large-scale conversion parties: all situations in which it

---

[132]Peyser (1997, p.77).
[133]Gauthier and Forsyth (1999).

may not even be possible to see what the sex partner looks like, let alone hold an intimate conversation.

There is a degree of debate surrounding the practice of bugchasing in relation to whether it actually happens (and to what degree) or if it is simply fantasy talk that has found a platform in online forums, blogs and websites. There is also speculation that bugchasing has neither increased nor decreased, but that interest in it has proliferated since academics 'discovered' it as a new area of research.[134]

Jargon and Search Terms

BB—bare back, denoting unprotected sex
Breeding—having sex with the intention of becoming HIV+
Bug brothers—men who are either friends or lovers and are HIV positive.
HIV+—HIV positive.
Poz—HIV positive.
Pump and dump—anonymous, unprotected sex.
Raw—unprotected sex.
Seroconversion—becoming HIV positive.
The gift—infection with HIV.
Travelling poz-delivery service—HIV positive man looking to infect others.
Wrapped—sex with a condom

---

[134]Gauthier and Forsyth ibid.

In Romantic Love with Things

Objects/Structures

> I have been in relationships with models of space-
> ships, the Twin Towers, a church organ and a ban-
> ister, though my main lover is a fairground ride
> called '1001 Nacht', located at Knoebels, an
> amusement park in New York State.
>
> —Amy Wolfe, Objectúm-sexual[135]

Objectophilia: object and philia (love of), is an erotic interest in inanimate objects. The intimate lives of these folk
revolve not around people but around objects or structures,
with which they profess to share romantic and sometimes
sexual love. The type of object varies widely according to
personal taste: from electronic equipment such as radios or
laptop computers, to musical instruments and even buildings.
Probably the best known object in this regard is the blow-up
doll; however, dolls are in a category of their own and are
purely a male interest, while the majority of object lovers
(excluding doll lovers) are female. Some women have been
known to go so far as to 'marry' their object—for example
American Erika La Tour Eiffel, who married The Eiffel Tower
in Paris and (as you do…) took the tower's surname.

People who have relationships with objects describe their
emotional and sexual attraction to them in the same way a
person will describe an attraction to another human being.
They believe that all objects are living and have a soul (the
basis of a type of belief system known as animism, which
maintains that inanimate objects are sentient beings with

---

[135]www.objectum-sexuality.org.

intelligence, feelings and the ability to communicate). The term used to describe lovers of objects is 'objectúm-sexual' and the most famous is Eija-Riitta Berliner-Mauer, a Swedish woman who believes herself married to the Berlin Wall (hence her surname Berliner-Mauer: Berlin Wall in English); which (who?) she maintains was murdered when it was dismantled in the 1980s. She lives with scaled wall objects in remembrance of the Berlin Wall, but admits being attracted to a number of fences though she does not consider her flirtation with palings as cheating (but I guess she is a widow, so is free to date). Ms Berliner-Mauer explains her relationships with objects on her website:

> If one can see objects as living things, it is also pretty close to being able to fall in love with them. After all, there are many different sexualities—if you care to look around. To make love with a thing isn't any more difficult than having sex with a man or woman. To be objectúm-sexual and having sex with an object, is NOT the same thing as masturbation, because in masturbation one doesn't see the object as LIVING, one does often dream about a person or something. In objectúm-sexuality one has sex with the object because one loves the object itself. That is a big difference.

> LOVE, the feeling of love is always the same—but the object of the love is different, but the FEELING itself is still the same. In my case I am in love with the Berlin Wall. WHY I love exactly the Berlin Wall, that I can only speculate on.[136]

---

[136]http://www.berlinermauer.se/.

In a recent newspaper interview, an English woman discussed her relationship with Jake, a hi-fi system,[137] whom she described as "beautiful" and someone who "wouldn't let her down". And it isn't just women that seek out unusual objects (thought they out-number men), as reported in a UK newspaper: [138] in March 2010, 28 year old Korean Lee Jin-Gyu married a large pillow with a picture of a woman on it.

Volkmar Sigusch, retired professor and former director of Frankfurt University's Institute for Sexual Science, has extensively studied an attraction to objects in his research into various forms of what he calls 'neo-sexuality'.[139] He considers the existence of objectophilia proves his hypothesis that society is increasingly drifting into a type of neo-sexuality, based on asexuality: the state of living happily without having sexual relationships with another human being. Sigusch maintains that "more and more people either openly declare or can be seen to live without an intimate or trusting relationship with another person. These gaps in human intimacy are then filled by some with an object."

How people interact with an object varies depending on practicalities. For some it can be kissing, cuddling or stroking it; for others it is finding ways to masturbate with it. When the object is large and cumbersome, such as a building or vehicle, the person may use a scale model or take one of its components to touch or fondle. The American sitcom *Boston Legal* dealt with this attraction throughout the 2007 season, when one of the characters tried to have a relationship with a woman who was dating a clock radio—she eventually rejected him for an iPod phone because it was "just so sexy".

As falling in love with objects or structures means the person can control the relationship, a significant number of people who maintain erotic relationships with objects appear

---

[137]*The Independent* newspaper (24/5/2008).
[138]http://www.metro.co.uk/weird/816601-man-marries-pillow.
[139]Sigush (1998).

also to suffer from Asperger's Syndrome, a disorder which causes people to have significant difficulties with social interactions.

Statues

Agalmatophilia: agalma (statue) and philia (love of)—also known as statuephilia—describes an erotic attraction to statues or mannequins. Sexologist Richard Von Krafft-Ebing noted a case in 1877 of a gardener who was found trying to have sex with an outdoor statue of the Venus de Milo. The famed fashion photographer Helmut Newton also had a pronounced interest in mannequins, photographing them in what were often such highly erotic or provocative poses that at first glance it was difficult to distinguish the doll from a human model. Newton engaged with the mannequins to the point that he believed some of them had personal traits and qualities, famously naming one very attractive mannequin who didn't seem to pose well, 'the idiot'.

This attraction includes a desire for sexual contact with the statue, the fantasy of having a sexual encounter with it, or sexual pleasure from thoughts of being transformed or transforming another into the preferred object. Robot fetishism is the most common form of this, but does form its own interest. When the desire is for a physical encounter with a statue, doll or mannequin, this is most commonly manifested in an interest in custom-made 'love' or sex dolls.

Related Interests

Robots, dolls.

Dolls

> It is a fact. Women are unobtainable for me, so
> having my girls simply makes life bearable.
> —45 year old owner of three RealDolls

Pediophilia pedio (doll) and philia (love of)—not to be confused with pedophilia (love of children)—is an attraction to dolls, including those that have been specifically designed for genital penetration and other forms of erotic interaction. There is a large market for what are known as love dolls, with human-sized dolls selling for thousands of dollars. Depending on what type of doll is required they can be a basic inflatable model (the plastic type cheaply and readily available in most sex shops around the world), or models constructed from very realistic material, with limbs that can be positioned like a real human. The top-of-the-range dolls sold by companies such Abyss Creations under the trademark RealDoll have pliable breasts, removable vaginas (for easy cleaning), opening mouths and lips and realistic pubic hair, and can be customised to the purchaser's specific preferences. They also weigh close to an average woman, which means there are practicalities concerning moving, transporting, storing and manipulating them. There are half-human-sized ones available from other manufacturers, which are easier to manage. Price and quality range from $US375 to $US7000, depending on the type of doll purchased and the customisation required. The US $375 dollar model from adultsextoys.net is described below:

> The Alexa vibrating love doll is a kneeling doll
> with Futurotic™ vagina, anus and mouth made of
> an almost seamless design, providing added
> strength and a soft realistic feeling skin. The Alexa
> vibrating love doll features a full mannequin head,

supple customized-to-fit noduled mouth, flowing hair, voluptuous breasts, movable arms with soft hands and painted nails, slender waist and a firm ass. Alexa is sensually scented and has 2 removable multi-speed bullets for maximum stimulation.

The Rolls Royce of dolls for the last decade or so comes from Abyss Creations in America, who have been selling their RealDoll products world-wide since 1996. The dolls are so realistic thanks to the use of Hollywood special effects technology, that men are purchasing them to act as partners, wives and girlfriends. The dolls feature completely articulated skeletons which allow for anatomically correct positioning, and the 'skin' is made from a blend of the best silicone rubbers, giving it a genuine flesh-like feel. Customers are able to purchase a number of faces, so that they can change the persona of the doll. RealDolls have a hinged mouth that opens and three different, interchangeable tongues. The oral and genital cavities are designed so that on penetration a vacuum is formed providing a powerful suction effect, and the dolls have stretchable vaginal lips and sculpted, realistic labia. They also come with 'awake' and 'sleeping faces' which owners can swap around to promote the illusion of the doll being a realistic partner. Abyss Creations sell around 400 units per year, mostly within the US, and while the basic model starts at US$5999 for a full doll, costs generally fall between US$6,500 and $10,000, depending on customisation.[140]

The RealDoll products have been the subject of a number of documentaries, including the 2007 BBC documentary *Guys and Dolls* which gives some unique perspectives on men who choose to settle with a doll for their life partner, and how they come to treat the doll as person rather than a sex toy. Davekat,

---

[140]Cost correct at time of printing. For more information see www.real.com.

a 29 year old Indian man who lives at home with his parents, is one of the four men featured in this documentary. Davecat qualifies his relationship with Shi-chan, his doll partner, as the difference between being alone and lonely, saying, "I don't mind being alone at all; however I cannot stand being lonely and this is something that I hope people would understand — that's why idollators have dolls." Idollator in this context is the slang term for a man who loves and lives with his doll or dolls. The men (many of whom call themselves doll husbands) do all the normal things a couple might do, such as taking a drive, eating opposite each other at the dinner table and sleeping together. Many of the men talk about the dolls as they would a real life-partner, with Davecat admitting that when Shi-chan first came it was just "sex sex sex", but now that they have settled into a relationship that aspect has tapered off and for him the most important thing is that they are there for each other. Shi-chan and Davecat both have their own Twitter accounts for anyone who is interested in following them.

A commendation from a satisfied customer on the Real-Doll website in November 2007 reads in part:

> To everyone at Abyss Creations: Hello again! Two years ago today, my beautiful RealDoll, Jenny arrived at my home. On that day, my life changed. So much so that I felt compelled to write this note.
>
> Jenny's presence here has had a dramatically positive effect on me psychologically and emotionally. A far more positive effect than I had ever expected. During this time, I have done many things that I feel I would never have done if I didn't have Jenny. I cannot recall any other purchase that has given me as much enjoyment as this sweet angel. You made her for me to love and for that, once

again, I thank you. You have created something truly wonderful.

In January 2010 a life-size robotic girlfriend complete with artificial intelligence and flesh-like synthetic skin was unveiled. Billed as a world first, the doll known as Roxxxy, is said to be unique in that she has been programmed with artificial intelligence; so that according to the designers at truecompanion.com, she can become "an actual companion":

> She has a personality. She hears you. She listens to you. She speaks. She feels your touch. She goes to sleep. We are trying to replicate the personality of a person.

As is the case with the Real Dolls, purchasers of Roxxxy can customise her features, including race, hair colour and breast size.[141] People ordering these robot dolls online can also specify their tastes and interests (much like online dating sites) and this information is used to sync the robot to her partner. So for example, if the purchaser follows a particular football team so does the robot; if the purchaser enjoys fishing, so does the robot. The robot is wirelessly linked to the Internet for software updates and technical support, so she can send her man email messages. Thanks to artificial intelligence programming, Roxxxy will also be able to chat with her flesh-and-blood mate, and touching her elicits comments varying according her personality.

These types of dolls obviously fill a gap for men who may have previously lived lonely and solitary lives. An Englishman in his early fifties who appeared in the *Guys and Dolls* documentary observed that once a person got past the fact that they "just lie there", they are certainly better than being without any

---

[141]A male sex robot named Rocky is in development.

female company, particularly for men like him who feel that for one reason or another women are simply unobtainable. This aspect was eloquently portrayed in the 2007 Canadian movie *Lars and the Real Girl*, featuring one of the dolls from Abyss Creations. The story is about an awkwardly shy young man living in a small town who suddenly brings home the girl of his dreams to his brother and sister-in-law's home— however, the 'girl' is a RealDoll whom he names Bianca. Lars is searching for a meaningful relationship and treats the doll as a person, cooking for her, taking her to social occasions and caring for her. To support Lars the entire town eventually goes along with this delusion and people invite Bianca to parties, church, and functions at each other's homes. The TV sitcom *Boston Legal* has featured a life-sized doll on a number of occasions, with one of the employees depicted as having what he considers a 'real relationship' with his doll. The American drama *Nip/Tuck* has also dealt with this subject.

As an offshoot of the doll industry, virtual pornography using life-size dolls has found a niche market on the Internet; but a fascination with mannequins or dolls is not a recent innovation: in the 1940s the German Bauhaus painter Oskar Schlemmer created a doll in the likeness of a girlfriend who jilted him, and regularly drove around the streets of Vienna with the doll for company.

Related Interests

Robots, dolls.

Jargon and Search Terms

Doll—with a capital 'D' in this context is short-hand for life-sized artificial human or, as others call it, a high-end love doll.
Doll husband—a man who owns a RealDoll and treats her as a human companion.

iDollator (pun on the word idolater)—people who are aficionados of high-end love dolls. They range from those who use them as sex toys to those who live with them as companions.

Robots

A robot fetish is fantasy and role-play related to either owning or being transformed into a robot. Robot fetishists may refer to themselves as technophiles or describe their interest as technosexuality.[142] Robot enthusiasts are not interested in sex dolls as they have no interest in the doll approximating reality; instead they are interested in the performance of robot-like behaviours. Robot fetishism is divided into two distinct but sometimes overlapping types of fantasies: the desire to have a ready-made android-like partner who will do as commanded (referred to as 'built'), or the desire to change into a robot known as 'transformation'.

Transformation role-playing includes starting up and shutting down the robot, done by pretending to turn a key (a common symbol of this fetish), pressing an attached button or knob worn on the clothing, or by pointing a remote control at the robot. Robot role-play also includes using robotic speech, achieved by speaking in a monotone or using clipped speech and phrases such as "yes master how may I serve you?" or "my circuits are overloaded." The role-playing robot may wear a robot costume—Lycra and the colour silver are highly popular—move in ways that are stilted, measured or jerky, and demonstrate a submissive mental state by taking commands from the master or being programmed. A highly popular aspect of robot play is the so-called 'malfunction'.

---

[142]Many of the long term robot fetishists still use the initials ASFR, which stems from the initials of the now defunct online newsgroup alt.sex.fetish.robots.

When the robot malfunctions, it loses control and may suddenly start twitching, melting, smoking or otherwise acting erratically. Robot lovers enjoy stories, videos and pictures depicting this because it confirms the fact that the robot is in fact…a robot.

When the robot fantasy is enjoyed online or in movies, aspects such as exposing the robot's circuitry or a depiction of the deconstruction of the robot (i.e. a limb becomes detached, or the head blows up) are considered highly desirable. Most robot fetishists are not really into graphic sexual scenarios, because provided the common robot themes described above are included, their desires are largely met. However, niche erotica for this group includes modifying conventional pornography so that one of the human models has an artificial robot hand or a computer panel attached to her midriff, or sports on/off buttons. This type of image modification is known by the term 'rasterbation' and is not limited to modifying pornography.

In response to feminist claims that this practice degrades women—when the robot is female—many robot fetishists argue that their interest is based on the feminisation of objects (i.e. a mechanical robot is given female characteristics) rather than the objectification of women. While the majority of robot fetishists are men, it is an interest shared by women. The android character Data from *Star Trek, The Next Generation*, Optimus Prime from *Transformers* and Arnold Schwarzenegger's character the cyborg assassin and soldier known as T-800 in all three *Terminator* movies are all considered by both male and female robot fetishists to be highly sexy.

Related Interests

Dolls.

It's an Animal Attraction

Zoophilia

Give a dog a bone....

Zoophilia: 'zôon' (animal) and philia (love of) describes a sexual or erotic attraction to animals by humans. People who love animals in this way are known as 'Zoos' and the practice is also known as Zooplay. Many Zoos actually find the term Zoophilia offensive, as they believe it describes a mental sickness rather than a simple sexual preference. For that reason they prefer the term Zoosexuality. The unnamed author of the Ultimate Zoo Page describes Zoosexuality as an orientation which is similar to being born heterosexual, homosexual or bisexual. To a Zoo, having a physical relationship with an animal, which includes having what they consider to be consensual sex, is simply another way of showing love. Sexual contact is defined as penile or vaginal intercourse or anal or oral contact between the animal and the human.

There is debate surrounding the terms bestiality and Zoophilia. Bestiality is commonly used to describe both states, although some Zoos find this an offensive term which does not describe the 'relationship sex' they have with their animal companions. While the term bestiality is commonly found on animal sex sites, Zoos consider it a term used for humans having non-consensual sex with animals to the point of raping or forcing an animal and therefore offensive. In bestiality, there is no requirement for the human to be familiar with the animal and so sex is considered to lack the 'relationship' aspect.

Zoos perceive the differences between animals and human beings as less significant than the average non-Zoo. For example, they often believe the animal has positive human traits such as fidelity or honesty. While many pet owners around the world also believe this, treating their pets as children or members of the family, they do not take the step of having a sexual relationship with them. Zoos view the relationship with their animals in the same way they view a romantic relationship with another human and consider having sex with the animal as a logical expression of love. On one discussion site I visited, a woman wrote:

> I love my dog deeply, he goes everywhere with me, sleeps with me, eats with me everything. I think that the first time I masturbated him was just an extension of stroking him and bonding with him. I don't really know why I did it; it just seemed at the time to be a natural next step in our relationship together. He liked it, and certainly didn't move away. I do it when he feels like it because I like doing it for him.

Groups such as The Animal Sexual Abuse Information and Resource Site[143] liken Zoos to pedophiles, arguing that they are nothing more than animal sexual abusers. While zoophiles defend their actions by saying that animals give consent by participating in the sex act, the animal abuse activists maintain that the behaviour of Zoos is abusive, because like children, animals are incapable of agreeing to sexual activity with an adult human being.

The most common animals that humans have sex with are dogs in cities and farm animals in rural communities.[144] According to a number of Zoo websites, dolphins, goats and snakes are also favoured as sex partners (or partners in

---

[143]Animal Sexual Abuse Information Resource Site: www.asairs.com.
[144]Kinsey and Pomeroy (1953).

fantasy). The type of sex varies according to the animal, but includes all the usual forms of human sexual contact and foreplay. This includes the giving and receiving of oral sex, masturbation, anal sex and conventional penis into vagina sex.

Sex with any animal poses health risks; in particular there are potential problems related specifically to the anatomy of a dog's penis. The dog gets what is known as a knot near the top of the penis when it is erect and this may get stuck in the human anus or vagina, becoming difficult to dislodge (dog penis dildos can be purchased in many online sex stores, complete with realistic knot). Online Zoophilia communities provide a lot of information related to health and safety to guide those interested, as well as explaining the methods and processes that must be used with each type of animal to ensure that sexual congress can be safely achieved for both parties.

Literature, myth and legends depicting erotic or sexual relationships between animals and people have existed throughout the ages. One of the most famous paintings depicting a woman and animal copulating is Michelangelo's Leda and the Swan, while ancient Greek myths contain many stories of gods who assumed the shape of animals in order to mate with mortals. Though sex with animals has been chronicled throughout history, there is very little documented research available, particularly large scale general population studies.[145] One of the few academic studies on zoophilia and bestiality is by Hanna Miletski.[146] She interviewed 92 people who had sex with animals (no distinction was made between beastophiles and Zoophiles, as Miletski, like most who write in this field, uses the terms interchangeably). She found that 48% of the men and 45% of the women were college graduates or above. Nearly 60% of those interviewed reported a higher interest in animals than in humans, 75% of the men described

---

[145]See older studies by Hunt (1974) or Kinsey, Wardell, Pomeroy and Martin study (1948).
[146] *Bestiality–Zoophilia: An Exploratory Study* (1999).

their sexual orientation as homosexual or bisexual and 32% of the males were currently married. Some Zoos will experiment with bisexual or homosexual activity with animals, but remain heterosexual with humans. A more recent survey of 848 people was conducted by a well known Zoophilia website in 2008. The results were as follows:

Male zoogay 24.47%, male zoobi 40.94%, male zoohetero 17.29%, female zooles 1.18%, female zoobi 5,29%, female zoohetero 8.35%, other 2.24%.(www.Beastforum.com, 2008).

The online Zoo communities are virtually closed to out-siders due to the social censure members face. Memberships are on a paid basis or via a barter system of exchanging animal sex pictures or videos. Discussion forums and chatrooms revolve around members sharing stories and posting pictures of a sexual nature involving themselves, their partners and their pets (mostly dogs). Pornography for this group involves an animal in a sex act with a human, or photos or drawings of the genitalia of animals in much the same way a sexually explicit website presents the genitalia of men or women. Sex with animals (whether consensual or otherwise) is illegal in many parts of the world.

Zoophilia is not related to pet play, which is role play by a human pretending to be a dog, pony or other animal.

Pseudozoophilia

Pseudozoophilia: pseudo (pretend), zoo (animal), and philia (love of) refers to sexual fantasy role-play in which one person pretends to be an animal. The person acting as the animal will make animal noises, behave like the animal (for example a dog), or wear an animal pelt, mask or custom-made outfit. This is different to pet play, as pseudozoophilia is only concerned with the fantasy of having sex with the animal. Pet play involves a range of other practices which are related to a specific animal, such as dog training or pony riding.

Insects

Formicophilia: Forma (ant) and philia (love of), is the practice of using insects for sexual purposes. These include ants, flies, snails, beetles or other crawling insects. The insect is placed on the genitals or sensitive parts of the body such as nipples and erotic stimulation comes from the creeping, crawling sensation of the insect on the skin. In some cultures men believe that getting a bee sting on the penis enhances their erection.

Arousal from spiders is known as arachnephilia. Insects or spiders are most commonly used in the form of domination or intimidation. The dominant partner ties down the submissive partner and the spider or insect is bought close to, or placed on the body of, the other person. The fear of the spider is intended to cause an adrenaline rush to the person who is being taunted and therefore increases arousal.

Safety

Care should be taken that no poisonous spiders are used in this type of play and that the people concerned do not have allergies to the insects.

Related Interests

Domination, submission, humiliation.

Crush Fetish

Crush fetishists are sexually aroused by the sight of a woman crushing small creatures such as insects to death. It is the animal version of a 'snuff film', the term for a movie in which the death of an actor is the pivotal part of the sex act. The most desirable scenario for crush fetishists is of an attractive woman crushing an insect with her bare foot; a platform shoe or an outrageously high stiletto heel is also favoured. Crushing small insects can be enacted in fantasy through story, cartoon or film, and the Internet is able to fill this niche as chatrooms and forums have made it relatively easy for stomp enthusiasts to communicate with others who share their passion. However some people prefer to watch an actual living creature being squashed, despite the fact that this practice is not legal in many parts of the world (the USA made it illegal in 1999). Crickets, worms and other such insects are common, but some individuals use larger creatures such as frogs or mice. The most common rule of thumb for those who enjoy crushing is that the animal should be no bigger than a shoe.

The crush freak typically fantasizes he is the insect as he masturbates. In his head, his orgasm is linked to the sudden, explosive mutilation of the insect's death.[147] In an interview with probably the world's best known crush freak, Jeff 'The Bug' Vilencia (publisher of *The American Journal of Crush-Freaks*) the experience is described by him as a substitute of what the animal is suffering, as he becomes symbiotically 'one' with it:

> At the point of orgasm, in my mind all of my guts are being squished out. My eyeballs are popping out, my brain comes shooting out the top of my head, all my blood squirts everywhere.

The crush fetishist is interested in the sounds, the visuals and the story leading up to the crushing and death of a small creature. Crush fetish porn always culminates in a scene of a female foot destroying some type of living animal. For those that enjoy the concept of crushing but draw the line at living

---

[147]Biles (2004, p.117).

animals, watching a woman stomp on plastic animals or fruit such as grapes, tomatoes or even sausages, fulfils the same needs. Because the focus is on the female foot, there may also be a foot fetish or an interest in trampling; see relevant sections.

Men who enjoy the fantasy of themselves as small and being crushed by a giant woman, for example under her foot, between her breasts or by being sat on, are generally attracted to the giantess fantasy.

Related Interests

Insects, feet, trampling, giantesses, wet and messy.

Jargon and Search Terms

Crush goddess—the woman doing the crushing.
Mash men—men who like to watch small creatures being crushed.
Smoosh videos—crush videos.
Stomp enthusiasts—crush fetishists.
Stomping—practice of crushing.

Furry Fandom

> My name is Xena, I am a cute Zebra with a nice markings and long ears. Looking to meet any type of large mythical creature such as a dragon or dragon hybrid (e.g. a driger), who is interested in online chat and attending real time fur meets.
>
> —advertisement on a Furry dating site

Furry Fandom, mostly just Furry for short, is a largely non-sexual subculture devoted to cartoon and fantasy characters who combine animal and human qualities, known as anthropomorphism. In art, it means to restructure the face and/or body of an animal, subtly or otherwise, to make it seem more human—think, Mickey Mouse or Teenage Mutant Ninja Turtles. A fusion of science fiction, comic book and animation fandom has evolved into what is known as furry fandom. The animal-type characters are known as furries, a term also used by people who are fans of furry art or have a spiritual connection with a specific furry character; however, it is generally capitalised when used as a form of identity. It is a diverse fandom, and many Furries take offence at the assumption by those either outside this practice or new to it, that it is predicated on a form of sexual practice, particularly as some Furries believe they are animals or have spirit animals.

Furry Fandom has a fairly young user base, with recent surveys conducted by a furry interest group finding that nearly 30% of Furries are aged between 15-19[148] and 20% are between 25 and 29 years old. Males make up 78.88% of the user base and females 20.38%. Various surveys have found that there are a high percentage of gay or bisexual people interested in Furry Fandom. For example, survey results from a poll conducted by Klisoura.com in early 2010 with 1998 respondents from the Furry community found the following in relation to sexuality:

Completely heterosexual	408 (20.42%)
Mostly heterosexual	376 (18.82%)
Bisexual leaning heterosexual	226 (11.31%)
Bisexual, no skews	220 (11.01%)
Bisexual leaning homosexual	197 (9.86%)
Mostly homosexual	311 (15.57%)
Completely homosexual	260 (13.01%)

---

[148] http://www.klisoura.com/ot_furrysurvey.php.

Furries (also known as furs or anthros) are very interested in (if not obsessed with) with fiction, art or discussion concerning the animals they admire or emulate. The nature of this interest means that most of the furry lifestyle is enjoyed online, so Furries have a strong online community which caters to both men and women. Furries routinely create fursonas (furry personas) that are based on either real creatures such as horses, foxes or tigers or mythical creatures or hybrid creatures such as unicorns or a drox (dragon-fox), driger (dragon-tiger), wolf-horse or any other another combination that people can think up. Foxes are particularly popular personas, which made the 2009 movie *The Fantastic Mr. Fox* a must-see for fox loving furries around the world. The most popular movie amongst furries is the 1973 version of *Robin Hood*, as it was (and remains) the only Disney movie to entirely feature anthropomorphic characters.

Many Furries do not see their interest as a hobby or a fetish, but rather as an actual identity. Helen is a thoughtful and socially aware 26 year old masters student at an American university. For her, Furry is both a passionate hobby and an accepting social group. She is saving for her own fursuit and her fursona is a winged wolf. This is how she explains her interest in Furry culture:

> I chose the fox as my fursona because I feel I share characteristics with the fox. A bit of a loner, crafty, clever, protective of its own. It was thoughts like this that made me think, "I bet if I were to be an animal I would be a fox". When combined with my love of vulpines, anthropomorphic films and my other diverse passions this created my fursona, who has various fur markings to express my love of sci-fi and Japanese culture.

Online communities exchange and discuss drawings, artwork, cartoons and stories that are furry, and will communicate in the style of their animal: for example, someone who is a unicorn may write 'stamping my hoof impatiently', or a wolf may write 'swishes his tail in delight'. These communities have an ongoing problem with what are known as fur-haters or trolls joining their sites and making disparaging remarks. This is because their interest is frequently confused by outsides with pedophilia (a sexual interest in children) or Zoophilia (a sexual interest in biological animals), neither of which is accurate.

Dressing up in character costumes is known as fursuiting and is a way some Furries choose to express themselves. Fursuiters make or purchase costumes—which are not cheap: a partial outfit starts at US$700—and enjoy attending conventions, many of which are held in North America and Europe every year. Disneyland is a mecca for furries, given the number of cartoon characters such as Pluto, Donald Duck or Minnie Mouse available for a photo or a hug.

Yiffy is another aspect of Furry Fandom, and is the term for sexual activity or sexual material within the fandom. Yiffy activity may be online in the form of cybersex, erotic furry drawings or art, or be real life interaction while in costume. A common assumption by both outsiders and those new to the community is that all fursuiters yiff. However, in speaking with Helen, a female Furry who has been in the community for a long time and has fursuit connections, this is not so. Given they are made of faux fur and not washable, fursuiters are not likely to damage their precious outfits by using them for sexual activities. According to Helen, the best way to think about yiffing is as you might with other interests in the broader community: so some Furries fursuit, some Furries yiff, some Furries yiff and fursuit, and some Furries do none of the above. Another young Furry explained it this way:

Furry is to yiffy, as anime is to hentai, dancers to strippers, or movie lovers are to porn addicts. The former is the broad interest and the latter is the sexual offshoot. Any group that grows large enough will spawn sexual deviations of the original.

The term yiffy comes from the word yiffing, which furries believe is the noise anthropomorphic animals would make if they were real and were having sex. Foxes have long been considered the most promiscuous of furry species within the yiffy community, but this has changed recently, with canine species in general becoming symbols of promiscuity. The attribution of sexuality to various species occurs only in the yiffy community.

Jargon and Search Terms

Anthro—anthropomorphic.
Personal furry/fursona—this describes a person's image of themselves as a furry, for example a 6-foot- tall Owl/Rabbit.
Fur-hater, fursecuter—someone who hates furries.
Fursuit—an animal costume.
Fursuiter—a person who wears and/or makes fursuits.
Furryphobe—someone with an irrational fear of furries.
Furvert—a person who is sexually attracted to furry characters.
Zoot—synonym for 'fursuit'.
Yiff or **yiffing**—sex between furries.
Zootaphile—a person who has a strong personal attraction to fursuits.

Related Interests

Soft toys.

Soft Toys

> I only come when I can think of my Jason, my
> beautiful, cuddly giraffe.

An erotic interest in soft toys is known as plushophilia: plush (soft toy) and philia (love of). A plushophile is an adult who loves stuffed animals either emotionally or in the literal sense. While the term plushie describes the soft toy, such as a teddy bear or stuffed rabbit, it is also s short-hand for describing plushophiles themselves. There appears to be no data on gender breakdown, but the Facebook plushie groups I visited have been overwhelmingly joined by women. Donna is an attractive 32 year old Australian woman who is tertiary educated, has a job in finance and looks that turn heads:

> I would definitely describe myself as a plush-a-holic, because I am so in love with my long-eared bunny Damien—I don't care who knows about it. I don't have a problem meeting men, the problem is bringing a non-plushie into my relationship with Damien. While these are grown men, feelings of jealously ultimately creep in. I can't believe an adult man would be standing there with a sulky look saying "why are you cuddling Damien instead of me?" Damien is a stuffed rabbit for heaven's sake. As I always tell them, "yes I sleep with him between my legs, but so what, it's me you have sex with, me who makes you toast, me who goes out for dinner with you—can't you just accept his little grey body sitting quietly on my pillows?"

How plushophiles express affection for their plushies varies from cuddling them, sleeping with them, having them present while having sex with a real-life partner, to using them as a type of sex toy. However, as I quickly learned, a plushophile takes offence to the inference that there is any 'use' of the stuffed animal or that they should be described as a sex toy. Instead, they much prefer to see them as companions who willingly participate in consensual sex. Those who love plushies describe enjoying the toys' visual appeal, softness, furriness and what they term huggability and cuddliness.

There are degrees of interest in soft toys, from those who enjoy them as foreplay or lone play, to those who call themselves plushisexual—a person whose primary sexual preference is for stuffed animals. When the plushie is part of sex between two human people, practices may include sitting the plushie in eyesight so it can be gazed at during sex, placing it in touching range or having it near the face so it can be smelled. The plushie can also be rubbed against a partner's body or placed between the two bodies having sex, known as a 'plushie sandwich'.

When a person has sex with the plush toy it is usually by hugging the plushie to the body while masturbating, or rubbing the genitals or other erotic parts of the body against the fur of the plushie until orgasming. Some men will modify their plushies for penetration by opening a seam, sewing in an insert, or constructing a penis-type attachment. Plushies with these types of professionally made modifications can also be purchased on the Internet, and instructions on how to modify a plushie can be easily found online.

Most plush lovers agree that it isn't easy being a plushie, because if they go public there is very little understanding of their interest. In particular 'plush bashers' as plushies call their detractors, accuse them of having pedophilic tendencies or just see them as those "who fuck children's toys". However this is not the case, as a plushie's interest stops at their toy. As one young man explained:

Whether we like it or not, people associate Plusho-philia with other things. When they complicate and dirty what should be a pure, natural, beautiful physical act it reminds me why I often avoid humans in my sexual life...

Jargon and Search Terms

Begging—when a plushie is posed with its legs spread or bum raised.

Biosexual—a person who prefers sex with biological partners.

Boink—the gender-neutral term for plush lovemaking.

Boinkable [by design]—a term applied to a plushie which is seemingly
custom-made for pleasuring. Also known as a talented plush.

Boink space—a place on a plushie that's pleasing to poke.

Mundanes - people who don't love plush animals the way plushies do.

Plushboink—having sex with a plushie.

Plushgasm—an orgasm elicited by making love with a plushie.

Plushie—interchangeable term for an adult who loves stuffed or soft toys, or the actual toy itself.

Plush rush—the rush of adrenaline or feeling of arousal that a plushophile experiences when they encounter an ideal plush partner.

White fuzzies—slang for the Fiberfill stuffing when it has adhered to one's penis after insertive plushie sex.[149]

Related Interests

Furry.

---

[149]Plush Central at: http://plushie.info.

Angela Lewis

Look, Touch, Show

Voyeurism

> Become the ultimate spy from the comfort of your
> own home.
> —advertisement for a webcam site

Scopophilia: scopein (watch) and philia (love of) refers to sexual arousal from watching or looking at particular events or people. While voyeurism is a synonym for scopophilia (and in more common use), voyeurism in its strictest sense refers to watching others without their knowledge when they are engaged in private acts such as undressing, bathing or having sex. Scopophilia refers to the enjoyment of watching per se— with or without consent. A situation where consent is given is paying sex workers to dance or strip, or visiting a club where it is acceptable to watch others having sex. A circumstance where consent is not given is spying on a person or people through windows or telescopes. The key difference is that in voyeurism, the voyeur does not interact personally with the person being observed.[150]

While pornography obviously appeals to voyeuristic desires, some advertising campaigns also leverage off voyeurism's appeal. A James Boag beer commercial, for example, exploits the power of 'watching' in a TV ad in which a beautiful woman spies on a man in a hotel room, through a key hole.

---

[150]Voyeurs are often called peeping toms, after the man who chose to look at the naked Lady Godiva during her 11th century ride through the mediaeval streets of London.

252

Some researchers[151] argue that voyeurism is in danger of going mainstream, given how readily popular culture has embraced reality TV shows. And it could be said that movie viewing is voyeuristic, given that the traditional movie viewer sits in the dark and observes the activities of people on a screen as they would through a window. The proliferation of Internet webcams has also created a new cultural arena for scopophilia which contributes to normalising voyeurism. If there is nobody to watch in the shower on *Big Brother*, there are online opportunities 24 hours a day to watch someone bathing, plucking their eyebrows or having intimate moments with a boyfriend in the privacy of their homes.

Commenting on this move towards normalisation, a fifty-something university professor agreed:

> I don't see what the fuss is about, I like to watch — so what. To my mind doing it occasionally doesn't make it a fetish, and I'm certainly not alone. Look at my own family: my wife is addicted to watching Gordon Ramsay scream at his staff; my kids are glued to morons flashing their boobs in *Big Brother* — while I like to view amateur webcams of ordinary girls flashing the odd boob or simply sleeping in their beds. It is no big deal.

Related Interests

Dogging, frotteurism, exhibitionism.

---

[151]Metzi (2004).

Exhibitionism

In its psychiatric definition, exhibitionism refers to a compulsion to expose genitalia in public for erotic pleasure; however it more generally includes displaying any body parts considered taboo in a specific culture, so in America or Europe this might include breasts or buttocks and in the Middle East hair, legs or face. Exhibitionism in this regard differs from the mainstream practice of showing off or behaving in such a way as to attract attention, which is also be referred to as exhibitionism. The colloquial term for displaying an intimate body part is flashing. Flashing is usually limited to simply exposing oneself and experiencing sexual arousal from the act, and there are no advances made on the other person. For men, flashing is the act of exposing the penis briefly to (in the majority of cases) a stranger of the opposite sex; while for women flashing involves a quick display of bare breasts with an up-and-down lifting of the top or bra. Mooning refers to either men or women displaying bare buttocks.

Exhibitionism is considered to be a predominantly male disorder, usually beginning in the mid-teens or mid-twenties;[152] while there are reports of women engaging in this behaviour they are not generally socially censored or reported to the police, as may happen to men. This may be because men do not feel threatened by the display of body parts in ways that women may be.

Exhibitionists may expose themselves to others of any age, with a study of college women finding that between 40% to 60% of those surveyed reported having been a victim of exhibitionism.[153] Some exhibitionists enjoy themselves by proxy, as they don't actually expose themselves but get a

---

[152]Berah and Myers (1983).
[153]Maletzky (1998).

vicarious thrill from having their partner do so. This includes encouraging a female partner to wear a top that shows outrageous cleavage, wear a super-short skirt, or go out in public without underpants. Exhibitionism by proxy can also include touching the partner intimately when in public or having sex where others can see, such as in a city lane or on a car bonnet.

Some exhibitionists, known as cyber-flashers or web-flashers, like to post their nude or semi-nude pictures on websites or social media such as Facebook or YouTube, email pictures of their breasts or genitals to unsuspecting recipients, or use webcam feeds to broadcast intimate images of themselves. The latest Internet fad is ChatRoulette, and a cynic could consider this custom-made for flashing. Users sign onto this easy to use, no cost website and switch on their webcams. By clicking the next button they can randomly look at other webcams, while broadcasting their own images. Not surprisingly lewdness and nudity are readily encountered in these random connections. Those who flash simply wait until the unsuspecting webcam viewer presses the next button and moves on. Flashing online offers the added benefit of anonymity (e.g. wearing a mask or pointing the webcam below the neck), which may explain its popularity to both men and women.

While generally considered exploitative, live sex performances can be a desirable way to earn a living for women who become aroused by having others watch them in sexually explicit positions or acts. Some exhibitionists wanting to display themselves sexually to other people, singly or in groups, will also participate in swinging or group sex or the more popular practice of dogging, described below.

Though it never caught on, sexologist John Money[154] tried to apply the term peodeiktophilia (peos – penis, deiknunain,

---

[154]Money (1986).

display, and philia love of) to exhibitionism, as he mistakenly considered it purely a male paraphilia.[155]

Related Interests

Dogging, carping, frotteurism, voyeurism.

Dogging: A Happy Meeting of Voyeurs and Exhibitionists

People who enjoy either voyeurism or exhibitionism may be drawn to the practice of dogging,[156] which refers to watching or being involved in sex acts which are deliberately exhibitionist. Dogging usually occurs in semi-secluded locations such as car parks or country parks. It is a well-known practice in the Western world and particularly popular in England and Wales. The original definition of dogging was spying on couples having sex in a car or other public place without their knowledge. However, dogging is now assumed to be a deliberate activity where all participants are aware of the circumstances, so participation is public, not furtive.

Dogging involves driving to parks that are known for this practice. Some folk have sex in the car, often with the lights on, while others arrive to watch and listen. Those watching may be invited to participate by the performing couples. The dogging community is well organised, using text messaging and the Internet to publicise dogging sites and events.There is a specific code of etiquette around dogging, which includes rules such as:

---

[155]Exhibitionism is also known as 'Lady Godiva Syndrome' in honour of the 11th Century English noblewoman who according to legend, rode naked through English streets to protest a toll imposed by her husband on his tenants.

[156] As in "I'm just taking the dog out for a walk dear".

- Let others find you. This means parking somewhere visible, flashing the car headlights or leaving the interior car light on. This signals that those inside are doggers and about to put on a show.

- Give them a clear view. It is suggested that when there are voyeurs outside the car watching, you roll down the windows so they get a better view of the action.

- Open your car door only if you wish to invite others in to share the activities.

Carping is engaging in conversation with a person on a mobile phone who is simultaneously having public sex. Some doggers invite carping by writing their telephone number on a cardboard box or large piece of paper and placing it on display inside their vehicle.

The term carping is also used to describe chatting to a person performing sex acts live on a webcam. When this is not practical, some webcam performers encourage online messages that compliment their performance. These messages are read and shared with those watching and often take the form of a commentary as well as requests for the performer to show a certain body angle or move a certain way.

Related Interests

Voyeurism, exhibitionism.

Jargon and Search Terms

Dogging—sex in parked cars, watching sex in parked cars.
Carping— having a phone conversation with a person who is simultaneously having public sex.

Frotteurism

Frottage (from the French 'frotter' to rub) is the act of rubbing one's body (generally the genital area) against another person whilst in a public place or crowd. This is most commonly a man touching or rubbing his body against a non-consenting, unfamiliar woman, though it can also occur with same-sex people in the gay community. An American study of male university students found that 35% of the men surveyed had engaged in this behaviour at some time in their lives.[157] Frottage generally takes two forms: the 'accidental brush', after which the man apologises to the woman; or the attack in a crowded public location when he rubs or touches the victim and then disappears into the throng. This has become such a problem on the crowded Japanese train system that some carriages have been designated women-only on peak-hour trains.[158] Nearly 64% of Japanese women in their twenties and thirties say they have been groped in trains, subways or in transit stations in the city, but are often too ashamed to speak out. Despite the fact that men face even more crowding as a result of the women-only carriages initiative, most support the concept as they worry about being falsely accused of groping if they accidentally brush against a woman in a packed train. Penalties include imprisonment for up to seven years as well as hefty fines.

It is believed that frotteurism generally begins in adolescence, and the behaviour tends to decrease when the man reaches his late twenties. There are no published accounts to date of female frotteurs,[159] but there have a been a number of studies that report if a man indulges in frotteurism then he

---

[157]Templemann and Stinnett (1991).

[158]'Tokyo Subway Experiment Attempts to Slow Epidemic of Subway Fondling' ABC news (2005).

[159]Penix and Pickett in Fisher and O'Donohue (2006).

usually also has an interest in either exhibitionism or voyeurism—if not both.[160]

Related Interests

Exhibitionism, voyeurism.

Mirrors

> Mirror, mirror on the wall, who's the fairest of them all….

Katoptronophila: katoptron (mirror) and philia (love of) is an erotic attraction to the presence of mirrors during sex. A person who is a katoptronophiliac may not be able to become aroused unless sexual play is in front of a mirror. An interest in mirrors will include having sex in front of a mirror, stripping or performing erotic dancing in front of mirrors. Some katoptronophiliacs find their own image so entrancing that they choose to masturbate in front of the mirror, while others may put mirrors all over their house so they can conveniently have sex in any room. Probably the most commonly known form of this interest is the 80s-style bachelor pad with a mirror on the bedroom ceiling.

Related Interests

Exhibitionism.

---

[160]See for example Freund (1990) or Abel et al (1998).

I'm a Lady and I Do Lady's Things

Transvestic Fetishism

The German physician Magnus Hirschfield (1868-1935) coined the term transvestism in 1910 and is credited with being the first clinician to make a distinction between this and homosexuality. In the DSM-IV definition,[161] Transvestic fetishists, or cross-dressers, are defined as heterosexual men who wear women's clothing for sexual excitement. Cross-dressers come from all walks of life, and despite a common assumption that men who cross-dress are homosexual, the average cross-dresser is said to be heterosexual and to marry and have children. My own experiences with meeting cross-dressers on social media sites has been that a reasonable number consider themselves bisexual with an attraction to men provided they are feminine in appearance or manner.

Homosexuals and women also cross-dress and have done so at various times during history, but the American Psychiatric Association[162] expressly limits the term Transvestic Fetishism to a paraphilia of heterosexual males.[163] This differs from the cross-dressing known as 'drag', worn by homosexuals or performance artists; which always includes behaving in an exaggeratedly feminine manner, wearing showy clothing, high-heeled shoes, obvious makeup and a wig. This form of cross-dressing is either a part of a performance or is done to attract other homosexual men—the female clothing and

---

[161]Morrison (2006, p.376).

[162]APA (2000 in Morrison 2006).

[163]Research by Bullough and Bullough (1997) 'Are Transvestites Necessarily Heterosexual' argues that the obligatory heterosexual orientation for transvestites needs reconsideration as they believe there is significant variation in sexual orientation for cross-dressers.

makeup used in this case to enhance sexual appeal and not for reasons of personal sexual stimulation or excitement.

Edward is a quiet, balding gay man in his early thirties who has been doing drag for years. He cross-dresses flamboyantly to be more attractive and to boost his self-confidence. His alter ego is Cara, a blond showgirl, and he often dresses as her to go to clubs and gay venues:

> My favourite thing about doing drag is the transformation. It never ceases to amaze me how I have the power to change my face, my hair—my whole demeanour—and in each little step Cara takes over more. Finally when she is done, a different persona comes out and that's really where the art is.

Transvestite heterosexual or bisexual men are more likely to limit their cross-dressing to the privacy of their own homes, when alone, or with a few trusted friends and family. They may spend several hours a week getting dressed or wearing women's clothing, or some have a specific room set up in the home where they go to relax or transform into a woman. Many cross-dressers and transgender women experience anxiety around whether their clothing and makeup are enough to make them look truly female. While some prefer to look like a genuine woman, practicing makeup, choosing clothing they consider a real woman would wear and generally try to blend in; others prefer a more sexualized version of femininity and choose provocative shoes and clothing; and many simply limit their cross-dressing to women's underwear that can be easily worn under male attire, allowing them to enjoy it discreetly in public.

The majority of cross-dressers that belong to social media sites use a female name and their ages range from nineteen to late fifties. Many looking for relationships specifically list they are not interested in men while others list themselves as open to male and female relationships. Those who are bisexual or bi-curious anecdotally prefer men who are less masculine in demeanor or appearance.

It is common for transvestite men to become aroused or feel excited when wearing their female attire, but while some masturbate or have sex when in female clothing, anecdotally many have sex after taking their female clothes off, as most of the men feel comfortable being male and have no desire to change gender—and whether they keep on their female clothing is also influenced by the wishes of their sex partners. Single cross-dressers almost always keep their cross-dressing to themselves and may never divulge their interest to the women they date as it isn't usually well received. Men who enjoy it say that cross-dressing is about a temporary transformation that they report as variously mentally, sexually, spiritually and even intellectually liberating, thrilling or intriguing.

Ken is 49, has been married for many years and has grown children. In the past year he has begun buying himself underwear from Victoria's Secret which he wears under normal clothing. He enjoys his new interest enormously and says it is not uncommon for him to wear something "pretty and frilly" and quietly play with himself under the cover of a blanket while watching TV in the evening with his unsuspecting wife nearby. He says the only drawback is the price of the underwear he favours, as well as finding ways to quietly launder it without his wife catching on.

Blanchard (2009)[164] makes the point that a problem with the DSM-IV diagnostic criteria (one which holds true for many other paraphilias), is that a man can cross-dress until the cows come home, but he cannot be clinically identified as a transvestite unless he is unhappy or it impairs his work, personal or social functioning. Money (1984) named an attraction to transvestites or male to female transsexuals by

---

[164]*The DSM Diagnostic Criteria for Transvestic Fetishism.*

men who do not cross-dress themselves as gynemimetophilia: gyne (woman), mime and philia (love of).

Autogynephilia

My therapist's advice to me was to try some cross-dressing, to see if it helped while I sorted out my feelings. It has had little effect, perhaps since my desires have always centered around possession of female characteristics. Cross-dressing always seems like a cheap imitation of the way things are supposed to be.

—*Thirty One New Narratives About Autogynephilia*[165]

Autogynephilia: from the Greek root auto (of oneself), gyne (woman), and philia (love of) is love of oneself as a woman. The term was coined by American psychiatrist Ray Blanchard some fifteen years ago to define what he saw as some men's erotic arousal from thoughts of imagining themselves as a woman, as opposed to the traditional assumption that all men who enjoyed cross-dressing did so because of its erotic stimulation. There is also continuing debate that autogynephilia should be contained within the definition of Transvestic Fetishism rather than to the side of it as is currently the case.

This phenomenon was original identified by Hirschfeld, who found that some men experience a type of personality split in which the masculine component of the psyche is sexually stimulated by the feminine component so that they feel attracted to the idea of what they believe is the woman inside them.[166] Eminent researcher Anne Lawrence, who is a

---

[165] www.annelawrence.com/31narratives.html.

[166] Hirschfield (1949, p.167) in Blanchard (2005,p.441).

male to female transsexual herself, has published an extensive collection of narratives by autogynephiles, and defines this paraphilia as men who love women and want to become what they love.[167] This excerpt from one of the narratives she collected illustrates the form this desire can take:

> There have been times in my life when I have enjoyed sex without fantasizing about being a woman—usually at the beginning of relationships. I call this being in my 'male mode'. At the very moment that most young males are first becoming aroused by the opposite sex, there are apparently a few of us who are becoming aroused at [the idea of] being the opposite sex. I remember this with a great deal of clarity—I became aroused by those blossoming young girls in their short skirts, wishing I was them (narrative 42).[168]

Sexual arousal for autogynephiles comes from impersonating or imagining a woman or female ideal they find sexually attractive. It manifests in behaving or fantasizing in ways they believe are typical of the woman they want to be, while continuing to be sexually attracted to women. Common ways this manifests (aside from cross-dressing) are that the man will fantasise he has breasts or a vulva, imagine that he is a woman while having sex with a woman, or enjoy anal sex with a man or woman (if bisexual) while imagining the anus is a vagina.[169] Michelle (see transsexualism below) is intersex and says she uses the fantasy of imagining herself fully a woman to enhance lovemaking and that mentally focusing on the female parts of herself ensures the sensations become very intense so she climaxes very quickly. The community of online cross-

---

[167]Lawrence (2007).
[168]www.annelawrence.com.
[169]Blanchard (2005); Lawrence (2009).

dressers with this particular interest commonly adopt female names and then add an appellation such as 'sissy' or 'whore' to their names—for example Natalie Sissywhore and they enjoy keeping on their female attire for sex. Their interests always include being dominated by a woman. Dennis has been married for many years and always enjoyed cross-dressing with his wife's full knowledge. His wife introduced him to cuckolding and in this arrangement she has sex with partners of her choosing while he sits in the room dressed in a sissy costume of choice and masturbates while fantasising he *is* his wife (see also Cuckolding). Related interests include rubber, adult baby play and sissification.

Transsexualism

Transsexualism, is known as Gender Identity Disorder (GID) and sometimes also Gender Dysphoria. It describes a person who has an overwhelming desire to be the opposite sex. The person may have had surgery or be debating it, but at the heart of the matter is the fact that they believe their body is the wrong gender They take on the dress and mannerisms of the opposite sex, and while cross-dressing, this not for sexual stimulation but generally a common first step in their quest to change gender. GID is reportedly rare (3 of every 100,000 men and 1 of every 100,000 women).[170]

Most transsexual men report growing up and living with a desire to be a woman is a difficult road to travel. According to Kay, who has been living as a woman for many years and is now approaching her sixties, many transsexuals attempt suicide and lead deeply unhappy lives, such is the burden of living with what she calls "the wrong body". More difficult again is wanting both equally. I need to tell Michelle's story,

---

[170]Morrison (2006, p.381).

but while he[171] has cross-dressed and has a female feelings and emotions, he does so because he was born intersex, the term used to describe a person born with reproductive organs, genitalia and/or sex chromosomes that are not exclusively male or female—the old term is hermaphrodite; so as a result he doesn't exclusively fit the transvestite, transsexual or autogynephile profiles.

Michelle is a 49 year old, happily married and monogamous father of three. He has had feminine or female feelings as well as a strong need to cross-dress throughout his life, but without understanding where these feelings came from. He fought against them, tried to ignore them and went to counselling. At 48 he finally had a bio-scan and it was discovered he had both a female and male signature. After speaking to his mother he discovered his parents were given the choice of surgery to define him as either a woman or a man and chose to have his vagina sewn closed at birth.[172] He also has breasts and at some point in his life took herbs and supplements to encourage them to grow, but is now ambivalent about them as they only feel suitable when he is in 'Michelle mode'. He routinely binds them as he has teenage boys and doesn't want to alert them to his biological makeup. He says his wife rarely touches his breasts but if she does, or if her breasts brush against his during lovemaking, it sends him "into an intense lovely place." His wife doesn't really acknowledge his female sexuality and despite being married for 25 years it is not something they discuss—she thinks he is 'healed' of cross-dressing, but what he has done is embrace spirituality and with the help of a spiritual counsellor and says he is now able to completely accept the two sides of his

---

[171] I am choosing to use the male pronoun because Michelle's dominant social position is male.

[172] This choice was also unusual, as intersex babies are usually gender assigned as female and have the penis and testes removed and a vagina created for them.

identity. He copes by not suppressing the female side in his head, heart and soul and speaks of himself in the plural, acknowledging and honouring his female side by allowing her to surface when necessary. Earlier in his life he would have coped by cross-dressing, but he has chosen to express himself internally now-days, instead of through physical changes. Accepting he is both male and female has brought him to a place of peace.

He has cross-dressed on and off for 34 years, beginning in his teens, however the ridicule that resulted from this stopped him from doing it publicly. He rarely cross dresses now, saying it has lost its thrill—as well as experiencing a certain disappointment that the clothing and makeup are never enough to make him look truly female—a fear and frustration that is common to most people who are transgender or cross-dressers, even the stunning ones.

During this research I was also approached by Ash, a beautiful 20 year old transsexual who lives and works as a woman. She has known all her life that she wanted to be a woman, and is saving for sexual reassignment surgery (having already had breast augmentation). While she recognises that she wants to be and is in her mind a woman, she is only sexually attracted to women—which puts her in an even smaller minority: a trans woman who is attracted to other women in a lesbian sense.

Transgenderist is a relatively new term for people living as their preferred as opposed to biological gender without resorting to genital surgery, though studies show that transgenderists employ other types of interventions such as facial surgery, mammoplasty and hormone therapy.[173] There is some debate in the transsexual community with regard to the term, as the argument is that they are not changing gender but changing sex; so for some the term is considered misleading.

---

[173]Bullough and Bullough (1997, p.9).

Sammi is a Eurasian transgender woman who prefers to use the term shemale to describe herself. While it is generally considered a slur or inappropriate label that is related to transsexual porn, some trans women use it because it is considered an apt description of the way their lives are split between two genders. He lives as a woman and describes himself as "a big haired, chick with a dick" and would not consider genital reassignment as he prefers to have sex as a man with biological or transgendered women.

The shemale concept anecdotally does well in the porn market, as heterosexual men who enjoy female domination, forced feminisation or are bi-curious can explore these interests without it being considered homosexual. Mal is a case in point. When he was 32 his wife became pregnant with their first child and came up with the novel idea that provided he didn't stray with heterosexual women he could go to brothels and have sex with transsexuals. He was initially shocked at the suggestion, but her background of working in the sex industry meant that she didn't have similar hang-ups and saw it as an ideal solution to keeping him happy while she suffered extended morning sickness. He was surprised and delighted at the level of attractiveness and femininity of the women he met, and ten years on continues to occasionally visit transsexual sex workers. Sexologists use the terms gynemimetophilia (Money 1984) or gynandromorphophilia (Blanchard and Collins 1993) to describe people who are sexually attracted to preoperative male-to-female transsexuals.

Thailand has a rich history of accepting what Richard Totman (who spent three years living in Thailand to research this topic) refers to as "the third sex" boys who grow up and live as women and who are known as Kathoey. The Kathoey (sometimes called ladyboys in English) form a significant subculture that is an acknowledged and accepted part of Thailand's history and life today. Some schools have so many Kathoey attending that they even have their own bathroom facilities and it is common for most Thai universities to have Kathoey cabaret troupes.[174]

Related Interests

To cross-dressing: rubber, adult baby play, sissification.

Jargon and Search Terms

Cosplay—costume play, cross-dressing in costumes that represent historical, movie or anime characters.
Crossdreamers—term used for either authogynephiliacs or cross-dressers.
Hawk—a heterosexual man who is sexually attracted to pre-operative male transsexuals.
Mtf—male to female.
Pansexuality—attraction to others regardless of their gender or sexual orientation, so this can be male, female or transsexual, pre or post operative. The slang term trisexuality is also used in this regard to denote that a person will try anything.
Passing—behaving and dressing as a person of the opposite sex.
Shemale—she plus male is slang for trans women with male genitalia and augmented female breasts. It is a term considered pejorative by most trans people.
T Girl—transsexual pre or post op woman.
Trannie chaser, transfans trannie chaser, trans catcher—men who are attracted to cross-dressing men or transsexuals.
Underdressing—the term used by male cross-dressers to describe wearing female undergarments under their own clothes.

---

[174]For more insights into the life of Kathoey, see *The Third Sex* (2003) by Richard Totman.

BDSM

The first time I logged onto alt.com (a deviant, membership only site), I knew I was home. I immediately found myself a Master and by the end of the week he had sent me to be measured for the sexiest red rubber skirt I had ever seen.

BDSM is an acronym for bondage, discipline, sadism and masochism. The three main categories are:

- **B&D** – Bondage and Discipline
- **D&S:** Domination and Submission (also commonly referred to as D/s)
- **S&M:** Sadism and Masochism (also called Sadomasochism).

In bondage and discipline (BD), the emphasis is on physical or psychological restraint. This can take the form of tying up a partner or disciplining them, physically or psychologically. Domination and submission (D/s) is based on power relationships where one partner assumes the role of powerful Dominant and the other the powerless submissive, frequently enacted within predefined roles such as Mistress/Master and slave/sub. Sadomasochism (SM) is the happy combination of sadism (the desire to inflict pain or punishment for pleasure) and masochism (the enjoyment of physical or psychological pain.)

In BDSM practices, the person leading or initiating the activities is often referred to as the top and the person following the top's lead or instructions as the bottom. It is believed these terms originated from missionary-position sex, where the male is literally on top of his partner; however, that is where the similarities with domination and submission (D/s) finish. A D/s relationship is mostly about power and including power in sex games, than about physical stimulation. While some choose to switch roles from top to bottom (particularly for pain play such as whipping or flogging), those who seriously pursue a D/s lifestyle would not consider swapping roles. People vary in how they enjoy a BDSM lifestyle: for a small number it can be a full-time, 24/7, lifestyle choice (see Total Power Exchange), while for others it is confined to the bedroom or reserved for special occasions.

The themes of BDSM are interrelated and will overlap, and individual preferences mean a person may choose to integrate aspects of any of them into his or her sexual repertoire. As well as the traditional activities of humiliation, bondage and punishment, many different fetishistic practices and fantasies may be incorporated into the world of BDSM; common ones include coprophilia, urophilia, and asphyxiaphilia.[175] People who enjoy any form of BDSM call it 'The Scene' or refer to it as 'being in The Lifestyle'; with the term 'scene' also used to describe the enactment of a sexual game.

The mindset called subspace is well known to both tops, bottoms, Dommes and subs, and is a state that is aspired to in most forms of BDSM play. It is described as a type of trance that results from receiving constant stimulus from the Domme or top (in the form of either humiliation or pain) which results in the sub or bottom obeying any command given by the Dominant. It manifests itself in a willingness by the sub to go past previously set limits so that nothing the Dominant commands seems too humiliating; for SM players it might mean enduring a more severe whipping or other physical punishment. For true aficionados, deep subspace is always the goal as it is believed to enhance both their experience of domination or pain as well as their orgasms.

---

[175]Love of human faeces, urine and being strangled respectively. See relevant sections for more details.

The most prevailing aspect of BDSM sex is the eroticisation and staging of power itself. In this context the intent is not 'power over,' unless implied by non-consensual consensuality,[176] but rather a 'power with' scenario where both partners agree who holds the power and how they will use it. Experts in the field such as Henkin and Holiday (1996) sum it up nicely as "consensual exchanges of erotic power".

What attracts people to this as a lifestyle or occasional practice is highly individual, but in terms of a common theme Baumeister (1997) describes it as a useful escape from what he terms "the stressful awareness of one's ordinary identity". He argues that Western lifestyles are so burdensome that a temporary escape from being yourself provides a useful way to relieve stress; citing examples such as the man or woman who spends the day as a powerful decision-maker and then becomes a willing and submissive servant at night.

A question that interests many people (including myself) is whether the BDSM dynamic can work in what I will prosaically call a 'normal' i.e. long-term or married, relationship. Experienced male subs believe it can, but only in the right circumstances. They say this passion is possible with wives or long-term girlfriends, but only if a mutual interest is established very early on—and in this respect actually forms the basis of the long-term relationship—as opposed to being an add-on that occurs later in the relationship. One long-term sub believes emphatically that the idea that wives magically discover dominance one day and then enslave the hubby is a myth—or is simply an interest of hobby BDSMers. This is because true subs tend to view their Dommes as Goddesses who live, to some extent, on a higher level than mere mortals. In the words of Joel, a mature, married male sub with whom I spent many hours in conversation:

---

[176]When one partner voluntarily gives up their right to consent and allowing the other partner to make those decisions on their behalf.

Having seen a wife sick, vulnerable, acting silly or using the bathroom like an ordinary person for so many years, sort of kills that fantasy — and if she is the mother of your kids that adds a whole other dimension. So we know that she is not Superior but rather an equal. But we view our Dommes as superior and i [sic] just don't think that switch can be turned on and off after living a long term relationship.

He concedes it may work if the Mistress/slave relationship is established early and so-called precautions are taken. Issues he believes need to be considered are that no woman can walk around in leather and heels, or mentally be in Mistress mode 24/7, so the sub needs to understand that he serves at her whim and must be deferential. It would also be a hallmark of this type of relationship that he would *of course* (sub's emphasis) do all of the household chores without expecting any special recognition and there would need to be regular so-called 'deprivation' of her presence — such as banishing him to a basement or rented apartment for a weekend or week at a time. The relationship becomes a balancing act as the Domme trains the sub-hub (submissive husband) to her requirements without allowing him to become too needy (which is — as any sub will tell you — his natural inclination). This is how Joel describes an ideal long-term partnership with a Domme:

It would also be assumed that she would establish very early on that She controls ALL of the money, what he makes and what she makes. If he has fetishes that she can use to control and weaken him (and it is a certainty that he does) such as a foot or high-heel fetish, She would want to use those judiciously as well. Not so much that he expects it or it loses its effect through overuse, but enough to keep him begging. She has to know him better than herself in order to make him live only for her.

Not all Dominants and subs are lucky enough to find a complementary partner, so they may pay for this service, join BDSM clubs or go to parties and nightclubs that cater specifically to BDSM interests. There are many different levels of clubs, from those that cater to 'newbies' to those that are as hardcore as publicly possible. The premise is similar to a party or nightclub event, with the inclusion of patrons putting on live shows, the possibility of BDSM play with strangers (either publicly or privately), and the opportunity to use the type of dungeon equipment that may not be feasible to set up in the average person's spare room (see the Bondage section for more information on equipment).

In regard to paying for a BDSM service, there are establishments in most capital cities of the world that cater for fetishes and BDSM play. In Australia they must generally be licensed as brothels, but negotiated BDSM scenes rarely involve paying for sex, as this is not what BDSM is about. Depending on the establishment, and if penetrative sex with the woman is requested, the Mistress may call in a sex-worker to perform that part of the service; otherwise the sub will take care of his own orgasm.

Salon Kitty's, [177] a BDSM establishment in Sydney, Australia, has been in operation since 1985. It is owned by Mistress Amanda, a Domme of some 20 years' standing. She prefers to charge based on content, with most sessions averaging out at around one and a half hours. Her website provides a comprehensive range of information on how sessions are conducted. As a example, an 'Introducing a Novice' session will cost between $330 to $380 per hour, while a session that includes anal sex, golden showers, electric play, cock torture, bondage

---

[177] www.salonkittys.com.

and physical punishment will cost around $440 for the hour. Prices vary depending on how much the client wants to get through in the session and whether one or more Mistresses are required[178]. Anal sex sessions are a more expensive area of content as not all women offer this service.

Fetish House in Melbourne, Australia, offers 'Fetish Sessions' (described as BDSM, fetish, fantasy, role-play, smothering, trampling, X-dressing) at prices starting from $80 for 15 minutes to one hour sessions costing $230.[179]

Popular literature for BDSM enthusiasts are Pauline Réage's *The Story of O* and A. N. Roquelaure's[180] series of *Sleeping Beauty* novels; movies include the *Blue Velvet* films directed by David Lynch, *Maitresse* starring a young Gerard Depardieu, *9MM* with Nicholas Cage and *Nine and a Half Weeks* featuring Mickey Rourke and Kim Basinger.

Domination and Submission

> I will do whatever you command, be your slave, a mere object with which you can do what you will—only don't send me away—I can't bear it—I cannot live without you.
> —Severin begging his Mistress, *Venus in Furs*

In a (D/s) dynamic a Dominant is the person in control, while the submissive is the one being controlled. Romantic love is not a cornerstone of D/s relationships, as the partners might be very much in love or have no romantic relationship at all. When the Dominant leads more than the sexual action and takes power in other aspects of the sub's life, then it

---

[178] Prices as published in 2010.

[179] Correct at time of printing, http://www.fetishhouse.com.au/Prices.htm.

[180] A pen name of Anne Rice.

becomes a D/s relationship, with the partners agreeing to an exchange of power that results in the submissive (sub) deferring to the Dominant (Dom or Domme)[181] and accepting any orders issued by him or her. The couple express themselves by commanding and obeying, in serving and being served; and this behaviour is considered more important to their sexuality than physical stimulation. The relationships they form are most often in the form of Master or Mistress and slave or sub.[182]

Female dominance in BDSM relationships is also known as Femdom. While either men or women can take the dominant role in BDSM acts such as spanking, wax play, electric play and humiliation, there are some practices where the dominant role is usually taken by the woman, such as foot worship, cuckolding, pegging, forced feminisation and financial domination (see the section on Femdom).

D/s activities vary from couple to couple, from something simple like being told to wear a particular outfit, or to go out to dinner without underwear, to being placed in various situations of physical or mental helplessness such as being tied up, locked out or locked in, or being punished or humiliated in some way. Other deferent activities such as being used as a footstool, kneeling at the Dominant's feet, being told when and how to take sexual pleasure and performing body worship or grooming are all common aspects of a D/s relationship. Role-play based on fantasies in which one person is powerful—say a jailer, parent, abductor—and the other is

---

[181]Dom is used to describe male dominants and Domme (sometimes also written as Dome or femdom), for women—the term dominatrix or Prodomme is usually reserved for the professional female. When writing about situations that apply to either Doms or Dommes, I have chosen to use the generic term Dominant for both male and female non-professional dominants.
[182]The terms Dom, Domme, Master and Mistress are always capitalised as a form of respect.

powerless as a captive or slave are also enjoyed by those in a D/s relationship. D/s remains, however, a relationship based on the permission of the sub, who has to trust the Dominant profoundly to make decisions on activities they are commanded to perform.

D/s is widely experienced by Dominants as making them feel high or aroused from exerting control and by submissives as arousal from being controlled. In addition, most Dominants who enjoy these relationships commonly report the experience of dominating as pleasurable not just from the action of dominating, but also because they are pleasing their partner as the submissive will have given permission for certain activities to begin with. Submissive partners also enjoy the complementary pleasure that comes from the lack of personal control as well as the anticipation of what experiences and sensations the Dominant has planned for them. In successful pairings, both partners report experiencing closeness brought on by the trust inherent in these acts, and for them BDSM is a successful, consensual power exchange between two people.

> Did I think I would grow up to be a Femdom? Well no. But here's the good news girls, being the Goddess I now am means I never go wanting on any erotic front. It gives me permission to have as much (or as little) sex or pleasuring as I want, when I want it and how I want it. Your sub is there for your pleasure, not the other way around—and trust me, these sorts of commands are ones that all subs are happy to obey!

Of course when the relationship is a professional one (with the Domme providing a paid service), the dynamic is different as the mutual pleasure aspect is not present; though one could argue that the pleasure the Domme experiences is from the income received from dominating the sub. Since the

Internet, the opportunity has opened up for men to easily indulge their submissive side and serve either Prodommes (professional dominant females) or what are termed lifestylers, women who while they do not consider themselves professional, have a relationship with a small handful of subs who provide them with gifts or money and keep them in an appropriate lifestyle. For their part, both Prodommes and lifestylers provide written or verbal humiliation and tasks as required by the sub. 59 year old Charles who is on his second marriage to an unsuspecting wife, is extremely happy serving his lifestyle Domme who occasionally sends him her worn panties and sets him tasks such as purchasing female panties, photographing himself wearing lipstick or a bikini (yes, I have to say he looks great in it), or using a dildo on himself. In exchange he pays her for setting these tasks, having initially given a broad idea of what he would enjoy; so it's win/win for all. Even his wife is said to benefit, as Charles reports being far more submissive with her, as his online mistress has set him the task of reading about how to treat women as goddesses.

Because many male subs are married, these online D/s relationships are reported to work beautifully[183] as the men are not in a situation where they can easily disappear to visit a Prodomme or do not have the discretionary income to pay the high cost[184] of a face-to-face session with a professional. Even if they have the freedom to visit a Prodomme, being online is financially attractive because for only a few hundred dollars they can experience submission from the anonymity of their own computers. It works for the Domme or lifestyler (there is a somewhat blurry line between where professional begins and ends) as well, because anecdotally there are far more subs than Dommes, so doing this online means one Domme can

---

[183] I have yet to encounter a sub who does this who is single, but I'm sure they are out there.

[184] In America anywhere from $500 - $1,000 and upwards depending on the service provider and what services are requested.

juggle multiple subs. The subs are aware this happens, and as Charles explained, a very real and hurtful punishment is being ignored by the online mistress for any period of time—not just because the subs crave her constant attention, but because they know there are more subs out there ready and willing to take their places. See also the section below for information on the somewhat contentious practice of financial domination, which always involves Dommes and male subs.

What precisely attracts a sub to being dominated is a question on many vanilla lips, and the best person to answer this is Joel, a married professional in his mid-forties. If you passed him on the street you'd probably look twice, as he is an attractive, well-dressed, self-assured Caucasian male, who stands at 194 cms or 6'4 and obviously works out. While he is not, as he says self-deprecatingly, George Clooney, his looks definitely tick all the boxes for what the average woman would consider an attractive man. But Joel is only attracted to women who will in his words "use and abuse him" and for this reason he has been serving Mistresses (nowadays always online) for years:

> It is definitely mixed with sexual feelings but not those caused by wanting to have sex with some-one. For subs (and certainly me), having sex with a Domme is so far removed from anything that is possible that i[185] [sic] don't dare even entertain the thought. Oh sure, i have great sex drive and would love to have sex with lots of Dommes i have served, but it doesn't seem right, doesn't seem submissive and i believe that my highest and best use to them is as labour slave or pay slave, not sex partner. And yes it can be trance-like especially in a real time session with a Dominatrix. After

---

[185]Submissives always use lower case in relation to themselves e.g. 'i', and uppercase for the Dominant, e.g. 'She, You, He', etc.

enough pain and humiliation, there comes a point
at which there is almost nothing that i would not
do for Her, no command that i would not obey.

The mental space that Joel is referring to is known as subspace, the holy grail of mindsets that submissive partners
(both male and female) universally aspire to. It is also known
as headspace, flying or floating, and describes a trance-like
state in which the person believes themselves to be mentally
separate from the environment. To many it is considered the
ultimate submissive foreplay.

Committed or career subs (as opposed to the role-playing,
weekend ones) are well aware that some sections of society
will find their behaviour weak while holding Dominants in
disdain. However, from their perspective the Dommes *are*
superior, which makes them winners in a Darwinian world in
which the weak serve the strong. As Joel commented:

Does the wounded Wildebeest hold the Lioness in
disdain for killing and eating it, or does it just accept that it is part of the circle of life? So it is for us
submissives.

As D/s mandates that one partner dominates the other
physically, mentally or both, contemplation of these practices
may appear alarming to those not drawn to them, particularly
given that they mimic situations such as slavery, abusive
parenting or misogyny.[186] However, the accounts of those who
enjoy voluntary D/s relationships are highly complimentary,
as power exchange for them is an important cornerstone of
sexuality. Some people find that the act of giving up power for

---

[186]Easton and Liszt (2000).

a pre-negotiated period of time and then taking it back[187] makes them ultimately wiser in the ways of handling power.

Total Power Exchange

Screw as I Say, Not as I Screw.

Some D/s relationships remain in the bedroom, and once the bondage toys are put away play is considered over and the couple return to an equal footing. For others it becomes a lifestyle that underpins the philosophy of how they view their relationship. For them it is necessary for the relationship to have a continuous thread of power exchange in which one surrenders and one controls. This type of arrangement is known as total power exchange (TPE) or by the acronym 24/7. It signifies a full-time arrangement in which the submissive gives the Dominant a very comprehensive range of rights to control their daily existence.

In TPE it is fairly common for the people involved to opt for a Master/Mistress and slave model, so while there is consent it is generally broader and assumed to be long-term and continuously in effect. Giving this type of overall consent is sometimes referred to as metaconsent, though this can be confusing as the same term is often used when referring to consensual nonconsensuality (described below), which operates on a slightly different premise. It is a common misunderstanding of those outside the BDSM scene that all D/s relationships work on the TPE model, but in fact these types of relationships are not at all common. Depending on the couple the sub may be a service or sex slave or both; and the sub is generally referred to as a slave.

People involved in a total power exchange relationship say that this type of lifestyle can only be successful when there

---

[187] Hardy and Easton (2004) refer to this as the currency of power

is a high degree of trust between the partners. It has to be a relationship in which the sub is comfortable enough to trust the dominant to be responsible for their psychological and physical well-being, and works best if the sub can honestly say they will do anything they are asked. This is a relationship that has to grow over time as the sub has to have a feeling of total trust and safety.

The reality of people's lives means that the word 'total' cannot really mean total unless the slave has no job, children or any other role outside the house. Even then it is not humanly possible for a Dominant to control every action or thought a slave might have during every moment of every day. Most Masters or Mistresses, even in these relationships, do not wish to micromanage the slaves[188] and generally do not expect them to be lolling around the house all day long in nothing but a bondage collar and frilly apron, preferring a slave to be fairly autonomous. For this reason many of these couples have the slave abide by a slave contract, a list of dos, don'ts and expectations. This can cover a diverse range of rules from sexual to the day-to-day of what to eat, how much exercise to do and when to go to bed. It is generally accepted that metaconsent does not mean 'with no limits', as the sub still has his or her own free will to withdraw consent if the lifestyle makes them unhappy or the Dominant gives orders to do something that is illegal or unethical, such as to kill another person or cut off their own leg.

However, power exchange does lie at the heart of this type of relationship, so the Dominant will usually modify the sub's behaviour (known as training) to suit his or her require-ments. Examples of training might be that the Dom expects observance of some type of etiquette, such as a preferred way of kneeling or way of greeting; or perhaps the slave is only allowed to wear certain types of underwear, styles of clothing or makeup. Training may become quite complex, so that the

---

[188]It is routine for a sub to known as a slave in TPE relationships.

slave must hold his or her orgasm back until they have the Dominant's permission, wear a chastity device or learn to orgasm on command (training is covered more fully in the Training section below).

While TPE is a concept that continues to attract debate both within and without the BDSM community, the concept of a Mistress or Master's right to complete control and decision-making power over a submissive remains for some an inspiring ideal. For the sub who willingly gives all financial control to a Mistress, financial domination can be a form of TPE, as it can include his entire salary, life insurance policies and even power of attorney, all of which tend to be irrevocable (see Financial Domination Online below).

The theme of TPE was also explored in the 1986 film *Nine and a Half Weeks* directed by Adrian Lyne.

Consensual Nonconsenuality

Consensual nonconsensuality is a mutual agreement to be able to act as if consent has been waived or given, and means that the dominant partner has permission to violate consent at any time. As such it may include giving up the use of a safeword, so is also known as 'no safeword play' or metaconsent. The practice involves a high degree of trust between the two parties as the sub has to believe that the Dominant will make the right calls. Because of this, it is a practice often limited to long-term partners who have a fairly comprehensive understanding of each other's personalities and psyches. In the words of one female submissive:

> It took me a long time to get to the point of hand-ing over all my consent (i.e. all my trust) to my Master. It is a curious feeling knowing that he now has control over every aspect of my life. But what a contradiction, to give consent to having no future

consent. It doesn't make me a non-person, it means
that I'm free to be me, because my Master under-
stands and embraces me along with my flaws and
weaknesses. He has to, because he now has responsibility for me.

People tend to assume the worst with regard to abuse or
domestic violence when consensual power exchanges occur
between a female sub and male dominant. Even male submissives tend to look at these types of relationships with some
trepidation, believing they leave the door open for women to
suffer harm. Given the social stigma against being a submissive woman, those who support these types of relationships
(whether male or female) believe that making this type of
choice requires courage. Consensual BDSM is not supposed to
be domestic violence or abuse, and The National Leather
Association has drawn up a type of charter[189] on how to
recognise the difference between consensual practices and
abuse, which includes a comprehensive list of questions to
help people make the distinction.

The attraction to taking this type of risk varies between
players: for some it lies in knowing that engaging in such a
comprehensive power exchange, where one partner has it all
and the other has none, demonstrates how much they trust
each other without the need for boundaries; so it becomes
symbolic of their love. For others the giving away of consent
means that they are signifying their trust in the partner to such
a degree that they can let down all defence barriers, based on
the belief that if the dominant partner takes responsibility for
both of them, he or she must love the sub enough to make
decisions that will not cause physical or mental harm. For
others, metaconsent is a way of having experiences that they
may be too scared to initiate or request. For example, a male

---

[189]Available on their website www.nla-i.com

sub may want to have sex with a man while his Mistress watches, and being told to do so by the Mistress enables him to have a guilt-free experience. There are of course people who are attracted to this precisely because the appeal lies in the uncertainty that the play may go too far, and they find the prospect of danger appealing. Consent can be given and revoked for short periods of time, for example an hour or an evening, and there are some subs who will take the risk of giving metaconsent in this fashion even to casual sex partners or paid Dommes.

David is a married submissive in his early fifties and has been paying professional Dommes (mostly online) for years. Very occasionally he will give up his safeword as he believes the risks are worth it:

> If i [sic] am in the right subspace and craving to serve a particular Domme, then I willingly up my safeword before any trust has had a chance to be established, it may even be the first time i serve her. i have done this twice before and both times were the hottest sessions ever. As well, my sexual release after taking this risk is always the most satisfying.

The classic literature on this theme of giving up all control is *Venus in Furs* by Leopold von Sacher-Masoch in which the hero signs an agreement with his lover which gives her the right to kill him:

> Mme von Dunajew is entitled not only to punish her slave as she deems best, even for the slightest inadvertence or fault, but also is herewith given the right to torture him as the mood may seize her or merely for the sake of whiling away the time.

Should she so desire, she may kill him whenever
she wishes; in short he is her unrestricted property.

It is a text that David discovered at university and can
recite almost word for word. He remembers reading it in
snatches while standing in the library; too scared to be seen
with it in his hands, as he didn't want to alert the world to his
secret submissive desires.

Training

Training in this context refers to the dominant partner
being given consent to modify the behaviour of the submissive
partner. It is generally an activity that takes place in an
established, as opposed to casual, D/s relationship, and
frequently marks a progression into a more permanent
association. A training collar (see Collaring) is often presented
to the submissive to formalise this stage of the relationship.
Training is a common hallmark of total power exchange
relationships.

Those who have experienced training believe it streng-
thens a relationship, by ensuring there is open communication
about both partners' wants and needs. As well, they believe it
can create a situation where the sub is able to relax and trust
the partner while the Dominant makes his or her wants and
needs obvious. They maintain this ensures there is less
guesswork than in a vanilla relationship, and helps to solve
problems more readily. What training occurs and how it is
done depends on the individuals involved, but it may require
the submissive to learn specific styles of etiquette that the
Dominant prefers, such as keeping the eyes downcast in
certain situations, particular ways of kneeling, sitting or
standing, a certain type of dress or undress for specific
situations or only orgasming when given permission. While
this type of controlling behaviour may sound harsh, the

partners believe the purpose of training is to bring out the best in the submissive.

Carol is a divorced mother of two young children and recently had herself placed on The Slave Register (TSR). The Slave Register is a website where Dominants register their slaves or subs, each of whom then receives a unique numeric code which signifies ownership on behalf of the Dominant and commitment on behalf of the sub. Carol's Dom has set out a comprehensive training schedule for her which includes the amount of exercise she must do daily, the types of foods she is allowed to eat and some goals for completing study. Carol does not live with her Dom—he in fact lives thousands of miles from her and they see each other infrequently, but she is as committed to her training program as she would be to a marriage.

What discipline is used in training depends on what the parties have negotiated as acceptable for various transgressions, and also takes into account what the sub finds repugnant, as imposing punishment that is enjoyed by the sub defeats the purpose of the training. If the activities used in training are those that the submissive enjoys, the sub will not modify the behaviour as they are being rewarded, not punished. The Dominant then has to administer punishments that the sub does not like, otherwise training simply becomes 'play' punishment, which serves a different purpose.

Some common training methods are the use of measured humiliation, restriction or corporal punishment. Humiliation might include making the submissive eat from a bowl on the floor, not allowing them to use the toilet so they have to wet their pants, or verbally disciplining them in public. Restriction can include making the submissive stand or kneel for long periods of time, tying their hands or locking them in a closet or box. Discipline comes in the form of being spanked or flogged.

Collaring for Commitment

In the D/s community collaring describes the commence-
ment of a relationship between a male Dom and a female
submissive, and while some subs wear a collar purely for
decoration or so that they may be led around on a leash this is
not collaring. An actual collar is the traditional item used, just
as a ring would be in an ordinary relationship, but there are
situations when it is simply not appropriate for a sub to be
wearing a collar—say at the office—so the couples choose
another item to represent the collar. This might be a decorative
chocker, bracelet, anklet, waist chain or ring, reserving the
collar for within the community or at private times. Carol's
Dom has given her a simple string of pearls which she wears
daily. They chose pearls because she has a middle manage-
ment job in sales and they fit in unobtrusively with her style of
dress. Carols takes her collar seriously, so she wears them to
the gym and on weekends to the supermarket. She tucks them
away when in casual clothing and laughs it off as being
straight from work when she finds herself doing a circuit class
in pearls. Carol justifies her behaviour by saying that she
wouldn't take off her wedding ring to go to the gym, and
therefore treats her pearls as collar with a similar respect.

Collaring has a number of stages, beginning with the collar of consideration, the first collar offered by a Dom to a sub.
This initial collar is given at the very beginning of a potential
relationship, and is somewhat like a friendship ring. While the
colour is unimportant, it is traditionally blue and made from
leather. This collar signifies a dating stage and an intention to
pursue a D/s relationship that is beyond casual play. It also
signals to other Doms that the sub is off-limits because she is
considering a serious relationship with someone, and this is
generally respected by others in the community.

After the collar of consideration comes the training collar.
This is like an engagement ring, and signifies that both parties

are serious in trying to work towards a permanent relationship. The training collar is usually plain, and has no particular colour.

The formal or slave collar represents the final stage of commitment, as it shows a desire to share in each other's lives in a power exchange dynamic and carries the same weight and symbolism as a wedding ring. There is generally some type of celebration or ceremony with close friends, family or the BDSM community when the collar is presented, as it is considered a serious undertaking. If it is to be an actual collar it is usually one that can be worn all the time, but if this is not practical the couple may choose to symbolise the collar in the form of jewellery that can be worn daily, or as a piercing or a tattoo. In all stages of collaring, if the relationship fails or goes no further the collar must be given back to the Dom.

Jargon and Search Terms

Body service—when the submissive takes care of all the Dominant's bodily needs, e.g. bathing, shaving, grooming etc.

Body worship—this is an oral service by the submissive to the dominant in which licking, sucking and kissing is performed on the Dominant's body.

Collaring—the giving of a collar as a sign of commitment. Also used to describe the ceremony held when a collar is given.

Dominant—a male or female Dominant.

Dom—male Dominant.

Dome, Domme, Domina, femdom—female Dominant.

Femdom—female domination.

Metaconsent, nonconsensual consensuality, noncon—when a partner voluntarily gives up their right to consent, allowing the other partner to make decisions on their behalf.

Prodome/Prodomme, Dominantrix—a female Dominant who provides paid domination services.

slave—a male or female submissive in a total power exchange relationship.

sub—a male or female submissive partner.

TPE—total power exchange.

Vanilla—a person only interested in mainstream sexual activities.

Femdom

As the name implies, Femdom is about female domination. While both men and women can and do take a dominant role in BDSM acts such as spanking, wax play, electric play and humiliation, there are some activities that only a Domme can control. These include cuckolding,[190] pegging, forced feminisation and financial domination (see relevant sections). Though they are not specifically Femdom activities, milking and facesitting are also common in this dynamic, so appear in this section.

Although not as well known, Loving Female Authority (LFA) also falls under the Femdom umbrella. LFA is a belief system and/or way of life based on female dominance as part of a broader lifestyle choice. While it does include sexual domination, it is based on the male being dominated within a loving, caring and intimate relationship. Self proclaimed female supremacist and Christian Elise Sutton is credited with coining the phrase, which is based on her theory that most men long to be submissive and are happier if they are dominated and disciplined by a woman within a relationship.[191] She explains the concept in her books, which are based on counsel-

---

[190]While some Doms will make the female submissive have sex with other men, therefore cuckolding himself, this is not commonplace and cuckolding remains more a dominant female activity.
[191]Sutton (2003, 2007).

ling couples in the BDSM lifestyle.[192] While the theory is broader than this, it encapsulates the idea that the wife takes as much power as she wants in the relationship; and while she takes on board the husband's input, he has to agree to her final authority. As well, the wife controls where, when and how they have sex and the husband is not permitted to masturbate privately or without her consent. It is common for there to be some disciplinary policy in place with punishment for broken rules—and spanking is common. A Google search for 'loving female authority' or 'female led relationship' (FLR) will unearth a large number of blogs on this topic.

Forced Feminisation

> I love it when my wife uses me as the little slut,
> sissy and whore that I am.

Forced feminisation, also commonly known as sissification, describes the so-called 'forced' switching of gender roles by a male submissive. It is not used to describe someone who is transsexual or a genuine cross-dresser (though cross-dressers may enjoy doing this with a partner). Forced feminisation, or feminisation for short, is played out between a dominant female and a male submissive, and while it is described as forced, it is an agreed game or behaviour between the two players. In a similar way to bondage, the submissive is coerced into an action, in this case wearing female attire of the woman's choosing. Men who enjoy cross-dressing but are not comfortable doing it voluntarily rate this activity very highly. Stockings, high heels, bras and panties are fairly common, and wigs and makeup are also worn. When a man cannot wear

---

[192]Amazon's author page states she has a bachelor's degree in psychology, but there do not seem to be any other professional credentials available.

these things in front of his partner, wearing female panties or a chastity device at the command of a Prodomme or Domme lover is the next best thing (see also Chastity Play).

Peter is a self-described 'sissywhore', with an understanding wife. She buys beautiful female undergarments which she mails to him, so it is always a thrilling surprise when he receives an unexpected parcel. While he can look at them, he is not allowed to touch or wear them until she instructs him, and this adds to the allure of the garments. He knows that he must put the underwear away; it won't come out until he has been naughty and she punishes him by making him put on his new frilly panties. Peter never knows when this will happen, so often does something deliberately to annoy her so he can put the panties on. As soon as he is wearing his panties he is referred to by his wife as a girl or sissy, and the power dynamic changes completely.

When in costume the sissy is required to take on tasks and behaviours of the stereotypical female, such as doing household chores like dusting, serving tea and biscuits (for this reason the maid's costume is highly popular), or grooming rituals such as giving a manicure or washing the mistress' hair. Unrealistic (or at least very strict) standards of appropriate feminine conduct and deportment may be insisted upon, and punishments using humiliating methods such as over-the-knee spanking are meted out for infractions. It is fairly common that the sissy is required to answer to a female name or be called explicitly female insults, such as slut or whore.

Charles is relatively new to serving a Mistress, but at 59 he has realised it doesn't no matter how beautiful, smart or sexy a woman is, unless she can dominate him the relationship will not survive. He has discovered that being feminised really works for him and says he is just sorry it has taken him until this late in his life to enjoy it:

> Having me go to an expensive lingerie shop wearing lipstick to purchase 3 pair of panties, having

someone take a picture of me there, sending her a picture of the panties and the receipt, and giving me just an hour or so to do it...that excites me, that she can make me do that...and that I want to, have to. It's do or die, as Her punishment is extreme...she will not talk to me and I don't know if she ever will again or not. The upside is that I got to wear the panties and play with her online as a reward for my humiliation...I got to soil my new panties...very exciting!

The male sub is also required to become sexually submissive. This may include having sex with arms or legs bound or having a rope tied around his neck so the Domme can use this to indicate he should move faster or slower. His penis may also be renamed a clit or clitoris, and the size mocked, his anus referred to as a vagina, pussy or hole, and his nipples as breasts. The man may be required to pleasure himself with a dildo, or he may be required to accept anal sex from the woman who will use a strap-on dildo. This practice is known as pegging and has become popular on Internet pornography. An interesting twist on the strap-on aspect is that some Dommes will also require the sub to perform oral sex on the strap-on dildo. While sucking on the synthetic penis cannot arguably give physical pleasure to either partner, those who practise this find that the mental thrill of having ones' 'penis' sucked and the total subjugation this causes the generally heterosexual man, creates a highly erotic, power-charged atmosphere. As is also the case with cuckolding, forced feminisation and acts such as forced anal and oral sex with a dildo can be a way for men who are bi-curious or have homoerotic fantasies to indulge their passions without actually having any male-to-male contact.

A number of heterosexual submissive men I have spoken with have fantasies of forced male-to-male sex. A 33 year old

IT professional who has been married for five years and has never been with a man sexually says his hottest fantasy is that a Domme rents him out as a gay prostitute. Charles also says he would do something similar for his Mistress:

> I will do anything to please my Mistress and I spoil her with gifts. It pleases her to make me do things that are beyond my boundaries. I am not gay and have no plans to be with a man. But my Mistress wants me to dress like a woman and perhaps have oral sex with a man on a webcam so she can watch. It would thrill her that she could make me do something like that…and I'm seriously considering it…just for her.

The Domme may perform prostate milking which, when it involves a feminised partner, is known as sissy milking. She inserts her fingers or a specially designed implement known as a prostate massager into the rectum and massages the prostate gland (see Milking). The Domme may insist the milked partner consumes the collected ejaculate as a demonstration of his lowly status (see also Erotic Humiliation); or as a gesture of humbleness he may be required to present it as a 'gift' to the Domme.

Feminisation role-play can be a genuine punishment to some male submissives as they find it difficult to cope with the loss of their manhood, which is precisely why dominant women consider it an excellent tool for subjugation.

Lift and Carry

Lift and Carry is a sexual interest in being lifted and carried by another person. It is most commonly enjoyed by men who are carried by women, but online content of women carrying other women is also popular.

Men who enjoy female domination are usually drawn to this practice, and while a small number of men appear attracted by the nurturing aspect of being carried or lifted, the majority are more attracted to the general idea of strong women overpowering men. This may also extend into other female dominant activities such as having a woman beat them in an arm-wrestling match or being trampled or smothered. For those aroused by lift and carry, it may be part of foreplay or be so erotic that they orgasm while being lifted.

The mechanics of a female lifting an adult male are influenced by the height and weight of both partners as well as the physical strength of the woman, and this dictates the type of lifts the couple are able to do. For this reason, women who provide the service professionally are often trained athletes, bodybuilders or dancers. Lift and Carry amateur video can be readily found on YouTube and there are several websites providing pay-per-view, some of which include nudity and sex. Websites such as liftgoddess.com, which is run by a woman who is an ex-dancer and body builder, offer real-time lifting sessions as well as video memberships.

There are numerous lifts that different people find interesting, including piggy-back, shoulder and pony rides, cradle carry, over the shoulder, around the waist, the traditional fireman's carry, the leg press lift, the scissor lift and simple lap holding. People who participate in lift and carry discussion forums are very interested in the height and weight differences of the couples, and it is common for the men to have a preference for strong, muscular or physically imposing women (often referred to as Amazon women) while they describe themselves as more diminutive.

Lapsitting is a more practical way for men who are taller or heavier than their female partners to enjoy the experience of being carried by a woman. Mark is 6' (180cms) and weighs around 175 pounds (80 kilos), and his wife is of average weight and height. They enjoy kissing and cuddling while he sits on her lap and treat it as part of their foreplay. Mark says that even without any stimulation, sitting on his wife's lap is a highly erotic experience.

Men who enjoy lapsitting do so for a various reasons. For some it is a thrill because it takes them out of their gender-determined role of the stronger partner, while for others it allows them to feel protected, nurtured or comforted. It can also be part of an adult baby fantasy; but there are many men like Mark who enjoy it for what it is and have no interest in role-playing mommy and baby.

Related Interests

Adult baby, trampling, BDSM.

CFNM

CFNM is short-hand for 'clothed female, naked male,' a specific interest in role-play, fantasy or erotica that is based on the man being naked and the woman or women remaining clothed. When it is done in real time it is generally between two partners, but online erotica on this theme is mostly based on a model of one naked man and a number of clothed women. The activities are same in either case, with the man being ordered around—for example being made to clean the house or serve, being sexually belittled and teased, subjected to medical examinations, or forced to masturbate with a vibrator. All or any of the ways a man can be humiliated in a female domination dynamic may be included, the only difference being that the man is naked. The male is denied the sexual pleasure of seeing the women in the same state of undress and is not in a position to dominate the scene, which is an enjoyable situation for men like Joel who enjoy a submissive/humiliating experience:

Aside from putting me in the more vulnerable position, the woman shows what she thinks of me by not even going to the effort to put on the fetish attire such as garters, leather or latex which appeals to so many subs.

While many submissive men enjoy CFNM, it is also attractive to men who have exhibitionist tendencies because as the only male and the only naked person, they become the star of the show. Richard is 32 and a self-confessed bisexual who enjoys the idea of CFNM with women (though he would consider it with men, when it would become CMNM). To date it has remained a fantasy, as is the case for most men, as it is difficult to engineer a situation where multiple women are willing to be involved with a single naked man and as a professional service may be cost-prohibitive due to the number of Prodommes involved.

This interest differs from Endytophilia: endytos (dressed) and philia (love of) which is a preference for sex with a partner who is fully clothed, as endytophiles generally prefer both partners to remain clothed during sex.

Related Interests

Exhibitionism.

Hand Over Mouth

HOM is short-hand for hand over mouth. It is most commonly enjoyed by submissive males and includes the tamer version of one hand over mouth as well as the more popular one hand covering the mouth and the other covering the nose, known as HomSmother. It is considered exciting because the sub feels he is putting his life into the hands of the Domme and enjoying the ultimate loss of free will.

Related Interests

Erotic asphyxiation.

Erotic Sexual Control: Milking

Milking—done by a dominant woman to a submissive partner—ensures the man no longer has the ability to orgasm conventionally. It is done by vigorously massaging the male prostate gland (a walnut-sized gland high on the rectal wall) so that ejaculatory fluid leaks out (like slow urination) without the man experiencing an orgasm. The massage can be done with two fingers or with the aid of a commercially available prostate massager, which is like a dildo with a handle on the end. Prostate milking can be used simply to intensify orgasm, and in that case it becomes more a case of prostrate massage, so the partner may also allow the penis to be stimulated. Otherwise it can be used as a control mechanism where the sole intention is to control the draining of ejaculate from the man without arousing or exciting the penis by touch, and therefore to deny him the pleasure of an orgasm. Some Dommes are known to place ice around the penis and testicles to further reduce any enjoyment the man may gain from milking.

While many who practise this report it to be a highly pleasurable and sought-after pastime, in this dynamic it is not done with the submissive's pleasure in mind but to either humiliate or control him (even though he may enjoy it). In relationships where partners use this as part of Forced Feminisation it is known as sissie/sissy milking. When milking is done as part of a systematic relationship control mechanism, for example in an LTA relationship where a wife has complete control over any sexual activity, it is common to make the man wear some type of chastity device between milkings to ensure he cannot get an erection or masturbate (see also Chastity Play).

Facesitting/Smothering

Facesitting refers to the practice of one person sitting with the full weight of their genitals and buttocks over the face of another person. It is most commonly done by a woman to man and is also referred to as either queening or smothering. While oral and/or anal stimulation are performed by the man this is not the goal of facesitting, otherwise it would be just straight oral sex. In facesitting her intention is to dominate him and by sitting her entire body weight on the man's face she has control of the proceedings and can position herself to maximise her pleasure and direct the events. The woman may be fully clothed, wearing pantyhose, leather or panties or have a naked bottom or crotch.

Depending on how she places her body she can engineer a situation where he is unable to breathe and for the some men the smothering aspect is the most exciting. Some men prefer to be chained to a chair or piece of furniture or being trussed up by some type of bondage equipment to further enhance the feeling that they are being forced and dominated. It is an interest that spans age groups and nationalities and many men use oral sex as a first step to having their wives or girlfriends perform it. Gary is in his thirties and says he has successfully introduced every new girlfriend to the practice. He believes the key to success is being accomplished at oral sex, but says that in most cases it takes months to encourage a woman to gradually rest her full weight on his face. He says women are eventually happy to participate, but are hesitant because they don't want to hurt or smother him, which is of course what he is after:

> My thrill from being queened or face-sat is the moment I feel I am being smothered, and comes from being helpless to stop it happening. When she starts grinding and controlling the action it is no longer up to me where I put my tongue or nose.

Do I really want to lick an ass? Perhaps, perhaps not. But to be made to do it, and be unable to stop it removes that question, and in my case heightens the thrill of being helpless. For me, I don't want a woman's ass in my face unless it's against my will.

In a professional establishment a custom-designed box known as a smotherbox may be used. The submissive partner lies down and the smotherbox is placed over his head. There is a second opening at the top of the box, and the dominant partner sits on this as if on a toilet, with the genitals exposed and accessible to the face of the submissive, who performs oral sex. While the submissive partner can be male or female, it is far more common for a Domme to have a male sub perform this service. It is a favoured device in BDSM circles, as it efficiently restrains the submissive while providing both comfort and pleasure to the Domme. Men who practice this report it as a very erotic experience:

> When that box is over my head there is nothing to focus on but her sweet juices. The darkness, the sensation of being trapped, feeling her body weight breathing in her female odours in such a close space and feeling the wetness, it just makes me want to adore her more. Sometimes she squeezes my balls or twists my nipples and that really gives me a jolt as I don't see it coming.

While similar in design, these devices differ from human toilet boxes, which do not allow for oral stimulation.

A Prodomme or Mistress will use facesitting as either a means of rewarding the sub for good behaviour or as a form of punishment, but either way the facesitting or smother session is often accompanied by harsh rebukes and sneering or scolding to ensure it is enjoyed as a form of humiliation. Facesitting is related to ass worship, where a Mistress or

Domme commands the submissive slave to lick, taste or smell her anus.

Jargon and Search Terms

Cock-mock—speaking derisively about the penis/slang for forced feminisation.
Facesitting—when one person squats or sits with their genitals over the face of another person.
Femdom, Loving Female Authority (LFA)—female domination.
Humiliatrix—a Prodomme who specialises in forced feminisation.
LFA—loving female authority.
Sissie/sissy milking—prostate milking.
Smotherbox—custom designed box used for facesitting.
WLM—wife led marriage.

Cuckolding: Please—Take my Wife!

> Nothing can intensify my passion more than tyranny, cruelty and especially the faithlessness of a beautiful woman.
> —Leopold von Sacher-Masoch, *Venus in Furs*

Originally, cuckold was a derogatory term for a man with an adulterous wife. In a modern D/s (domination and submission) dynamic it refers to a relationship in which the woman has sex with as many different men as she wants with the full blessing of her partner. He generally does not participate in the sex act and may or may not be physically present— whether he is allowed to watch depends on the wishes of the couple and the agreement of the woman's sex partner. He may continue to have normal sexual relationships with his partner, but it is fairly common for him no longer to have sex with his wife. It is still considered cuckolding if the female partner has sex without his knowledge, provided she comes home afterwards and tells him about it and he finds it arousing. Simply seeing other men behind the partner's back without sharing the experience is considered cheating.

Survey data collected by one cuckolding site shows that education levels for both men and women who cuckold is high and that most men are employed in IT, followed by education and health. While male ages were not published, the majority of wives were thirty-six or older.

Jinxypie is a sweet, petite, 30 year old self-proclaimed Cuckoldress[193] and her husband is a cuck—a man who derives sexual pleasure from seeing his wife or girlfriend have sex with other men. She is a mother with young children and runs a website that invites men to pick a date on the website's calendar to have sex with her. She sells video subscriptions of her various flings, and would-be sex partners are made aware of this. Her husband organises the filming of her dates which are mostly held at their home, and while not present in the room, he will watch remotely as they are being filmed, or later during masturbation. Jinxypie and her husband still have sex together, but she is very frank in admitting she prefers a larger penis than her husband's, so this is a criterion for her partners. Other than that she is simply open to new experiences:

> I don't want to have sex with someone too old or really young (they just don't seem to have much of a clue, honestly)… and yes while looks matter a bit, they have to fall into a penis-size category that's bigger than my husband's 3 inch penis. All I really want is a good sexual experience. It's also exciting to have a bunch of men want me (who doesn't want to be wanted?)… I just crave the attention!

---

[193] As is the case with Mistress, Cuckoldress is often capitalised as a form of respect.

The cuckold community is largely accessed via online forums and meeting sites where couples can advertise for partners. Many of the cuckolding sites require a submission fee and mandate that membership is only granted once couples provide proof of their identity with photos that include placards saying something like "I'm a cuck" or showing the name of the website written on their bodies with marker pen. This stops the sites from being used as a free source of porn, as members enjoy posting video clips of their wives having sex with the Bulls.[194] The Craigslist website also contains regular advertisements from Bulls looking for so-called hotwives, another term for Cuckoldresses. Depending on the sites there are various categories including inter-racial dating, with lots of advertisements for well-endowed black men (referred to as Mandingos) to have sex with the wives of white couples.

For those unwilling to take the step into cuckolding but who enjoy it as an erotic concept, there are plenty of sites offering videos and stories related to the cuckolding theme. How they cater to an interest in cuckolding, as opposed to simply two people having sex together, is to ensure the videos have a home-made quality in terms of style and background (i.e. nothing too professional), ensuring images include the wife's wedding band, often with that hand wrapped around a large penis, or with semen dripping off the ring; or images that show a white wife next to a black man. In American cuckold culture there is a definitely a preoccupation with black men being better endowed fulfilling the need of some caucasian husbands to be sexually inferior to the Bull.

Men overwhelmingly instigate the cuckolding lifestyle. It is rare to find anecdotes of women suddenly coming up with the idea of introducing new men into the marriage while the

---

[194]The cuckolding community always capitalises Bull when used to refer to male sex partners.

husband remains faithful. Women on the whole have difficulty coming to terms with or understanding why their husbands would want to pursue such behaviour. A common fear (aside from believing it is unacceptable for married women to behave like this) is that it will lead to the end of the marriage or relationship; or that it is some type of trap that the husband is laying and if the woman goes ahead she will have failed the test and proven she is a slut. When they do try it, it is frequently after a lot of convincing and because they can see how important it is to their husbands—though they may not understand his reasons and sometimes never do.

I spent some time as a guest blogger at JustJinxy.com so that I could get to know some of the cucks and ask what drew them to this lifestyle. One man who had been married for 30 years wrote to describe his experiences when, after 15 years, his wife instigated cuckolding. After the initial shock he made peace with it, and they are both happy with the outcome:

> It took me a while to come to terms with it. But I never for an instance doubted her love for me or her commitment to our marriage or to our family. And there was absolutely no denying how much pleasure and joy she received from her lover.

> For me that has been the biggest turn on, seeing my wife come home from a visit with her lover literally glowing. She has a look and smile on her that I just can't feel anything but elation for her.

The husbands who responded to my request for feedback on what cuckolding meant to them were honest and soul-searching. Some of the reasons that husbands nominated for pursuing cuckolding were that they had esteem issues because of their penis size or sexual prowess, or that they did not have a high sex drive and becoming a cuck allowed them to satisfy their wives and preserve the relationship—and take pressure off themselves, as one older husband described:

> This has been an ideal solution for us. My wife is beautiful and while I am not ugly, I am more the quiet, geek type and I've always worried about the day she finds someone better. While other men may worry that their wife is cheating because she is sexually frustrated, I can sleep soundly knowing that mine is satisfied every time she has sex because she can pick whoever she wants. She would never sneak around to sleep with other men because she knows she doesn't have to and this way I always know where she is and who she is with. I know I am first in my wife's heart, her best friend, her confidant, the one she turns to for comfort and support and the one she relies on the one she wants to wake up next to in the morning. But I also know that when she is horny and really needs to get laid, that I am definitely not her first choice. They satisfy her sexually but I satisfy her emotionally and that is more important to me.

For the man who has homosexual fantasies or is bi-curious, homoerotic thrills can be enjoyed by proxy, as watching his wife in the act provides an opportunity to vicariously experience homosexuality. When they are allowed to be physically present, some men will give oral sex to the Bull or touch him under the guise of pleasing the female partner; but they do not consider this homosexual activity.

A common outcome of the cuckolding lifestyle is that sex with the husband or partner generally drops off or becomes non-existent. In some cases this is because the man gets enjoyment from what his wife is doing and she becomes the source of inspiration for his masturbation fantasies—some liken it to having their own private porn star. This then allows him to have highly selfish sex during which he no longer has to provide his partner with sexual with attention:

> I believe I feel more attracted to her since she stopped having sex with me. I can't explain the thrill I still get from actually watching her have sex with another man, whether on tape or if I am allowed to be there. She is still the object of my desire, but my desire is turned to being something different. Now we share it organically as I get the wonderful pleasure of dressing as a sissy and playing with myself while my wife is being satisfied completely. (Married 17 years)

For others the erotic thrill is tied to the intense humiliation they feel in knowing what their wives are doing. The need for humiliation can be so strong that some men insist on performing oral sex on their wives afterwards (known as clean-up duty or a creampie) and report a deep thrill in going "sloppy seconds". While many Cuckoldresses (including Jinxypie) practice safe sex, it has to be said that given the interest in creampies, sex without condoms is not unusual in the cuckolding lifestyle.

Despite all the thrills that cuckolding can bring, in some instances the shine can go off the apple fairly quickly as the reality of unexpected emotional entanglement with the new male partner surfaces. Kate has been cuckolding for a fairly short period of time and already finds herself at a crossroads in her marriage as a result of unintended romantic feelings:

> Yes, oral sex afterwards was one of hubby's big turn-ons and in the beginning I let him do it. I saw it as him showing me that he really accepted the whole setup (and it made me feel less guilty). It was quite powerful knowing he would do this

with the full knowledge that another guy had been there. But after awhile it became tiresome, particularly once I started seeing my boyfriend regularly and I was sexually worn out by the time I got home. Things also got complicated in my head when I started to have feelings for my boyfriend as I felt it was disloyal to him, so I stopped allowing hubby to touch me there afterwards. We need to work this out as it is doing my head in.

Kate's situation is not unusual, as other women who see their Bulls regularly and start to see them as boyfriends have also found themselves emotionally conflicted as sex with the third party leads to commitment and a desire for exclusivity (by either party). This is at odds with how cuckolding is meant to work, as in theory cuckolding is based on the idea of the woman having lots of sex without emotional attachment because her main relationship is with her husband. She enjoys a rich sex life, he gets his pleasure from her activities and they both view it as giving something to the other. Couples such as Jinxypie and her husband who have managed to separate sex from other aspects of their relationship appear happiest, likening it to the usual give-and-take in normal sex. As Jinxy points out, a Cuckoldress doesn't cheat on her husband; she shares everything with him.

Jargon and Search Terms

BBC—black bull cock.
Bull—the male cuckolding sex partner.
cuck—male who is knowingly cuckolded.
Cuckoldress—the female who is adulterous with her partner's knowledge.
Mandingos—well endowed black men.

Financial Domination

> Hey little piggie...I WILL take your wallet, I WILL
> drain you dry..., you will spoil ME and you will
> get trained to be My perfect human ATM.
> —Mistress Michelle, drainyourwallet.com

The practice of financial domination has its roots in the traditional dominance and submission dynamic, based on the power exchange that occurs when the dominant partner controls the willing submissive and compels him to be in service to another. Financial domination, also known as money slavery, describes the practice of a man giving money or gifts to a woman he has generally never met (or will ever meet[195]) in return for being psychologically dominated. It came into being in the late 1990s and is the first real information-age fetish, as it is played out through online interaction. In a real-life BDSM relationship a slave shows his or her submission by acts such as surrendering to a beating, being tied up, cleaning the toilet or running errands. In a financial domination dynamic the woman who is known as a Mistress (or Princess)[196] and the slave or sub (the terms are used interchangeably) have a relationship that is based on the sub submitting to the Mistress by giving her regular sums of money, buying gifts or paying her rent or bills. While this may sound exploitative, the men approach the women and choose to give the Mistress unsolicited worship and devotion or prefer role-playing what is known as voluntary duress—pretending to be coerced to gift or tribute the Mistress. Some Mistresses do take this further and exploit the slave for more and more money until the domination becomes sadism and the man experiences financial

---

[195]They may live on other sides of the world.
[196]Money slaves always capitalise the titles Mistress, Goddess and Princess as a form of respect in the same way that Dominant and Domme are capitalised.

difficulty or finds he is living off an allowance while sending all his money to the Mistress. When it gets to this point, what started out as role-playing can become the sub's way of life; some report relying on and craving this type of psychological and emotional humiliation. There is also some argument in the BDSM community that financial slaves are not actually truly submissive given that they are 'paying to play' and as such hold the dominant hand. However, there is no denying that for some money slaves financial hardship becomes a state they have difficulty reversing.

A variety of terms are used to describe this type of relationship, including money slavery, financial servitude, cash fetish, financial domination, financial rape, wallet raping or extreme spoiling. The women who offer these services refer to themselves as a Money Mistress, Money Domme (using the female form of dominant in the BDSM sense), Findomme, Hypnodomme or Money Collector. They also commonly refer to themselves with a title such as Mistress, Princess or Goddess, which fits nicely their core business activities of engendering subjugation, worship and adoration. There are many online advertisements for these types of services, at websites such as YouTube, Nightflirt, Talksugar and Clips4sale. Mistresses—both financial and in real time—have also embraced social networking tools such as Twitter, so it is now possible for subs to follow their favourite Mistress' tweets. Facebook is also used by both Money Mistresses and money slaves looking to make mutual contact.[197] Some of the Facebook pages are very simple and to the point with requests for cash or goods—such as this one by Coco from the UK which offers nothing more than email domination and no visual or verbal contact:

---

[197]Searching for financial domination, money slaves or human atms will bring you to the Facebook pages of both mistresses and money slaves.

Looking for financial slaves and slaves who want email tasks, with a tribute of course. DO NOT DO WEBCAM OR PHONE CHAT, MY SERVICES ARE VIA EMAIL ONLY.

Which begs the question: is Coco a man, is she a woman, is she gay or straight or she is a composite created by 3 nerds in someone's bedroom? While some subs will be content to be manipulated and defrauded simply by the idea of a Money Mistress, there are enough Money Mistresses in business who will provide all that as well as providing proof of their female identity. Much as they enjoy being exploited, all the subs I interviewed said they expected some proof of legitimacy before handing over cash and being willing to worship.[198]

The majority of Money Mistresses carry out their financial domination businesses online, but occasional financial domination relationships occur in real time, where a man approaches a woman he knows or has admired, or in the context of a relationship. That being said, most money masochists would consider this inappropriate or unappealing, as financial domination is not about a sexual relationship but about desire, want and obedience directed at a person who is unobtainable and superior.

Many Mistresses begin their careers as phone sex workers or use this avenue to attract new customers. The terms of engagement generally involve a first step of sending the Money Mistress an initiation fee (the amount varies), so she may consider whether she wishes to begin a relationship with the man. Once she takes him on as her slave she expects various forms of remuneration ranging from regular tributes, pre-set amounts ranging anywhere from $25 to $200, to

---

[198] When the Internet first came into popular use and webcams were unheard of, one veteran money slave funded his own mistress habits by going online and pretending to be a Money Mistress—easy to do as he knew exactly which buttons to press to make other subs pay.

requiring the money slave to make regular monthly payments for her manicures, pedicures, hairstylist, phone bills, rent, utilities and gym membership, or contributes towards her holiday expenses. Some Money Mistresses maintain gift lists at various department stores similar to a wedding registry, and the money slave can use these to order online and have articles delivered to her. Amazon's wish list service is a favourite for many Mistresses, with their lists of requested and received items going for pages and including such diverse items as a Toyota Rav4, depilatory kits, books, cosmetics and airline vouchers. At least one Goddess boasts of having received over 2,400 items that were purchased from her Amazon wish-list. Transactions and money tributes are done online through a third party such as PayPal or credit card debit, or the mistresses get cash sent to a post office box or via a money order. Another method of payment that has increased in popularity is the Green Dot Visa used with MoneyPaks. The Mistress buys a Green Dot Visa card (US $9.99) and the slave then purchases MoneyPaks for varying amounts (up to $1,000 a time) and gives the Mistress the code so she can load the money onto her Visa card. For the married slave this is an attractive option as it is an anonymous cash transaction with no paper trail to credit cards or PayPal.

The exchange of money or goods between Mistress and slave involves no sex or physical interaction, given that it is very rare for a money slave and Money Mistress to meet. Their relationship is limited to emails, online chat, web-cam or the mistress sending photos or allowing telephone calls—all dependent on whether the man has gifted or paid amounts that have pleased her. The men willingly trading cash and gifts for the opportunity to be psychologically humiliated in ways that they find erotic, with the humiliation governed by the size of their tribute or gift. As one man neatly sums it up:

The idea of submitting to an otherwise normal woman, and throwing wads of your hard-earned cash at her while she laughs at your stupidity is really the punch line to the whole thing. Its about humiliation, plain and simple.

When and if the Mistress gives the slave any attention it may be to talk with him about how what he is doing is benefiting her life ("I just had a wonderful holiday, thanks Loser"), or to belittle or degrade him. Attention from the Mistress always involves humiliation, which while it takes various forms depending on the people involved, commonly includes the money slaves being told to perform degrading tasks, being verbally castigated, having derogatory comments about them posted on her website, being constantly harangued for more money, being told to wear women's panties or clothing, not being allowed to climax, being made to eat dog food on webcam, or some other humiliating task or activity that the Mistress believes the slave craves. It is common for most slaves to request the Mistress's permission to climax, and to pay her for the privilege of granting it (known as a wank tax). For some men the mere process of making payments to a strange woman is reported as completely arousing, as this money slave observed:

> The act of paying is just so mind-blowing. When I see how much I have paid her I always masturbate with the credit card statement wrapped around the hand that is holding my dick.

Money Dommes have their own version of cuckolding, which in the traditional sense is a wife having adulterous sex.[199] To Money Dommes cuckolding means taunting subs

---

[199]See Cuckolding for more information.

and making them pay for activities that benefit the Domme and her boyfriend or husband; so this might be dinners, holidays or even renovations to the house. As one Mistress writes in her blog:

> I took the new boyfriend out for dinner last night, or should I say my latest sub did. I made the stupid Loser ring the restaurant, book a nice table, arrange a good bottle of wine and leave his credit card open to pay for us to have a great night, while he sat at home thinking about it. I did send him a text to let him know how delicious my steak was. Thanks you pathetic Loser!

While the relationships always operate in a strictly one way dynamic and a money slave is unable to ask anything in return from the Money Mistress, the professional Mistresses ensure they tailor a program around each slave, ensuring his needs are met and he remains a worthwhile and paying client. For example, a man may want to wear a nappy in his private time; however he only feels able to enjoy this if the decision is taken away from him and he is dominated or forced into doing it. He would let the Mistress know of his requirements and then after he pays her the financial tribute she might tell him he must wear a diaper, take a photo of himself and then send it to her as proof.

The more extreme Mistresses may require the willing slave to perform 'forced' bisexual/homosexual activities (or when this is not possible, have him perform with a dildo) and provide photographic evidence of his compliance. The aspect of photographic evidence or webcam performance can be extremely erotic because as one slave explained to me, he never knows who else is watching the webcam or who the mistress has shown this to, which adds further to his humiliation, and therefore arousal.

'Forced intox' has also become very popular with both Mistresses and slaves. Short for forced intoxication, it refers to a Domme getting a sub on webcam and then ordering him to do shots of alcohol. As he becomes drunk and slowly loses his inhibitions she instructs him to click her tribute buttons to send cash or click on her wish-list items. Dommes will brag about these sessions on their blogs or websites, and subs reading about them find the idea a turn-on and also want to experience it or spend time with such a mean Mistress. If the sub has given over remote access to his computer to the Mistress (and this is not uncommon), the Mistresses may also take the opportunity of deleting data and contacts from the sub's computer—notably videos, pictures and details from other Mistresses.

Some Money Mistresses provide a blackmail domination service. How this works is that the man voluntarily fills out an application form with his name, address, employer details, the phone number of his wife or girlfriend and discrediting information of his choosing, which he submits to the Mistress. The money slave is then required to pay the Mistress to avoid having this information revealed publicly. For a submissive who has an intense need to be shamed and degraded, being made to put the Mistress before his family and confess to it while she laughs at him fills that need. The Mistresses of course do their homework and learn about the money slave's weaknesses in order to exploit them as much as possible. Some Mistresses have been known to make a slave spend more money on her children than on his own at Christmas time and have them prove this with receipts, creating a particularly intense form of humiliation for certain subs. Disturbing as this sounds, the blackmail is generally always negotiated to run for a specific time, with a buy-out clause at the end.

It is accepted by the money slaves that in most cases the gifts or money they pay garner very little attention from the Money Mistress or $adist as some call them. This means when they do receive a mention on her website (a common practice is to list what each money slave tributed or gifted in a type of honour roll) or perhaps a brief text, they are motivated to spend more in order to receive continued attention—or even be acknowledged with a personal email or a webcam session. And of course in this way the process continually feeds into the money slave's masochistic tendencies.

The money masochist who is universally a man, is referred to by a variety of terms, including money slave, human ATM, pay-pig, paybot, pay piggie, servant, cashpet, sissie, cash cow, walletworm, zombie, sucker and Loser (generally with a capital L, the only capital letter ever used in relation to a money slave). There is no typical profile for a money slave, but he is generally in the 35 plus age group, as he needs to earn a reasonable salary in order to pay the Mistress regularly. Anecdotally he is usually a white-collar worker, such as lawyer, accountant, salesman or manager, and may be married or single. It can be a highly seductive addiction, as this educated and high earning money slave frames it:

> i[200] adore greedy, manipulative women that use me without regard to my well-being or that of my family. God help me, but i truly worship those women and I live for the moments I can serve them.

Another money slave I interviewed said that the greatest problems occur for single men as they are more likely to be exploited and get into financial trouble (even bankruptcy) because a skilled Money Mistress will ensure she becomes his primary financial obligation. This can be a state of affairs that the men themselves engineer, as this blogger on a human ATM website explains:

---

[200]Submissives or slaves generally use lower case for personal pronouns such as 'I'.

i [sic] have had the experience, in my past of handing a Woman[201] an envelope with all my most personal details—bank account numbers and online access passwords; credit card details and balances. The first time you log on and realize that She has been prowling through your bank accounts and credit cards—it is the most amazing feeling. A real, to-the-bone experience of being utterly owned.

On any given day advertisements by money slaves looking for Mistresses and Mistresses offering their services can be found in the personal section of the Craigslist website:

Demanding, Controlling, Dominant? Let's get in touch, please:

Yes, this would be STRICTLY PLATONIC, so I post here...I seek to be in contact with a suitably selfish lady. Your color, size, looks etc.. are all unimportant. What matters to me is how much you want to control me, and how selfish you are. It is important to me that you are in control, so some form or coercion is needed and I cannot just stop because I have changed my mind. I would expect this primarily to be remote control humiliation, chastity, extortion - but most importantly, I need to know that SHE is also enjoying this, and I am doing things that give her some buzz. (Craigslist.com Knoxsville, Mass.)

The now defunct Money Masochism group on Yahoo ran a poll among members, and in response to the question "How

---

[201]Money slaves always use deliberate capitalisation for any female noun or pronoun such as woman, goddess, she, etc.

much attention does an MM REALLY need from his $adist?"
50% of the money masochists who responded said they only
needed attention once a week or less, while almost 25%
responded that once every other week or less would sustain
their obsession and the relationship. An overwhelming 85% of
those surveyed said that phone, email and chat were sufficient,
with no 'in person' contact with the mistress deemed necessary. When asked what type of communication a money slave
needed from his Money Mistress, 47% agreed with the
statement that "acknowledgement of receipt of their payment
or completed assignment", would be an acceptable amount of
contact from a Mistress. Based on this poll, it would seem that
many money slaves can exist on very little attention or contact
and therefore do 'get what they pay for'. As one devotee
explained it:

> Because i [sic] am an absolutely worthless pile of
> shit, i will devote my entire being to worshipping
> and serving my Goddess, whether she acknowl-
> edges my worthless life or not. i live to serve her.

Money Mistresses are well aware of the level of excitement experienced by some men when paying them and many
make references to 'wallet raping' as a sales pitch on their
websites, as well as making frequent associations between the
giving of money and sexual fulfillment. One question that I
know many people would be curious about is whether the
money slave/Mistress dynamic can operate in a traditional
marriage. Unless the relationship begins in that dynamic, the
answer is generally no, as the money slave needs to feel the
Mistress is a superior being he can worship, not a fallible
human being he lives with day to day (see also the section on
Domination and Submission).

A common complaint in the community, including forums where Dommes meet to talk about their business, is that

financial domination attracts what are derisively called "insta" or poser Dommes, operators who have no real understanding of, or skills in, negotiating a power exchange or creating a power dynamic, and who simply join the industry because of the perception that online domination is an easy way to make a lot of money without much effort. In fact, according to some Mistresses, they have to work harder at being creative with men who wish to be blackmailed and become financial slaves than in a real time dungeon session. As one Mistress explained, it is not exciting enough to simply say "give me all your money", and most men won't do it anyway—they expect the Mistress to be very creative in her demands and make it fun, dangerous, exciting, humiliating or whatever it is that pushes their buttons. As this Mistress commented:

> It's the same with your ordinary sub serving in dungeon. He wouldn't pay for a session and then spank himself while the Mistress sits on her ass. The girls who just put up ads saying "I want your money" don't get it. At the end of the day we are still a service industry, so we have to give them something for their money.

At a glance money domination looks like a tempting way to make easy money, but the reality of the effort and skill required to do this properly (often coupled with their own preference for physicality), means many Mistresses choose to work with punishment and humiliation that is based around traditional BDSM and physical pain. Still, it is no exaggeration to say that quite a few skilled Dommes make a very nice six-figure living from money slavery. These Dommes know that a simple but well-timed text message to a slave's phone such as "pay me now pig" can result in an immediate delivery of several hundred dollars to their Visa card or bank account.

Jargon and Search Terms

CPA—certified paypig abusers.
Cumtax—paying money in return for being allowed to climax (alone).
FinDom/Findom—financial domination.
Human ATM, money slave, pay pig, pay pet, wallet worm, Loser—money masochist.
Money Mistress—a woman who is given money, gifts or tributes voluntarily by men who she may never have met in real life.
$erve—the act of paying money to serve.
Slut—a money slave who is incapable of loyalty to one Money Mistress and pays/serves many Dommes.
Sub—a male or female submissive partner.
TPE—total power exchange.
Whore—a money slave in a relationship with a Money Mistress.
Further Search Terms: ruination, powershopping, extreme spoiling, mind control.

Erotic Humiliation

> For a heterosexual male, swallowing your own cum is an extremely humiliating experience, but still extremely hot.
> —male sub, private exchange

Erotic humiliation, also known as emotional humiliation, can be present in both D/s and SM. Erotic humiliation is when humiliation is deliberately and consensually used in a sexual context, for the pleasure of either or both partners. It is not the same as dominance, though the dominant partner will be the one to humiliate the submissive partner. Some of the behaviours will be recognised as routinely employed in ordinary vanilla relationships as they include things like flirting with another person in view of the partner, doing something that is known to make the partner jealous, showing deliberate indifference to the partner or name calling.

More extreme forms of emotional embarrassment or humiliation may include verbally belittling the man's penis or sexual performance, making the man consume his own sperm or posting demeaning photos of him on BDSM community sites (men in women's underwear or wearing chastity cages are favourites). Activities for either sex include writing demeaning comments on the partner's body, spitting on them, making the partner shave their genitals, having the partner do something that is known to make them feel uncomfortable, such as urinating in public, having sex in public places, masturbating in front of strangers, eating from a dog-bowl or being led on a leash. The enjoyment is not from performing the act, but from the sexual feelings that result from the humiliation or belittlement. What makes one person feel sexy and another completely degraded varies widely, so partners should discuss the acceptable boundaries for these types of play.

> Being made to stand in the corner like this at my age is very embarrassing and humiliating, almost as much as being spanked like a naughty 9 year old. But deep down I know I need the control and discipline and it always gives me a hard-on. (Male, fifties)

Humiliation is present in a wide range of interests, including foot fetish, trampling, spanking, cuckolding, financial domination, facesitting, ravishment and forced feminisation/sissification.

Sadism and Masochism (Sadomasochism)

> To derive from the real or imaginary suffering
> which is thus inflicted upon you, a feeling of
> pleasure which constitutes an exciting addition to
> normal enjoyment, and sometimes takes the place
> of this enjoyment, to which it is completely equiva-
> lent; this is masochism.
>
> — Dr. Jacob X, *1900*

People in the sadomasochistic community are sexually aroused by consensual acts which involve some sort of pain or anticipation of pain (see also Algolagnia). The DSM-IV (the premier textbook authority on sexual disorders), published by the American Psychiatric Association (APA 2000), continues to label these practices as sexual disorders despite recent studies showing that most self-identified sadists and masochists are well educated, well adjusted and sexually creative individuals[202] who generally enjoy a reasonable level of wealth and status.[203]

In a purely sadomasochistic dynamic the receiving partner is known as the 'bottom' and the giving or doing partner the 'top', and the terms Dominant and submissive are not used. This distinction is important[204], because it indicates they are seeking a hedonistic experience as opposed to the power-play dynamic that is inherent in a Dominant/submissive relationship.[205]

While sadists will sometimes use non-consenting victims, sadomasochism is overwhelmingly a consensual practice. The

---

[202]Sandnabba, Adademi, Santtila and Nordling (1999)

[203]Baumeister and Butler (1997).

[204]Though of course the terms top and bottom may be used to describe Dominants and subs.

[205]Brame (2000).

sexual sadist derives sexual pleasure from inflicting physical or psychological suffering or pain on another person, who is generally a masochist. The masochist in turn gets his or her pleasure from receiving the pain, making the behaviour of the sadist complementary to the needs of the masochist. Some masochists prefer just one form of pain, such as spanking, and may limit their requirement for physical punishment solely to one area of the body—say the buttocks—and have no interest in other forms of punishment. Where a masochist varies from someone with algolagnia is that the algolagnist needs the physical experience of pain for arousal whereas the masochist may not enjoy physical suffering but finds the mental thrill of experiencing pain or even just the thought of pain to be sexually arousing. Most sadomasochists prefer the pain be inflicted or received with love or affection and for the mutual pleasure of both participants—certainly never in the context of abuse. In the words of Tom, a male masochist in his late fifties who has his wife beat him regularly:

> The actual pain gives me no pleasure, yet the idea of pain does, but only if inflicted by way of her loving heart and head and it has to be for the eventual good of the person suffering it, not just for the sake of hurting someone.

Masochism only became a so-called perversion in the last few hundred years after being indentified as such by the psychiatrist Kraft-Ebbing. Freud made similar claims and this has remained the status quo. Interestingly, religious history is predicated on pain, suffering, humiliation and punishment. The New Testament, for example, makes frequent mention of flagellation and physical pain, and it was part of the Jewish tradition for the deeply religious to lash one another with scourges after they had finished praying and confessed their sins. The Passion play that is re-enacted in Catholic communities every Easter involves bondage, flagellation and crucifixion, which signify being subjected to the will of a higher power; many of those who participate will flagellate themselves to the point of collapse. Western religion has a long history of connecting pain with religious ecstasy, and most of the early Christian orders routinely using flagellation as part of their spiritual discipline, believing that it brought about a state of oblivion and liberation so that the individual came into union with something higher.

The descriptions that masochists today offer for the psychological space (usually referred to as subspace) that they strive to enter are very similar to the descriptions of religious ecstasy that come from days of old—in the words of this male masochist:

> Experiencing the pain provides not so much a state
> of weakness to me, but a sense of surrender, recep-
> tivity to the universe around me, a total being in
> the moment type of headspace, a time out from the
> normal me. I come back refreshed and at peace.

The terms sadism and masochism as used for sex-related activities were coined by the 19th century psychologist Krafft-Ebing. He drew on the names of the 18th century French writer de Sade, whose novels such as *The 120 Days of Sodom* and *Justine and Juliette* are provocative portrayals of sexual violence and degradation, to describe sadism; and used a version of the Austrian novelist Leopold von Sacher-Masoch's name[206] for masochism. Krafft-Ebing believed both to be mental disorders, and in his well-known writings on the subject[207] postulated that sadism was essentially a masculine disorder and masochism a feminine disorder—despite naming it after a man. The

---

[206]He most famously wrote about a mistress and slave relationship in the cult novel *Venus in Furs*.

[207]His best- known body of work is *Psychopathia Sexualis* (1886).

number of submissive men paying for female domination services online would probably disagree. The American Psychiatric Association[208] notes that approximately 5% of sexual masochists are women and while a small proportion, this still makes masochism the only paraphilia in which appreciable numbers of women participate.

British sexologist Havelock Ellis observed that for many who enjoy sadomasochistic activities, the pain and/or violence is usually for the benefit of the masochist, who controls what is done, and how, through communicating subtle emotional cues to the sadist. It is not unusual for the male partner to coax or persuade the woman to try a dominant role, so in this way he is both the submissive and the voice of authority who engineers the situation according to his own needs. Ellis was ahead of his time in arguing that no clear distinction should be made between aspects of sadism and masochism, as they were complementary states. He also made the point (which is still considered correct) that sadomasochist behaviours are only concerned with pain in relation to erotic pleasure and should not be confused with general cruelty, as argued by Freud.

Bondage

Bondage refers to any type of consensual restriction or immobilisation employed by a Dominant on a submissive partner. What is used as a bondage tool takes many forms, but includes the use of scarves, belts, elaborate specialty store-bought ropes, or straps of leather or webbing. There are various levels of being constrained or tied up, and those participating choose whether they wish to be lightly tied up or put into discomfort or severe pain. Generally, hands are bound to each other, either behind or in front, or the person is tied to a chair or other item and the feet may also be bound.

---

[208] APA (2000).

Why bondage is practised also varies according to the partners. While it is mostly used for pleasure, it can also be used for correction, punishment or training. During a bondage session the Dominant has complete control over the submissive partner, and given this situation there must be pre-negotiated boundaries and safewords in place (see Safewords). The level of responsibility carried by the Dominant is high, given that if something goes awry the submissive partners may not be in a position to defend or assist themselves; and this means the sub must have a high level of trust in the Dominant's judgement. Because of this, bondage is reported by enthusiasts to engender a state of dependency by the sub and dependability on the part of the Dominant. Many BDSM partners believe that foregrounding feelings of mutual trust, vulnerability, desire and love in this type of play is partially what makes BDSM so attractive. As Mary, a female sub who only experienced her first bondage session five years ago after coming out of a seventeen year marriage describes it:

> For me, the allure of bondage is in being owned and possessed. Experiencing that feeling of helplessness and allowing myself to trust and be cared for is a deeply intimate act and for me there is no obvious counterpart in vanilla sex.

For those without regular partners, most capital cities around the world have bondage clubs, nightclubs or parties that cater to BDSM enthusiasts. Different theme nights are common and might cover violet wands, electric play, doctors and nurses, or ropes. Different clubs cater to different levels of interest, from those that are ideal for newcomers to those that are strictly hardcore. A club in Melbourne called Purgatory has a sample of pictures on its website so patrons can see what they might expect on various nights.[209]

Bondage represents different things to different people. Some enjoy the inherent trust they place on their partner; for others it may be the simple physical pleasure of being bound; for still others the enjoyment lies in the sense of freedom that comes from having to do nothing and having no responsibility while in a helpless state. The most frequent reason cited for enjoying bondage is that in giving up physical power a person is able to experience freedom from inhibition, sexual or otherwise.

Some people report that the pressure or pulling of the bonds intensifies their orgasm, while others just like to live dangerously and see bondage as a risky practice. Being bound and then sexually pleasured, violated or overpowered can also present a guilt-free way for some people to have experiences which they might consider forbidden or feel unable to request. What is used to restrain a person is up to the players, but the following are some of the common items and methods. Regardless of what is used, there are very real risks for those who are unsure of how to use restraints correctly and improper use can lead to permanent injury or even death.

Breast Bondage

Breast bondage involves binding the breasts tightly with some type of restraint such as rope or rubber used to encircle each breast tightly where it joins the chest. This causes the nipples to become engorged with blood and highly sensitive to the slightest touch. Nipples may also be bound, but require a finer material given the size of the area. While some people use rubber or elastic bands or even dental floss, experienced practitioners caution against this, because as the nipples swell it may become difficult to loosen or remove the binding

---

[209] http://www.purgatory.com.au/gallery.html.

material without causing damage. Fine bindings also run the risk of becoming so hidden in the flesh that it may be impossible to remove them without cutting the skin. Some practitioners take this to another level by also clamping or whipping the breast, causing intense pain and/or pleasure.

There are custom-designed stainless steel devices on the market that work like a vise for squeezing breasts. The device is placed so that one bar is above the breasts and one below, then the apparatus is screwed down so that bars close in on the breast.

Bondage Furniture and Fittings

Rooms set up specifically for BDSM play (either professionally or in the home) are known as bondage dungeons.[210] The bondage space usually includes specialist fittings such as bondage chair, bondage wheel or rape rack. The bondage chair is a piece of furniture that may look like a normal chair but has special devices for tying or strapping the submissive partner's legs or arms to the body. The bondage wheel is a piece of furniture featuring a revolving round plate (generally with a diameter of two to three metres), which is installed against a solid wall. The wheel is designed with grips for hands, arms, legs and ankles, and fixed body straps to hold a person to the wheel. The victim can be strapped facing the wheel if they are to be whipped or facing out for genital stimulation or torture.

Colloquially known as a 'romance chair', a rape rack is a description given to specially-rigged tables, beds or saw horses that anchor people in a sexually vulnerable position with custom-designed straps or chains (the term is also routinely used for the restraints used on cows or pigs for artificial insemination). The bondage swing is a special type of strap-on device that is attached to a stand or the ceiling, and is intended

---

[210]Though they are generally not in a basement or dungeon, but in someone's spare room.

to facilitate sex in unusual positions. It consists of a number of nylon or leather straps for the feet, ankles, and thighs, plus a seat like a normal swing.

Bars, also known as spreader bars, are used to separate extremities such as arms or legs. They are around a metre long and are attached to the cuffs on leg or arm restraints. The bar holds the legs apart or spreads the arms away from the body, rendering them immobile and alleviating the need to tether someone to a chair or bed. This practice appeals to those who enjoy exhibitionism.

Collars

Neck collars are widely used, either as a form of restraint or as a way of indicating affiliation to the BDSM community (see Commitment Collaring for more on the latter). Collars are generally made of leather or nylon, and are often used with a bondage leash. A bondage leash is essentially the same as a dog-lead, and is made of rubber, nylon or leather with a snap hook, Velcro or D-ring on one end and a loop on the other end, which can be used as a handle or attached to a collar; so the dominant partner can then lead the submissive around. There are also heavy duty collars known as posture collars which are for the specific purpose of disciplining the submissive. The sub must keep his head upright under the collar's heavy weight and any neck drooping invokes a punishment.

Crucifixion Bondage

Crucifixion bondage is so termed because it mimics an actual crucifixion. It utilises a stationary cross which has been created especially for the purpose of holding a human body. The person's arms and legs are tied (not nailed) to mimic Christ's crucifixion. This is said to have particular appeal to those who have had some type of Catholic upbringing or influence in their lives.

Chains

The chains designed for bondage play are a series of cus-tom-made connected rings made from metal, plastic or other materials. They can be purely ornamental, acting as a visual display of a submissive's humiliation, or may be used to attach a submissive by their cuffs or shackles to a wall or piece of bondage equipment. They are not normally applied directly to the body as they may twist or pinch the skin. Heavy duty chains designed specifically for the purpose are used for suspension.

Cuffs

Cuffs are applied to restrain wrists and arms; if the leg or ankle is cuffed then the device is known as a shackle. Cuffs or shackles are made from various materials such as nylon, leather or metal and, depending on a person's requirements, may be lightweight, heavy-duty police-style or lined with silk, fur or padding. They come with options such as padlocks or other fasteners. Those in the BDSM community caution that police-style handcuffs should never be used as they may cause skin or tendon damage. Most cuffs have ring attachments so that they can be attached to furniture or bondage equipment to facilitate leaving a sub unsupervised for a period of time; or a leash can be added to the ring so the sub can be paraded.

Toe cuffs are also available. These are used to tether the big toes or thumbs together, or to attach a thumb to a toe so the wearer must be doubled over.

Hair Bondage

Also known by the term 'hair tie', hair bondage refers to any technique in which rope, twine or other material is used to tie up the hair so that the head is made immobile.

Predicament Bondage

Predicament bondage is so called because the intention is to place the bound person in an awkward or difficult situation by setting them a task or challenge which is difficult to accomplish when bound. For example, a person may be bound in such a way that his or her hands are partially immobilised, and then be required to pour the dominant partner a glass of wine. If the bound person spills it, he or she is punished. Or a weight connected to nipple clamps may be placed in the sub's mouth, and if the weight is dropped it will yank on the nipple clamps.

Nose Hooks

These consist of a set of rigid, blunt hooks, about two centimetres long, which are connected to a length of rope, cord, or chain. The hooks are inserted into a person's nose to anchor them and then the rope is tied above or behind the person, forcing the head into an upwards posture. If the head droops the hooks dig into the delicate nose tissue. Nose hooks are most often used in Shibari (see Japanese Rope Bondage).

Japanese Rope Bondage

Those who are highly experienced in BDSM may participate in some of the more dangerous forms of bondage practices such as Shibari or suspension bondage (se below). These types of bondage require a high degree of knowledge and experience, given the possibility of harm and even death. It cannot be emphasised enough that these types of practices are quite complicated and can be dangerous; they should not be explored by inexperienced people.

Japanese rope bondage, also known as Japanese bondage art or Kinbaku, is most commonly referred to in the West by the term Shibari, although it also goes by the slang term 'erotic macramé'. It is a type of bondage that not only tethers a person but does so in a way that is said to be aesthetically pleasing. Shibari has a long history in Japan, beginning in medieval times when rope restriction and suspension were used as punishments for various crimes. It was favoured because it could create poor circulation, immobility and humiliating positions for prisoners, so that punishment was both physical and mental.

Shibari is a highly refined skill, often performed by rope masters or artists who demonstrate their prowess to large audiences in the same way as does, say, a popular musician. Hallmarks of this type of bondage include using specific lengths of rope, using only natural rope such as hemp, relying on very few knots, and tying to age-old patterns such as capturing the upper body, breasts and arms in a specific U shape behind the back, tying in a style called Kikkou which ends up with a tortoise shell design on the torso, or creating a body harness known as Karada, which ends up with the wearer in a rope dress.

Suspension Bondage

This is, as the name implies, bondage equipment that involves suspension of a human body. It is done with the aid of custom-made equipment consisting of weights and pulleys which allow a person to be hung off the ground by their feet or wrists from one or more overhead suspension points. Suspension bondage can take a number of forms: vertical suspension, in which the person is lifted off the ground by the wrists and with the aid of special suspension cuffs; horizontal suspension, in which the person is suspended face down; or inverted suspension, in which the person is hung upside down by specialist ankle cuffs. This last is the most dangerous form of bondage as the blood rushes to the head and a person can quickly black out. Suspension bondage is considered to carry a higher risk than other forms of bondage. Some of the many risks associated with suspension bondage include nerve compression and other ancillary damage including circulation problems and fainting, and the recently-recognised 'harness hang syndrome' (HHS),[211] also known as suspension trauma or orthostatic intolerance. HHS occurs when a person is forced to stay upright without the ability or room to move; it can be fatal, as this posture pools blood in the feet and disturbs blood flow to the heart.

Mummification Bondage

All wrapped up and nowhere to go...

In mummification bondage the person is completely re-strained by being wrapped in various materials and ends up looking somewhat like an Egyptian mummy. The materials vary from plastic or cling-film, rubber strips, bandages, duct tape and traditional bandages to actual body bags (which are known as a sleep sack and may only be fitted with breathing holes), or straightjackets that can be purchased in specialist outlets (see also Rubber Fetish). Straightjackets are generally made from leather and are modelled on the basic straight jackets used in last century's lunatic asylums. The garment straps up the back, between the legs and crotch and around the middle, to hold the arms behind. The hood may have eye blinders which adjust with side buckles to block out light and may also include a mouth cover to stop speech. Often used for mummification, the mono-glove is a piece of attire consisting of a single glove for both hands and arms, somewhat like a straightjacket in that it severely restricts the movements of the wearer. The glove is closed by zipper or straps, and keeps the arms together behind the person's back.

---

[211]Seldon (2000).

People who enjoy mummification say it enhances a feeling of total bodily helplessness. Others report pleasure from the experience of sensory deprivation, while for others the fun comes from being sensually stimulated while completely bound and inert. Experts caution that prolonged mummification, particularly with materials like cling wrap or latex, will cause sweating and consequent dehydration in the person being wrapped, so they must have access to water.

When heavy binding is not possible in real life, people turn to the online community to swap stories and art on the topic of mummification, join groups such as the boundforum.com and visit YouTube, which hosts many user-posted videos on the topic.

A related interest is known as 'buried alive', or Taphephilia; taphe (burial) and philia (love of) in which people mummify themselves first and then have someone bury them in the ground if doing it in real-life[212], or view video or art related to this theme.

Jake is a German man in his late twenties. His fascination with buried alive is so strong that seeing any type of hole in the ground or watching construction workers digging, actually gives him an erection. For as long as he can remember his fantasy has been to be buried in the woods after being tightly bound in bandages After watching a number of buried alive videos on YouTube he decided to make his fantasy reality with the help of a willing friend. Digging in a forest wasn't practical so they etched out a grave size site on a friend's country property and constructed a breathing tube, the only aperture in his cloth binding. As soon as the first few clods of earth were thrown on him he began to feel like he was choking and had a panic attack, calling a rapid an end to the whole thing. Despite this experience he continues to find the concept erotic.

---

[212] While they are genuinely buried, there are of course airpipes attached to the person's mouth.

Trashbag play, where one partner is put into a large garbage or trashbag also appeals to folk who enjoy encasement play. The plastic trashbags provide a sense of confinement, a threat of air loss (though all practitioners say air-holes must be punched into the bag for safety) and while giving a sense of permanent encasement they can be easily opened by the person inside.

Related Interests

Trashbag play, rubber.

Jargon and Search Terms

Bondage bunny—a person who enjoys bondage.
Dungeon—a space or room intentionally set up for bondage play with all the equipment and furniture.
Encasement—covers bondage, mummification or tight clothing.
Erotic macrame—Japanese rope bondage.
Packaged—a person who is heavily bound or mummified.
Mummee—the person being wrapped in mummification bondage.
Zentai—skin tight garments that cover the entire body.

Safety

Whatever sort of bondage or encasement is chosen, the universal rule of safety is never to leave a bound person unattended. This is considered dangerous due to the risk of heart attack, panic attack, fits, vomiting or entanglement in bindings; to name but a few potential problems. Experts caution that when someone is mummified they must obviously be able to get air and they must have access to water so they do not become dehydrated. Care must be taken not to risk the health of the person being mummified or bound by prolonging the wrapping, and they must be constantly monitored for any signs of distress. The dominant partner should also be aware of basic first aid principles should the bound person require immediate medical help.

Discipline

> Just hearing words such as discipline, naughty, smack etc, make me very hot and excited.
> —female submissive, 46

Discipline, the other widely practiced component of B&D, traditionally covers all manner of punishments. It may be physical or psychological and is used to either keep a partner in control or as punishment for broken rules. There is often confusion around punishment, as there are two types: (1) 'Play' punishment is a style of play in D/s relationships where situations are engineered so that the submissive can be disciplined in a way that pleases both participants. In these scenes the sub may be asked to do something which is not achievable, or will accidentally or deliberately transgress rules set by the Dominant and therefore need to be punished. (2) 'Real' punishment is for the involuntary transgression of rules and belongs under the category of Training (see relevant section).

Real and play punishments can be of the same type, whether the intention is to control the behaviour of a submissive or simply to have fun. Discipline is meted out when rules are broken or commands disobeyed—for example the submissive is commanded to kneel for 2 hours and failure to do so is punished. The punishment is chosen by the Dominant so it might be a caning, humiliation such as having to clean the toilet with their own toothbrush, having a public enema or being made to ass worship the Mistress' or loss of freedom— for example being locked in a cupboard or handcuffed to the toilet.

Although the Dominant chooses the punishment, it will
have been negotiated between the partners and previously
agreed to by the submissive as an allowable option, unless the
partners are in a metaconsent relationship and the Dominant
has cart blanche. A common problem related by Dominants is
that the submissive will have vetted a list of punishments that
includes activities he or she craves, and may engineer situations where they are can be indulged. As this submissive
woman explains it:

> I'm trying to be a bad sub so he will get pissed at
> me and see that i [sic] really do need a little disci-
> pline. I like a good paddling that leaves a few
> welts, but my Master prefers not to leave marks, so
> i have to really annoy him to get the belting I like.

The way a punishment scene is acted out depends on the
players and their level of expertise, whether it is in the home
or in a club that has many pieces of equipment, or whether it
occurs in front of others: these are all down to the personal
preferences of those involved. A description of a scene enacted
by a middle-aged man and his Domme girlfriend posted on
one of the many BDSM websites reads:

> There I was, a 42 year old husband and father,
> kneeling on the floor, hands tied behind my back,
> naked, gagged with a big red ball in my mouth
> and nipple clamps on my chest. I had to remain
> upright and still, because sitting in the chair in
> front of me using me as her footstool, was my Mis-
> tress. My Mistress is not a particularly beautiful
> woman, but she is strict and I worship her. We get
> together once a week or so, or when she has time
> for me. Today she had a couple of girlfriends over
> and they were also using my back as a side table
> for their ashtrays and glasses.

Now and then once of them glanced my way if I make a tiny adjustment or movement. To them I don't really exist except as Mistress' possession, so of course they didn't acknowledge me. Sometimes if one of them crossed her legs or moved to reach for her drink she might give me a little nudge or push with her high heel and if they spoke it was only something cruel or demeaning about how poorly I was doing my job. But I was used to that and secretly happy that they even noticed me. I really deserved my punishment today, because Mistress had specifically told me to be on time, but I had been very naughty and was 2 minutes late.

Physical discipline involves flogging, whipping, caning or spanking, and is always administered by a Dominant to a submissive or a top to a bottom with the intention made clear by the Dominant prior to the act. That way the submissive knows ahead of time whether the discipline will be followed by sex or sensual play, or will be given as a punishment only. Spanking is generally done with the palm of a bare hand, and flogging or whipping with some type of instrument.

Spanking

Spanking can also relieve stress, improve my mood, make me feel energised and in our relation-ship, enhances communication.

Consensual spanking between adults, also known as erot-ic or sensual spanking is when one adult strikes the buttocks of another and generally no other parts of the body are involved. Purist spankers will only accept spanking as spanking when it is done with the bare hand, but the back of a hair-brush, a table-tennis or ping-pong bat, slipper or school ruler are also commonly used.

Spanking is not an activity confined to the BDSM community, with sensual spanking generally always done for the pleasure of both parties and not intended to be a genuine punishment for infractions. The most common position adopted for spanking is over-the-knee (often abbreviated to OTK). The spanker takes a seat and lays the person to be spanked over his/her lap, face down and bottom up; in this position the palm of the hand or any other short implement such as a hairbrush is comfortably used. Some people prefer to use a piece of stationary equipment with attachment points designed to secure a person in preparation for a spanking; this is known as a spanking bench. The spanking skirt is a popular outfit worn by women for a spanking session. It is a conventional skirt with cut-outs over each buttock, so that the skirt falls away when the person is bent over a lap or spanking bench, allowing easy access to bare-skinned spanking. Others prefer to begin the spanking over clothing and then tease the submissive by lifting the skirt or slowly pulling down the pants. A big part of the enjoyment comes from the anticipation of when the skirt will be lifted or the panties removed, and players capitalise on this by talking about it as they build up to bare flesh.

Jane is a mother of two grown children and about to become a grandmother. Nothing about her hints of her love of being a naughty girl who loves a spanking:

> When he says "young lady bring me that ruler" it sends a shiver of anticipation down my back. Getting the ruler doesn't mean the fun will begin immediately, it could be now or in an hour, so part of the excitement is not knowing. At some point he will tell me to get into position which is over the couch arm. He always makes me wait by having a glass of wine or fiddling about, but the waiting

isn't long anymore as I'm not that young and hanging over the couch isn't so easy for me. Waiting is fun though, as I can't see what's going on and don't know when the first slap will come. It may be with the ruler, it may be with his bare hand, it may be over my clothing or he may rip down my panties and do it on bare flesh, he might start a slow rhythm, he might start hard. We always make love afterwards, sometimes on the couch.

People familiar with spanking suggest that it is best done methodically and rhythmically. The spanker should keep a steady pace without using too much force, as it is the quantity of slaps, not the impact and force that should be the focus. For safety's sake spankers should concentrate on the fleshy parts of the bottom and stay away from the tailbone and any region above that.

Corner Time

People who enjoy spanking often also enjoy a bit of corner time. This is when the person is made to stand or kneel in a corner before or after their spanking. A man in his late forties with teenage children and a responsible job describes his experience:

My wife is a firm believer in the use of corner time as part of the punishment process. Very often I will be made to stand in the corner for 15 minutes prior to being spanked. All corner-time is done while the bottom is bared for her viewing pleasure.

Upon completion of the spanking, I am returned to the corner where I must remain for up to thirty minutes, with my bare and very red bottom in full view. If I am caught looking around or fidgeting, I am given extra spanks and more corner-time.

Corner time is said to enhance the spanking session psychologically, as the person placed in the corner enjoys the nervous anticipation of not knowing how long they must wait, or of not knowing what the other person is up to behind them.

Whipping, Flogging and Caning

A dear one's blows hurt not long.

—old Russian proverb

Both whipping and flogging mean to be struck with a specially designed instrument in a considered manner that has been negotiated between the two parties. Specific instruments such as whips, canes and paddles are most commonly used.

The difference between whipping and flogging is in the implement used. Flogging is done with a flogger, a whip with a number of leather tails attached to a handle, based on the old 'cat o' nine tails' used in prisons. The style of flogger varies, based on the type and weight of the leather used for the tails and how the tips of the tails are shaped. The floggers are designed to deliver light sensations when the leather tails are very light-weight, and actual pain without any major damage when the tails are made from a stiffer and thicker leather. If a person is flogged with a light flogger, the punishment can actually look far more painful than what the person is experiencing. Some of the implements used to strike a person include:

- The traditional cane made from flexible rattan or bamboo. Rods are canes but made from plastic, rubber or fibreglass. As they are denser than rattan, they can inflict deeper damage and the feel is described as 'cutting'.

- The crop: a rod with short leather strip on the end, modelled on a horse rider's crop.

- Straps or belts (either from specialty shops or normal household items).

- The Hog Slapper: This implement consists of a strap of thick, heavy rubber, often wrapped in burlap or some other coarse material.

- The Cable Loop or Slapper: one or two loops of thick wire, coated with plastic, rubber, or leather and affixed to a handle. A cable loop can be used much like a crop or similar implement, and is said to produce intense sensations.

These implements are all generally purchased in adult sex shops, although some people construct their own from household items or purchase items intended for horses from tack shops.

A popular practice during whipping, flogging or caning is the ritual of the submissive or bottom counting the strokes received. Depending on the couple, the submissive may be required to thank the Dominant with each count; so each time the whip falls he or she may say something like "one, thank you Sir/Master/Mistress. two, thank you Sir" etc. The count starts again each time a mistake is made, whether it was deliberate or not.

Early Christian orders used flagellation as part of their spiritual discipline and in the Catholic faith in particular, priests would not only flagellate themselves but lash the church community as part of their penance. It was believed by holy men and followers alike that humiliation and physical pain provided a way in which one could become fully human and experience religious ecstasy.

Jargon and Search Terms

English—a code word for spanking or corporal punishment sometimes used in advertisements when discretion is required.
Figging—The practice of placing a piece of carved ginger root into the anus or vagina. The result is a burning sensation which many people claim can intensify orgasm, and which other people use as an adjunct to physical discipline such as whipping, flogging or caning.
German—a code word for sadomasochistic desires.
Pervertibles—tools used for BDSM play derived from ordinary household items (e.g. clothes pegs, brooms, hairbrushes).
Tickler—a whipping implement.
Whacker—a spanking implement.

General BDSM Activities

There is no way to separate out what practices or toys are solely the domain of sadists or masochists or just for dominants and submissives—or even whether a practice is discipline or reward, given there is such wide overlap. This overlap also includes partners incorporating activities into BDSM play that may have a fetishistic following of their own, such as human cow, enemas or pony play. For these reasons, the following section simply describes some of the ways that BDSM followers report enjoying themselves. Regardless of what practices people indulge in, the universal rule in the BDSM world is that people remain sober and un-drugged so that they are aware of their environment and watchful of the health and safety of all concerned.

Chastity Play

The chastity device is a special belt or cage worn on the genitals by either men or women with the purpose of preventing sexual relationships. The device is usually locked and the key carried by the dominant to prevent the partner from having intercourse or masturbating. A large part of the attraction to this practice is in giving one partner complete control over when the other partner may orgasm or enjoy sex. The dominant will sexually tease or excite the sub, who is physically prevented from any sexual gratification; or they may take the chastity device off and instruct the partner to masturbate, stop them before climax, and fasten them back in. Many female key-holders who practise chastity play will deny their partners penetrative sex but enjoy watching their man masturbate for them. Another chastity game involves the man's penis remaining locked in the chastity device while he is required to wear a strap-on dildo and have sex with his partner so that she is fully pleasured and he is not, or else the female partner wears the strap-on and anally penetrates the male who must continue to wear the chastity device (see also Forced Feminisation and Femdom).

The classic chastity belt for women consists of a leather belt around the waist connected to a leather band running between the legs with openings for toileting. The belt is fastened and then connected to the band with a lock. There are also variations on the chastity belt known as a chastity panty, which is aesthetically more pleasing but still works on the locked genitals principle, such as this one advertised for sale online:

> This leather G-string chastity panty is sure to keep her from enjoying herself until you are ready for her. Leather with a secure two -way crotch zipper which can be accessed from front or back Waistband locks in the front and comes with one lock

and two keys. Comes in small/medium or larger/extra large.

The male versions work on the similar principle of a waist belt, but with a penis tube or cage made from steel, leather or plastic attached, into which the flaccid penis is inserted. Variations include a metal or plastic ring which slips over the flaccid penis and attaches to leather straps which lock around the scrotum. The wearer is unable to have an erection due to the confining nature of the device. A US$325 deluxe device for sale online[213] is described below:

> This intriguing chastity toy is a hollow container in the shape of cock & balls. It is made from a strong metal alloy which is tinplated for a shiny, durable finish. The cave completely encompasses the genitals and is designed to fit average-sized men snugly. The inside diameter of the opening which is lined with soft black leather, measures 1 5/8". It is also hinged at the bottom & closes around the cock & balls in clamp-shell fashion. There is a lockable hasp at the top for security.
>
> The Cave is designed to prevent erections, orgasms, masturbation, etc. and to stand up to a certain amount of activity & wear. The tin-plating inserts will not rust if exposed to water or other fluids. There is a small hole in the end which would permit fluids to flow in or out.

Many of both the male and female chastity belts have options of attaching vaginal or anal plugs which remain in place while wearing the chastity device. As some belts are unnotice-

---

[213]www.erosboutique.com.

able worn under the clothing (e.g. the panty or jockstrap styles ones made from leather), the Dominant may instruct the sub to wear the device to work or out in public. Chastity games are also played online, with the willing submissive male instructed to put himself into a chastity device and then being held to his word not to take it off unless instructed.

Prostate milking may be included in chastity play (as well as a cage or instead of it) as the man is unable to sustain an erection after being milked and so remains chaste. When milking is combined with chastity devices, the penis is not touched and usually remains locked within the chastity belt or cage throughout the milking.

Erotic Sexual Control: Forced Orgasm

Forced orgasm is a form of play in which the Dominant partner attempts to bring the submissive partner to orgasm but the submissive tries to delay the orgasm for as long as possible. Forcing orgasms can be practised by males on females and by females on males. The submissive is usually restrained, with legs spread so the genitals are exposed, giving the Dominant carte blanche in how stimulation will occur. The forced orgasm is helped along with toys such as vibrators or through oral or digital stimulation. Once the person has climaxed, a feature of this play generally includes continued stimulation, which may cause irritation or discomfort to the submissive due to the sensitivity of their genitals post-orgasm. However, the intention is to arouse the submissive past this stage so they may orgasm again. For submissives, part of the reason for enjoying this practice is that they can be completely selfish, as their orgasm is in effect served to them on a platter and they do not need to worry about the partner's needs. As well, for people who may have some inhibitions or guilt issues around letting go and enjoying themselves sexually, having the responsibility taken from them can be a very liberating experience.

While it can be a form of play all of its own, it is common to force orgasms as preparation before orgasm denial play, so that the submissive partner builds up a level of addiction to the feeling of orgasm by being forced to orgasm many times over a period of several days or weeks. This means that when orgasm denial begins and no more orgasms are allowed despite being stimulated, the submissive feels the frustration all the more keenly.

Erotic Sexual Control: Orgasm Denial

Orgasm denial also known as cum restriction or tie and tease, is the practice of restraining a willing partner then repeatedly or continually sexually arousing them but denying them an orgasm. The restrained partner may be gagged or blindfolded to increase their sense of helplessness. The partner may have been subjected to milking or forced orgasm in the weeks prior, so that they are receptive to orgasming but denied relief by the circumstances.

Jargon and Search Terms

CB—chastity belt.
Cage—any male chastity device.
Cum restriction/tie and tease—stimulation but denying the partner an orgasm.
EC—enforced chastity.
Keyholder—the dominant partner holding the key to the chastity belt.
Milking—forced male ejaculation.

Clamps

Placed on the genitals or nipples (though they can be employed on other parts of the body as required), clamps are used as bondage, pleasure or punishment devices. While they are similar to a basic metal clamp used on paper, they are specially designed for use in sex play with rubber padding on the ends to protect the skin. Some people choose to use ordinary household items such as washing pegs or binder clips, but these offer no protection to the skin and there are risks of breaking or bruising the skin of the wearer.

Nipple clamps are items that specifically pinch the nipples. Some have adjustable settings so the pressure can be customised or varied. Nipple clamps may be simply attached to the nipples or they may be squeezed, ripped off or have chains attached to them. There are many uses for chains when attached to nipple clamps, including hanging weights from them and leading the wearer along. Experts caution that just like any other tight bonds, nipple clamps will reduce circulation, so the recommended usage is no more than ten minutes at a time to avoid damage to the area. Users should be aware that coldness, numbness, or discolouration of the area are all signals that it is time to release the clamp. There are also a variety of lightweight clamps available which serve merely as decoration and are intended for comfortable wear as opposed to physical sensation.

Sensory Deprivation: Blindfolds and Hoods

Sensory deprivation is a frequent element in bondage. Common devices include gags and blindfolds, while some participants enjoy using a full head harness or leather hood with openings for eyes, nose and mouth. Temporarily blocking the sense of sight is a common technique in SM scenes. It can make the bottom or submissive feel more vulnerable, increase anticipation, help them concentrate or 'get into the headspace', enhance sensations by removing one of the senses and, is said, to be essential in abrasion or surface play games where everyday objects (e.g. ice) are used to give unexpected sensations. Those who use them regularly recommend the basic traveller's blindfold, which is made from nylon and makes a useful, inexpensive everyday blindfold. Other blindfolds include scarves, handkerchiefs, long socks or even masking tape or bandages, which can be wound around the head and easily removed (tape of course can be tricky if it gets stuck to facial or head hair). If a more professional blindfold is required, specialty outlets sell a wide range designed specifically for BDSM play. They can be made from rubber or leather and purchased with padding or fleece lining, padlocks or ties.

A bondage mask is one that hides all or part of the face. It is generally made from leather, nylon or latex, and includes straps, buckles or Velcro to fasten behind the head. Masks are often accompanied by mouth gags especially designed for the purpose of stopping speech. These can be purchased in leather or rubber, and consist of a ball that goes in the person's mouth and ties behind the head. Some of these are designed with an inverted rubber penis that sits in the wearer's mouth.

When a blindfold or mask is not enough, a full hood is worn. Hoods are used for the same reason as blindfolds, to block vision, as well as to complement the outfits or particular personas people adopt in play. Most hoods are made from either leather or latex, with black leather being the most common. Where a Dom may choose to wear something like a crafted black leather hood known as a 'Master's Half', which covers the head but allows full sight and leaves the mouth exposed, a submissive is more likely to wear a fully enclosed hood or a hood with a zippered mouth area.

Abrasions

Abrasion play refers to rubbing another person's skin with some type of abrasive item. This may be twigs, leaves, sand, thistles or other materials such as an ordinary kitchen pot-scrubber. Abrasion play is often carried out when the partner is blindfolded, to encourage them to focus on the abrasive sensation. Whereabouts on the body this is done depends on the players, but regardless of whether it is on the arm or the genitals, care should be taken in abrasion play not to break the skin. If this occurs, steps should be taken to disinfect and clean the area to avoid infection.

Cock Rings

Cock rings are not limited in use to the BDSM community and are known as one of the oldest mechanical sex aids employed for sustaining an erection for an extended period. A cock ring is a device that is placed around the base of a man's penis and serves to slow the leakage of blood from the erect penile tissue, therefore maintaining an erection for longer. Rings are commonly made from leather, rubber or silicone, though nylon and metal may be used. The cock ring is placed on a flaccid penis by inserting first one testicle through the ring, then the second; finally the flaccid penis is pulled through.

A leather snap-on cock ring is placed around the base of the penis below the testicles and adjusted by using the attached snaps, which make the ring fairly safe because it is easy to remove. Metal rings may also be used in specialist sex games, when cords or ropes are passed through the ring for bondage purposes or electricity is conducted through the metal for cock torture games. A cock ring must be removed if the penis begins to tingle or burn, as prolonged venal constriction can cause thrombosis of the veins. Male strippers in gay clubs routinely use cock rings, as patrons prefer an erect to a flaccid penis.

Caging

In BDSM culture a cage is an enclosure used to restrict the freedom of a submissive partner. Most cages are built in a box shape, but they also come in other forms, such as a pyramid, dome or sphere. They can be made of metal bars, chicken wire or wood, and have connotations both of animal husbandry and of prisons. Cages vary from the size of a coffin to something that holds several people. Very small cages restrict the enclosed person's movements to the point that the person may only be able to lie or squat. The term 'cage of little ease' describes a cage which is so small that the submissive cannot rest in a comfortable position; so this type of cage is always used as a punishment device. As it can be damaging to blood flow and circulation, is it is essential that confinement in very small spaces is not for any period of time.

Cages are used to punish submissives or as part of acting out a role-play (e.g. captive prisoner or naughty puppy). How long a person stays in the cage depends on the partners and what they have negotiated, as this is a consensual practice. Forced caging is not endorsed by ethical BDSM practitioners, as imprisonment is illegal. Time spent in the cage may be a couple of hours; or there may be an ongoing arrangement in which the submissive uses a cage set up nightly in the Dominant's home for sleeping. Others enjoy caging of several hours or even a day while the Dominant goes to work. In these cases the submissive must have access to an emergency key so that if the building catches on fire or some other emergency occurs they are able to release themselves.

People report various reasons for enjoying this practice. For some submissives, it can be a welcome time-out from real life; for others it connotes a private place of safety; others say caging shows they are worthy of being kept—a special gift that must be safely guarded. For some Dominants the thrill comes from a feeling of control and ownership and the knowledge that the other person's freedom is contingent on their permission, while for others enjoyment comes from knowing that the submissive is all nicely packaged up and waiting just for them.

Fetish Clothing

Fetish clothing is often designed not just to look good and feel good to the wearer, but to act almost as bondage in its own right. It is a common assumption that women only wear fetish clothing to please men, but through history high heels and tight clothing have remained in vogue despite health warnings and feminist claims of oppression, and in donning such items it is possible that women choose to perceive themselves as sex subjects rather than sex objects.

Hobble skirts are a perfect example of fashion as bondage. These are skin-tight skirts fitting very snugly from waist down to ankles (think Morticia Addams of *The Addams Family* TV series, who was always seen in a black hobble skirt dress). As the wearer can only step a few inches at a time while wearing the skirt, the term describes how she hobbles along. When combined with a pair of high heels, these skirts can be almost completely immobilising, even without any other bondage. Leather or rubber are (again) the preferred materials, though some people tailor their own from elastic, or more sensual materials such as velvet or satin.

Trash or garbage bags are considered by some folk as ideal fetish outfit material, particularly those who enjoy rubber, Lycra or PVC. As plastic trash bags are glossy and thin those who enjoy wearing them say they are sensual on the skin and have the ideal bonus of being cheap and with just a pair of scissors, allow the wearer to design outfits to suit the occasion Designers on the fashion show *Project Runway* have previously used trash bags as working material.

Corsetry refers to garments that place a restriction around the waist, diaphragm or abdomen. Depending on its style, a corset can decrease the size of the waist and make breathing difficult. Tight-laced garments have long been reported as a factor of sexual excitement and an oblique method of masturbation for the wearer. Feminist Beatrice Faust[214] argues that most analyses of corsets and high heels have concentrated on men's visual experience of women's rolling hips and jutting breasts in these garments, without considering that women may actually choose to wear them for their tactile stimuli. She maintains that for women in the fifties and sixties the tight girdle may have been 'as pleasing as geisha balls in the vagina' because a tight garment can encourage pelvic tumescence and, if the garment is long and tight enough, may also provide some labial friction. British sexologist Havelock Ellis similarly argued that women have continued to wear waist cinches, tight girdles or corsets because, for some, this favours pelvic congestion while exerting pressure on the abdominal muscles, bringing them to a state similar to orgasm.

BDSM Negotiation

However it is enjoyed, BDSM play must have some rules around a scene to ensure partners feel safe (emotionally and physically) and so that accidental physical harm is not caused over and above the pain a person is willing to tolerate. The BDSM motto of 'safe, sane and consensual' is highly regarded in the alternative sex scene. The BDSM community existed long before the Internet, and as a subculture is extremely well organised in terms of guidelines, rules and practices. Responsible discipline or bondage occurs with the mutual consent of both partners, which means that BDSM players negotiate how

---

[214]She made this claim in the highly controversial (at the time) book, *Women Sex & Pornography* (1980).

they will play a scene and are clear about what is acceptable to both of them. It is not unusual for participants to complete a negotiation questionnaire or co-sign a consent form which details what activities they are both willing to participate in. Many BDSM community websites[215] publish downloadable forms which allow both parties (e.g. Master/slave, top/bottom, Dom/sub) to clearly indicate which activities are acceptable to each and the document is then signed by both players. Part of this negotiation process includes being made aware of any physical limitations or medical conditions (e.g. heart condition, epileptic fits, etc) that either partner may have and being clear about birth control and safe sex. While negotiating sex activities may sound impersonal or embarrassing, it is necessary to ensure that no misunderstandings occur and unintentional harm is not caused. Some scenes may involve being gagged or tied up and can last for several hours or even over a weekend; so consent and rules have to be clear to avoid potential problems such as a submissive being left tied up and mute by a Mistress for six hours when he thought he could leave after 45 minutes to attend a meeting.

Safeword

An important aspect of engaging in BDSM involves partners choosing a mutually agreed word or signal, if one partner is to be gagged. A safeword (generally written as one word in the BDSM community) is a word or phrase that has been negotiated between the players to be used if either person seriously wants to stop an activity. This must be a specific word that would not normally come up in sex play. Given that sadomasochistic sex is a clear-cut example of when no can often mean yes when pretending not to consent, words such as

---

[215]www.alt.com, offers a very comprehensive negotiation document.

no or stop are never used. As the SM manual *The New Bottoming Book* explains:

> The reason we need a safeword is that lots of us
> like to pretend we don't want to have these amaz-
> ing things done to us and we may pretend by joy-
> ously shrieking "nonononononono", so we need
> another word to mean that.[216]

Because no in these situations almost always means the opposite, unusual words such elephant or radish are used, because hearing an out-of-context word is both jarring and disconcerting—and most importantly leaves no room for ambiguity. The use of traffic light colours is also common, with yellow meaning slow down, green for keep going and red for stop. Safety is often referred to by the acronym SSC, standing for safe, sane and consensual, though others use the term RACK, meaning risk-aware consensual kink. However it is described, rules of play exist is to ensure that all participants are aware of their responsibilities and the inherent risks of what they are doing.

Aftercare

> He had smacked my bottom harder than I had ex-
> pected. I felt a bit weird about it at the time and it
> was almost like I didn't know him. But afterwards
> we lay quietly together and as he stroked my hair I
> could feel his love and the feel strange feeling went
> away.

In a BDSM context the term aftercare refers to the interaction and communication that occurs between the Dominant

---

[216]Easton and Hardy (2001).

and submissive after a scene has finished. It is considered an essential last step after BDSM play, because as well as having minor physical injuries people may experience feelings of anxiety, exposure, embarrassment, guilt or emotional over-load, depending on what has transpired. The emotional lows after a scene are colloquially known as 'top' or 'bottom' drop.

BDSM play can take people out of their comfort zone, par-ticularly if they are new to it or have just tried something different. This can leave one or both of the partners mentally drained, physically exhausted or with some injuries that need attention, such as rope burn that needs ice or a cut that needs a band-aid. This is considered an important time to wind down, comfort a partner if necessary and talk about the experience that has just been shared. It typically includes some cuddling, quiet words and refreshments such as some water and snacks, in an environment that is quiet, warm and private. Couples may choose to nap or chat, but the important thing is that both people have space to process what has occurred.

When couples take time for some aftercare they common-ly report feelings of protection/protectiveness, caring, grate-fulness, and a deepening of mutual understanding. Important questions for the partners to discuss include whether the scene was effective, if it was moving, if it went too far or had some distasteful aspects; these can be a basis to talk about what elements might be changed, explored further or improved on next time.

Regardless of what the dialogue covers, the purpose of aftercare time is for the partners to be clear about how they experienced the scene and how they wish to structure it the next time, ensuring that both partners' needs are met. As one experienced BDSM player frames it, "To skip it altogether is as rude as having dinner at a friend's house and bolting once you've eaten your last mouthful".

References

ABC News (2005). 'Japan tries women-only train cars to stop groping'
<http://abcnews.go.com/GMA/International/story?id=803965>, accessed 13 December, 2009.

Abel, G.G., Becker, J.V., Cunningham-Rathner, J., Mittelman, M., and Rouleau, J.L. (1988). 'Multiple paraphilic diagnosis among sex offenders'. *Bulletin of the American Academy of Psychiatry and Law*, (16), pp. 153-168.

Alfred C., Pomeroy, B., Wardell, C., Martin, C. E. and Gebhard, P.H. (1953). Sexual Behaviour in the Human Female. W.B. Saunders, PA.

American Psychiatric Association (2000). *The Diagnostic and Statistical Manual of Mental Disorders* (4th ed). American Psychiatric Association, Washington DC.

Anderson, M. Gaman, W, Gaman, J. (2010). *Stay Young, 10 Proven Steps to Ultimate Health*. George Publishing, NY.

Au, W. and Cannon-Au, N (2006). *The Discerning Heart*. Paulist, NY.

Bancroft, J. (1989). *Human Sexuality and its Problems*. Churchill Livingstone, Edinburgh.

Baumeister, R. F. (1997). 'The enigmatic appeal of sexual masochism: Why people desire pain, bondage, and humiliation in sex'. *Journal of Social and Clinical Psychology* vol 16 (2), pp. 133–150.

Beckford-Ball, J. (2000). 'The amputation of healthy limbs is not an option'. *British Journal of Nursing* vol 9 (4), pp. 188–190.

Behrendt, N., Buhl, N. and Seidl, S. (2002). 'The lethal paraphilic syndrome: Accidental autoerotic deaths in four women and a review of literature'. *The International Journal of Legal Medicine* vol 116, pp. 148–152.

Benamou, P.J. (2006). 'Erotic and sadomasochistic foot and shoe'. *Foot, Medicine and Surgery Journal* vol 22, pp. 43–64.

Berah, E.F. and Myers, R.G. (1983). 'The offense records of a sample of convicted exhibitionists'. *Bulletin of The American Academy of Psychiatry and Law* vol 11, pp. 365–369.

Biles, J. (2004). 'I, insect, or bataille and crush freaks'. *Janus Head* vol 7 (1), pp. 115–131.

Blanchard, R. (2005). 'Early History of the Concept of Auto-gynephilia'. *Archives of Sexual Behavior* vol 34 (4), pp. 436-439.

Blanchard, R. (2009). 'The DSM Diagnostic Criteria for Transvestic Fetishism'. *Archives of Sexual Behavior,* vol 38 (4). <http://www.springerlink.com/content/9267212375m4n40r>, accessed 2 January, 2010.

Blanchard, R., and Collins, P. I. (1993). 'Men with sexual interest in transvestites, transsexuals, and she-males'. *Journal of Nervous and Mental Disease,* vol 181, pp.570–575

Blickenstorfer, C. H. (ed) (1996). 'Where big is beautiful'. *Dimensions,* Issue 12.

Brame, G. (2000). *Come Hither.* Fireside Books, NY.

Breslow, N. (1989). 'Sources of confusion in the study and treatment of sadomasochism'. *Journal of Social Behavior and Personality* vol 4 (3), pp. 263–274.

Bridy, A. (2004). 'Confounding extremities: Surgery at the medico-ethical limits of self-modification'. *Journal of*

Law, Medicine and Ethics vol 32 (1), pp. 248–259.

Brownmiller, S. (1975). *Against Our Will: Men, Women and Rape.* Simon and Schuster, NY.

Bruno, R.l. (1997). 'Devotees, pretenders and wannabes: Two cases of factitious disability disorder'. *Journal of Sexuality and Disability* vol 15 (4), pp. 243–260.

Bullough, B. and Bullough, R. (1997). Are Transvestites Necessarily Heterosexual?' *Archives of Sexual Behavior* vol 25 (1), pp.1–12. <http://www.springerlink.com/content/lk064v4j383555 62/>, accessed 27 January, 2010.

Chalkley, A. and Powell, G. (1983). 'The clinical description of forty-eight cases of sexual fetishism'. *British Journal of Psychiatry* vol. 142, pp. 292–295.

Chapman, G. (2010). 'World's first sex robot Roxxxy unveiled'. <http://news.ninemsn.com.au/article.aspx?id=992547>, accessed 15 January, 2010.

Clark, P. and Davis A. (1989). 'The power of dirt: An exploration of secular defilement in Anglo–Canadian culture'. *Canadian Review of Sociology and Anthropology* vol. 26 (4), pp. 352–371.

Clinard, M.B. and Meier, R.F. (1998). *The Sociology of Deviant Behavior.* Harcourt Brace, NY.

Comfort, A. (1972; revised 2008). *The Joy of Sex.* Pocket Books, NY.

Critelli, J.W. and Bivona, J.M. (2008). 'Women's erotic rape fantasies: An evaluation of theory and research'. *Journal of Sex Research* vol 45 (1), pp. 57–70.

Dailey, M.D. (1989). The Sexually Unusual: Guide to Understanding and Helping. Hawthorn, NY.

Denko, J.D. (1973). 'Klismaphilia: Enema as a sexual preference. Report of two cases'. *American Journal of Psycho-therapy* vol 27 (2), pp.232–250.

de Sade, D.A.F. (1930). *Justine, Philosophy in the Bedroom, and Other Writings.* Republished 1994 by Grove Press, NY.

de Sade, D.A.F. (1904). *The 120 Days of Sodom and Other Writings.* Republished 1994 by Grove Press, NY.

Dotinga, R. (2000). 'Out on a limb'. *Salon,* August 29.

Easton, D. and Liszt, C.A. (1997). *The Ethical Slut.* Greenery, San Francisco, CA.

Easton, D. and Hardy, J.W. (2001). *The New Bottoming Book.* Greenery, San Francisco, CA.

Eby, C. (1999). Hemingway's Fetishism: Psychoanalysis and the Mirror of Manhood. State University of New York, Albany, NY.

Ellis, A. and Brancala, R. (1956). *The Psychology of Sex Offenders.* Charles C. Thomas, Springfield, IL.

Ellis, H. (1906). *Studies in the psychology of sex* (vol II), Project Gutenberg <http://www.gutenberg.org/etext/13610>, accessed 14 January 2010.

Ellison, J. (2008). 'Cutting Desire'. MSNBC. <http://www.newsweek.com/id/138932>, accessed 28 May, 2008.

Faust, B. (1980). *Women, Sex and Pornography.* Penguin, Victoria, Aust.

Fenichel, O. (1945). *The Psychoanalytic Theory of Neuroses.* W.W. Norton, NY.

Freud, S. (1905). 'Three essays on sexuality'. In J. Strachey (ed), *The Penguin Freud Library* (1991), vol 7. Penguin, London.

Freud, S. (1928). 'Fetishism'. *International Journal of Psycho-*

Analysis vol 9, pp. 161–166.

Freund, K. (1990). 'Courtship Disorder'. In W.L. Marshall, D.R. Laws and H.E. Barbaree (eds), *Handbook of Sexual Assault: Issues, Theories and Treatment*, pp. 195–207. Plenum, NY.

Freund, K., Scher, H. and Hucker, S. (1984). 'The courtship disorders: A further investigation'. *Archives of Sexual Behavior* vol 13 (2), pp. 133–139.

Freund, K. and Seto, C. (1998). Preferential rape in the theory of courtship disorder'. *Archives of Sexual Behavior* vol 27 (5), pp. 433–443.

Friday, N. (1976). *My Secret Garden*. Hazell, Watson, Bucks, Great Britain.

Gamman, L. and Makinen, M. (1993). *Female Fetishism*. New York University Press,. NY.

Gauthier, D.K. and Forsyth, C.J. (1999). 'Bareback sex, bug chasers and the gift of death'. *Deviant Behavior* vol 20 (1), pp. 85–100.

Gendin, S. (1997). 'Riding Bareback'. *POZ*, pp. 64–65.

Giles, F. (2004). 'Relational and strange: A preliminary foray into a project on queer breastfeeding'. *Australian Feminist Studies* vol 19 (45), pp. 369–405.

Gregson, I. (2002). 'The Apotemnophile: An amputees perspective'. <http://www.amputee-online.com/amputee/wannabee.html>, accessed 12 November 2009.

Grimm, I. and Grimm, W. (1975). *The Complete Grimm's Fairy Tales*. Routledge, London.

Hardy, J. and Easton, D. (2004). *Radical Ecstasy: SM Journeys to Transcendence)*. Greenery, San Francisco, CA.

Harpers Bazaar (2007): 'Jennifer Hawkins Graces Cover'

<http://www.news.com.au/dailytelegraph/story/0,2204
9,22346458-5001026,00.html>,accessed 9 August, 2009.

Hays, S. and Warren, T. (2003). 'Human pheromones: Have they been demonstrated?' *Behavioral Ecology and Sociobiology* vol 54, pp. 89–97.

Hazen, H. (1983). Endless Rapture: Rape, Romance, and the Female Imagination. Scribner, NY.

Henkin, W.A and Holiday, S. (1996). *Consensual Sadomasochism: How to Talk about it and Do it Safely*. Daedalus, Los Angeles, CA.

Herrick, R. (1891). *The Works of Robert Herrick*, vol 1. Alfred Pollard (ed) Lawrence & Bullen, London. http://www.luminarium.org/sevenlit/herrick/nipples.ht m>,accessed 9 January, 2010.

Hill, D. (2000) 'Bug Chasers', *Alternative Magazine*

<http://www.alternativesmagazine.com/15/hill.html>,accessed 11 May 2009.

Hirschfield, M. (1956). Sexual Anomalies: The Origins, Nature and Treatment of Sexual Disorders (2nd ed). Emerson Books, NY.

Hopkins, J. (2000). 'A case of foot and shoe fetish in a 6 year old girl'. In Lubbe, T. (ed), *The Borderline Psychotic Child*, pp.109–129. Taylor and Francis, Philadelphia, PA.

Hunt, M. (1974). *Sexual Behavior in the 1970s*. Playboy, Chicago, IL.

Janus, S., and Janus, C. (1993).*The Janus Report on Sexual Behavior*. John Wiley & Sons.

Jenkins, P. (2000). 'When self-pleasuring becomes self-destruction: Auto-erotic asphyxiation paraphilia'. *The International Journal of Health Education* vol 3 (3), pp.

208–216.

Jung, C.G. (1954). *The Archetypes and the Collective Unconscious. Collected Works* vol. 9 Part 1 (2nd ed, 1981), Bollingen, Princeton, NJ.

Jung, C.G. (1963). *Memories, Dreams, Reflections.* Vintage, NY.

Kafka, M. (2009). The DSM Diagnostic Criteria for Fetishism. *Archives of Sexual Behavior.* <http://www.springerlink.com/content/c6678382t185t12 1/>, accessed 12 January, 2010.

Kendall, P.C. and Hammen, C. (1999). *Abnormal Psychology: Understanding Human Problems.* Houghton Mifflin, Boston, MD.

Kimmel, S., Cameron, J. and Aubrey, S. (producers); Gillespie, C. (director), (2007). *Lars and the Real Girl* [motion picture]. MGM: USA.

Kinsey, A.C., Wardell, C., Pomeroy, B. and Martin, C.E. (1948). *Sexual Behavior in the Human Male.* W.B. Saunders, Philadelphia, PA.

Kinsey, A.C., Pomeroy, B., Wardell, C., Martin, C.E. and Gebhard, P.H. (1953). *Sexual Behavior in the Human Female.* W.B. Saunders, Philadelphia, PA.

Kleinplatz, P. J. (2001). *New Directions in Sex Therapy: Innovation and Alternatives.* Taylor and Francis, Philadelphia, PA.

Krafft-Ebing, R. (1886). Psychopathia Sexualis (12th ed, 1965). Pioneer, NY.

Kringelbach, M. (2006). 'Bodily Illusions'. <http://www.kringelbach.dk/Preprint_Beagle_BodilyIll usions.html>, accessed 2 January 2008.

Langer, W.C. (1972). The Mind of Adolf Hitler: the Secret Wartime Report. Basic Books, NY and London.

Latteier, C. (1998). Breasts: The Women's Perspective on an

American Obsession. Hawthorn, NY.

Lawrence, A. (2009). 'Anatomic Autoandrophilia in an Adult Male', *Archives of Sexual Behavior* vol 38 (6), pp.1050–1056.

Levin, R.J. (2006). 'The breast/nipple/areola complex and human sexuality'. *Sexual and Relationship Therapy* vol 21 (2), pp. 237–249.

Levin, S.B. (2003). 'The nature of sexual desire: A clinician's perspective'. *Archives of Sexual Behavior* vol 32, pp. 279–285.

Longhurst, R. (2006). Pornography of Birth, Crossing Moral Boundaries'. *ACME International e-Journal for Critical Boundaries,* vol 5 (2) pp. 209–229. <http://www.acme-journal.org/vol5/RLo.pdf>,accessed 14 December 2009).

Love, B. (1992). *Encyclopedia of Unusual Sexual Practices* (2nd ed, 1999). Greenwich, London.

Lowenstein, L.F. (2002). Fetishes and their associated behavior'. *Sexuality and Disability* vol 20, pp. 135–144.

Maletzky, B. (1998). 'The paraphilias: Research and treatment'. In P.E. Nathan and J.M. Gorman (eds), *A Guide to Treatments that Work,* pp. 474–500. Oxford, NY.

Malin, M. and Saleh, F. (2007). 'Paraphilias: Clinical and forensic considerations'. *The Psychiatric Times* vol 24 (5), pp. 671–682.

Masters, W H., Johnson, V.E. and Kolodny, R.C (1992). *Human Sexuality.* Harper Collins, NY.

Metzi, J. M. (2004). 'From Scopophilia to Survivor: A brief history of voyeurism'. *Textual Practice* vol 18.(3) pp. 415–434.

Miletski, H. (1999). *Bestiality–Zoophilia: An Exploratory Study.* The Institute for Advanced Study of Human Sexuality,

San Francisco, CA.

Money, J. (1977). 'Paraphilias'. In J. Money and H. Moustapha (eds), Handbook of Sexology. Excerpta Medica, Amsterdam/London/NY.

Money, J. (1980). Love and Love Sickness: The Science of Sex, Gender Difference and Pair Bonding. Johns Hopkins University, Baltimore, MD.

Money, J. (1984). 'Paraphilias: Phenomenology and classification'. American *Journal of Psychotherapy* vol 38, pp. 164–179.

Money, J. (1986). Lovemaps: Clinical Concepts of Sexual/Erotic Health and Pathology, Paraphilia and Gender Transposition in Childhood, Adolescence and Maturity (2nd ed 1993). Irvington, NY.

Money, J., Jobaris, R. and Furth, G. (1977). 'Apotemnophilia: Two cases of self-demand amputation as a paraphilia'. *Journal of Sex Research* vol 13, pp. 115–125.

Morris, D. (1967). *The Naked Ape*. Jonathan Cape, London.

Morrison, J. (2006). *DSM-IV Made Easy: The Clinician's Guide to Diagnosis*. The Guildford Press, New York, London.

Moser, C. (2001). 'Paraphilia: A critique of a confused concept'. In P.J. Kleinplatz (ed), *New Directions in Sex Therapy: Innovation and Alternatives*, pp. 91–108. Taylor and Francis, Philadelphia, PA.

Moser, C.(2009). 'When is an unusual sexual interest a mental disorder?' *Archives of Sexual Behavior* vol 38 (3), pp. 323–325.

Munroe R. L. and Gauvain, M. (2001). 'Why the paraphilias: domesticating strange sex' *Cross-Cultural Research* (34), pp. 44–64.

Murphy, W. (1997). 'Exhibitionism: Psychopathology and

theory'. In D.R. Laws and W. O'Donohue (eds), *Sexual Deviance: Theory Assessment and Treatment*, pp. 22–39. Guildford, NY.

National Association for Fat Acceptance Website: <http://www.naafa.org/documents/policies/fat_admirer s.html>, accessed 3 March, 2008.

Pate, J.E. and Gabbard, G.O. (2003). 'Adult baby syndrome', *The American Journal of Psychiatry* pp. 1932–1936 <http://ajp.psychiatryonline.org/cgi/content/full/160/11/ 1932>, accessed 11 May, 2009.

Penix, T.M. and Pickett, L. (2006). 'Other paraphilias'. In J.E. Fisher and W.T. O'Donohue (eds), *Practitioner's Guide to Evidence-Based Psychotherapy*, pp. 478-493. Springer, NY.

Peyser, M. (1997). 'A deadly dance'. *Newsweek* Sept 29, pp. 76–77.

Pfafflin, F. (2008). 'Good enough to eat.' *Archives of Sexual Behavior* vol 37, pp. 286–293.

Piven, J. (2000). 'The weirdness of history'. *The Journal of Psychohistory*, vol 28, (1). <http://primal-page.com/piven.htm>, accessed 17 December, 2009.

Prescott, J. (1989) 'Genital pain vs. genital pleasure: Why the one and not the other?' *The Truth Seeker* vol 1 (3), pp. 14–21. <http://www.violence.de/prescott/truthseeker/genpl.ht ml>, accessed 9 January 2010.

Prins, H. (1985). 'Vampirism: A clinical condition. *The British Journal of Psychiatry*. (146), pp. 666–668.

Prins, H. (1985). 'Vampirism: A clinical condition'. *The British Journal of Psychiatry* vol 146, pp. 666–668.

Rachman, S. J. and Hodgson, R. J. (1968). 'Experimentally

induced sexual fetishism: Replication and development'. *The Psychological Record* vol 18, pp. 25–27.

Ramachandran, V.S. (2002). Encyclopedia of the Human Brain. Academic, San Diego, CA.

Real Doll Creations website. <www.Realdoll.com>, accessed 9 August 2007.

Richo, D. (1999). Shadow Dance: Liberating the Power and Creativity of Your Dark Side. Shambala, Boston & London.

Rosen, I. (1964). *Pathology and Treatment of Sexual Deviation.* Oxford University, London.

Seldon, P. (2002). 'Harness suspension: Review and evaluation of existing information'. *Contract Research Report 451,* UK Health and Safety Executive. <http://www.scribd.com/doc/10564050/Forensic-Pathology-of-Trauma>, accessed 12 December 2007.

Sigusch, V. (1998). 'The Neosexual Revolution'. *Archives of Sexual Behavior* vol. 27 (4), pp. 331–359.

Spectrum (2004). *The Toybag Guide to Hot Wax and Temperature Play.* Greenery, San Francisco, CA.

Stoller, R. J. (1968). Sex and gender: On the Development of Masculinity and Femininity. Macmillan, NY.

Sutton, E. (2003). *Female Domination.* Lulu.com.

Sutton, E. (2007). *The FemDom Experience.* Lulu.com.

Templeman, T.L. and Stinnett, R.D. (1991). 'Patterns of sexual arousal and history in a normal sample of young men'. *Archives of Sexual Behavior* vol 20, pp. 137–150.

Tollison, C.D. and Adams, H.E (1979). *Sexual Disorders: Theory, Treatment and Research.* Gardner, NY.

Turner, V.W. (1969). The Ritual Process: Structure and Anti-structure. Aldine, NY.

van Gennep, A. (1909). *The Rites of Passage*. Macmillan, NY.

Wiederman, M.W. (2003). 'Paraphilia and Fetishism'. *The Family Journal: Counselling and Therapy for Couples for Families*, vol 11 (3), pp. 315–321.

Wyatt, A. and Tristram D. (2003). *Pheromones and Animal Behaviour: Communication by Smell and Taste*. Cambridge University, Cambridge.

Zillmann, D. (1998). *Connections Between Sexuality and Aggression*. Lawrence Erlbaum Associates, NY.

Appendices

Selected groups and sites consulted along the way:

www.adultfriendfinder.com

www.ampulove.com

www.armpit-sex.com

www.asexuality.net

www.alt.com

www.beastforum.com

www.bmezine.com

www.boundforum.com

www.castfetish.com

www.cryingappreciationforu
m.com

www.cuckold.org

www.cuckyboy.com

www.dailydiapers.com

www.darkerpleasures.com

www.dwarfdate.com

www.drainyourwallet.com

www.ebanned.net

www.erotichumiliation.com

www.extremerestraints.com

www.femaletongue.org

www.footdirectory.com

www.hairpersonals.com

http://groups.yahoo.com/gro
up/humanatm/

www.humiliation.me

www.jinxypie.com

www.mistressdestiny.com

www.medicaltoys.com

www.mukiskitchen.com

www.nightflirt.com

www.objectum-
sexuality.org

http://plushie.info/

www.rubberist.net

www.secondlife.com

www.tsr.com

www.tonguefetish.com

http://www.velocity.net/~gal
en/

www.Yahoo.com/group/dev
otee-of-women-on-wheels/)

www.zoophilia.com

Index

Freud, 13, 14, 17, 151, 214, 324
Frotteurism, 258
fur, 36, 149
Furries, 245, 247
Furry Fandom, 245
Furry play, 244
fursona, 246
fursonas, 246
fursuit, 246

G

gainer, 80
garbage, 100, 101, 137, 334, 351
garbage bags, 351
gas-masks, 153
Gender Identity Disorder, 265
genital waxing, 66
gerontophilia, 88
giantess fantasy, 79, 177
glasses fetish, 154
GOC, 155
golden showers, 116
gunging, 205
guns, 210
gynemimetophilia, 263, 268

H

haematophilia, 123
hair, 57
hair blow job, 58
hair bondage, 329
hair cutting, 58

hair fetishism, 57
hairless genitalia, 66
hairy armpits, 63
hand over mouth, 297
harpaxophilia, 206
Havelock-Ellis, 189
headspace, 280
height, 87
high heels, 36
hircusophilia, 63
HomSmother, 207, 297
hoods, 348
hoof hugger, 22
hooks, 330
hoplolagnia, 210
human cows, 168
human footstool, 28
human hair, 57
humiliation, 287, 294, 306, 320
hybristophilia, 215
hygrophilia, 94
hypoxyphilia, 206

I

inanimate objects, 227
inflatables, 201
inflation fetish, 197
inflatophilia, 197, 198
insects, 242
intersex, 264, 266

J

Japanese rope bondage, 330
Jung, 14

Angela Lewis holds a PhD in education and has worked in IT for many years as a provider of various learning programs to both the government and corporate sector. She is a qualified counsellor and has acted as IT Adviser to the *Australian Counselling Association* for the past 10 years, publishing extensively in the ACA's journal on the intersection of society and technology. While exploring and then writing about how people expressed their sexuality she found that community attitudes towards anything other than mainstream sexual practices remains deeply suspicious and judgemental. So began a 4 year project of gathering narratives and interviewing people who enjoyed a wide range of alternative sexual practices, resulting in her first book, **My Other Self**, the stories of ordinary folk quietly leading extraordinary private lives.

Contact her at angela.lewis@myotherself.com.au.

CPSIA information can be obtained at www.ICGtesting.com
Printed in the USA
LVOW10s0813191214

419577LV00006B/97/P

9 781921 791284